| exploring |

D1308904

Photoshop CS3

| *exploring* |

Photoshop CS3

Annesa Hartman

Ken Sholar

Exploring Photoshop CS3

by Annesa Hartman and Ken Sholar

Vice President,
Technology and Trades ABU:
David Garza

Director of Learning Solutions:
Sandy Clark

Managing Editor:
Larry Main

Senior Acquisitions Editor:
James Gish

Product Manager:
Nicole Bruno

Editorial Assistant:
Sarah Timm

Marketing Director:
Deborah Yarnell

Marekting Manager:
Kevin Rivenburg

Marketing Specialist:
Victoria Ortiz

Director of Production:
Patty Stephan

Production Manager:
Andrew Crouth

Content Project Manager:
Andrea Majot

Technology Project Manager:
Kevin Smith

Cover Image:
Hilltoppers © David Arsenault, oil on canvas

Library of Congress Cataloging-in-Publication Data:
Hartman, Annesa.
   Exploring Photoshop CS3 / Annesa Hartman Ken Sholar.
      p. cm.
ISBN-13: 978-1-4180-5259-1
   (adhesive/perfect soft/case : alk. paper)
ISBN-10: 1-4180-5259-0
   (adhesive/perfect soft/case : alk. paper) 1. Computer graphics.
   2. Adobe Photoshop. I. Sholar, Ken. II. Title.
T385.H34745 2007
006.6'86--dc22
2007015523

ISBN-13: 978-1-4180-5259-1
ISBN-10: 1-4180-5259-0

NOTICE TO THE READER

For my mother, Carolyn Murov

For my parents, Johnnie and Chiyo

contents

| *contents* |

contents

CONTENTS

| *preface* |

"The universe is full of magical things, patiently waiting for our wits to grow sharper."
—Eden Phillpotts

INTENDED AUDIENCE

Quick, grab a seat. The show is about to begin, and it is full of a wonderfully mischievous cast of characters you do not want to miss. They call them "pixels," magical spirits brought to life by digital mayhem and transported by light. They are the muses of the digital artist, the star performers on the Photoshop stage, and the lead actors in this book, *Exploring Photoshop CS3*.

Whether a new student to computer graphics, a computer arts educator, a professional visualizer, animator, designer, illustrator, photographer, or just plain curious dabbler, *Exploring Photoshop CS3* has something for you. It offers a practical and straightforward introduction to the essentials of digital image creation, compositing, and photo retouching; comprehensive step-by-step lessons; easy reference to commonly used tools and features of Photoshop; and plenty of encouragement for artistic exploration.

EMERGING TRENDS

In today's world, the amount of data that moves through our consciousness is overwhelming. Some of this information we manage to absorb into knowledge and understanding, and it enhances and improves our lives. Other data comes to us as fluff; we hold on to or let go of it as our interest wanes.

More so than ever, graphic designers have the tools and resources to bring data to visual life in diverse ways.

Thomas L. Friedman, author of *The World is Flat*, says, "The world is being flattened. ... we are now connecting all the knowledge centers on the planet together into a single global network ... , which could usher in an amazing era of prosperity, innovation and collaboration. ..."

A high-speed flow of digital information is prevalent and far-reaching to all corners of the world like never before. In our case—as graphic designers, artists, developers, students and educators—this digitally connected world opens up a level playing field, where we can explore endless new ways to research, use, and effectively design our creative visions.

The need to find the best solutions for the effective, horizontal flow of data is not being over-looked. Adobe's new creative software suites are designed for easy transfer of visual and textual content between different software programs, allowing quick workflow processes between varies designers and developers. An illustrator can draw a logo in Illustrator, add effects to it in Photoshop, and then send it to an animator. The animator can make it move in After Effects, and then send it to a printer or the Web or a mobile device content developer.

As well, today's successful graphic artists realize the importance of not just having a foundation in design principles and knowing the tools, but also having the skills to communicate clearly and collaboratively with others in the innovation process. The artists highlighted in this book were asked, "What suggestions for success would you give to the emerging graphic artist?" All emphasized the need for one to be adaptable to change and alterations; to be professional, organized, and prompt in all matters of his or her business; to be personable to others, and yet persistent in self-promotion; and to keep learning, exploring, and engaging with all that this expansive world offers.

BACKGROUND OF THIS TEXT

"Any sufficiently advanced technology is indistinguishable from magic," says Arthur C. Clarke, author of *2001: A Space Odyssey* (1968) and astrophysicist.

Aptly, Photoshop is an example of such a technology. For Photoshop, or any other current computer graphics software program, it is not uncommon to describe what it can do and how it is embraced by the user as anything but amazing, magical. Without lessening the impact Photoshop has made in the graphics and photographic industries, and the continual advancements occurring with each new version, this book is intended to demystify what ostensibly seems complicated but is really quite engaging and accessible. After all, as automated as the program can appear, it is still a product of the mortal mindset, which we can assume understands some method to the madness.

As is *Exploring Illustrator CS3*, and in purpose all the books in Delmar Learning's Design Exploration series, the objective of this text is to be clear and no-nonsense in approach, never negating the practical—yet vastly experiential—aspects of the program. You could say it is the "Penn and Teller" method of instruction. Yes, for the outside viewer it appears all magic (and we want to keep it that way!), but for the magician it really is just practiced tricks that can be easily explained and enacted.

TEXTBOOK ORGANIZATION

As you learn in Chapter 1, Photoshop is a "must-know" program for the graphic artist, with the ability to retouch, blend, composite, layer, and add effects to photos and digital imagery, draw and paint, and save in different image formats for different purposes, such as for use on the Web, for print, or in other programs.

The way in which this book has been conceptualized and organized derives from the following intentions:

▶ Explore the questions that face today's Photoshop artist and provide some educated answers through the use of Adobe Photoshop's digital tools and features

▶ Offer process-oriented lessons developed from actual implementation in the classroom and production firms

▶ Develop an understanding of core concepts related to digital artwork and image creation through fundamental design principles and methods

▶ Provide an inside look at how artists working in the field come up with ideas and inspirations

▶ And, most importantly, open the door for continued, self-guided discovery

The textbook contains common features found in each of the Design Exploration books, but specifically this material is presented in a need-to-know basis and so each chapter builds upon itself. This eliminates the amount of information the reader must know to successfully complete a task. Each chapter also accommodates those who appreciate alternative methods of learning information, providing both textually and visually succinct explanations of important concepts, step-by-step experiences, or for those who prefer to wander around, final project files, samples, and a section for further exploration. The following is a brief rundown of what is learned in each chapter:

Chapter 1: A Discovery Tour Right away, retouch a photo in Photoshop and discover the purpose of the Photoshop program.

Chapter 2: The Staging Area Take center stage and explore the workspace and navigational features of the program.

FEATURES

The following list provides some of the salient features of the text:

▶ Learning goals are clearly stated at the beginning of each chapter.

▶ Written to meet the needs of design students and professionals for a visually oriented introduction to image composition and the functions and tools of Photoshop.

▶ Client projects involve tools and techniques a designer might encounter on the job.

▶ Full-color format provides the most accurate depictions of software screen shots and contributing artists' works.

▶ "Exploring on Your Own" sections offer suggestions and sample lessons for further study of content covered in each chapter.

▶ "In Review" sections are provided at the end of each chapter to quiz a reader's understanding and retention of the material covered.

▶ A CD-ROM at the back of the book contains the support files to complete the exercises.

E.RESOURCE

This guide was developed to assist instructors in planning and implementing their instructional programs. It includes sample syllabi for using this book in either an 11- or 15-week semester. It also provides answers to the "In Review" questions, PowerPoint slides highlighting the main topics, and additional instructor resources.

ISBN: 1-4180-5260-4

FILE SETUP

Located in the back of this book is a CD-ROM containing all files for completing the lessons. These lesson files are compatible with Photoshop CS3. For a trial version of Photoshop CS3, visit *http://www.adobe.com/downloads/*.

Before starting the lessons, create a folder on your local computer. Name it **My Lessons** (or whatever name you prefer). From the CD, drag a copy of the lesson files to the folder. As you work on the lessons, open the lessons, assets, and sample files from this location. You can save your work in the same place.

HOW TO USE THIS TEXT

The features discussed in the following sections are found in the book.

▶ Charting Your Course and Goals

The introduction and chapter objectives start off each chapter. They describe the competencies the reader should achieve upon understanding the chapter.

▶ Don't Go There

These boxes highlight common pitfalls and explain ways to avoid them.

▶ Explorer Pages

These sections showcase the imagery, insights, and work-flow processes of successful graphic artists.

---

charting your course

If you were at a carnival, Chapter 1 would be the enticing gyp sy beckoning you into the tent of digital enchantment. It was only a teaser, offering a small taste of what Photoshop has to offer. In this chapter you will pull back the curtain, step inside the tent, adjust your eyes to the darkness, and become a part of the performance rather than remain a spectator. Here, you take center stage—where all the action happens—and explore the workspace and navigational features of the program.

goals

In this chapter you will:

- **Get comfortable with the Photoshop interface**
- **Set and delete preferences**
- **Navigate the workspace**

▶ Don't Go There!

Once you have an area selected, whatever you do next in the program—move, add a filter, paint, etc.—will be applied to that area only. On occasion, you might select something inadvertently (or forget it was selected) and then attempt to do something else, like paint on another layer. When this happens,

a warning circle comes up. See Figure 4–21. Do not freak out. Choose Select > Deselect from the menu bar to remove all selected areas (even those you cannot see), and then make sure the layer you want to modify is highlighted in the Layers panel.

figure | 4–21 |

Warning: You cannot do that! Deselect all and check to be sure you are on the layer you want to modify.

Explorer pages

NATASCHA ROEOESLI

About Natascha Roeoesli

Besides the fact her parents are photographers, Natascha has not had any specific art education. She did consider attending art school in Switzerland but felt it was not good enough even though she did make the acceptance test. Most of her knowledge comes from observing her surroundings. She loves to try to figure out why something works the way it does. Physics are an important part of understanding how colors work or how we see shapes and much more. Being self-educated is, in her opinion, a great advantage because it forces you to really understand what you are painting instead of learning theory by heart. "However, there are books" Natascha claims, "—like *Exploring Photoshop CS3* or theory books—that help you fill in the gaps you might not have elsewhere."

Natascha has worked for over two years for the game industry and, in addition, several fantasy authors and private clients.

To view more of her work, visit http://www.tascha.ch/.

Wax Dragon. Compliments of Natascha Roeoesli. In the tutorials section of her Web site (http://www.tascha.ch/), Natascha shares her techniques for creating such effects as the silky fabric on the female character in *Wax Dragon*.

About Natascha's Work

In her own words Natascha shares her artistic process in the creation of *Can't Stand the Light*.

"*Can't Stand the Light* started as normal pencil sketch where I brainstormed a few compositions and character tryouts.

"Once I had the general idea I used Adobe Photoshop and my Wacom tablet to rough in some guidelines to work from using a hard-edged brush, which imitates a ball pen or ink pen.

"I am much more of a painter than a drawer and think in shapes than lines. This is the reason I am normally not taking much time for sketches. The lines, however, help me to not make big anatomical mistakes and stay somewhat true to my initial idea.

"Once I do have the rough layout I copy this layer and hide it as a backup and create a new background layer, which I fill with the color I want to use for my ambient light (green for forest, blue for sky, and so on). The original sketch layer now gets painted on, starting with roughing in color using a brush with special settings, like 80% flow. This helps me to not paint-ing full opacity and lets the background color get mixed into everything I paint (most important: skin color). Switching the brushes during painting is also quite important.

"My paintings develop a lot while I work. They constantly change as I am trying out different hairdos or clothing com-binations for my characters. Even the color scheme for this changed drastically during the process. Using Photoshop's amazing color adjustment tools I shifted the colors of the almost finished painting and then worked some more with the changed color scheme.

"Using the Color Picker is something I do almost without a break. Picking colors from my background and mixing them ever so slightly with the main objects (or the other way around) helps to unify the painting.

"I also use a lot of layers. Mainly to keep the background, foreground, and main objects separated from each other. In this case I was able to correct a compositional error and move the character slightly more to the right from where she started out. I did this to give more focus to the hand and more space to the left."

Can't Stand the Light. Compliments of Natascha Roeoesli.

Summer. Compliments of Natascha Roeoesli.

▶ In Review and Exploring on Your Own

Review questions are located at the end of each chapter. They allow readers to assess their understanding of the chapter. The section "Exploring on Your Own" contains exercises that reinforce chapter material through practical application.

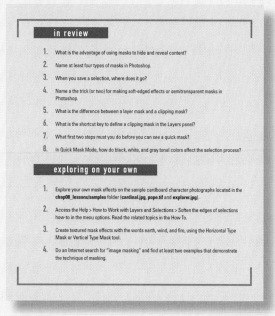

in review

1. What is the advantage of using masks to hide and reveal content?
2. Name at least four types of masks in Photoshop.
3. When you save a selection, where does it go?
4. Name a trick (or two) for making soft-edged effects or semitransparent masks in Photoshop.
5. What is the difference between a layer mask and a clipping mask?
6. What is the shortcut key to define a clipping mask in the Layers panel?
7. What first two steps must you do before you can see a quick mask?
8. In Quick Mask Mode, how do black, white, and gray tonal colors affect the selection process?

exploring on your own

1. Explore your own mask effects on the sample cardboard character photographs located in the **chap08_lessons/samples** folder (**cardinal.jpg, pope.tif** and **explorer.jpg**).
2. Access the Help > How to Work with Layers and Selections > Soften the edges of selections how-to in the menu options. Read the related topics in the How To.
3. Create textured mask effects with the words earth, wind, and fire, using the Horizontal Type Mask or Vertical Type Mask tool.
4. Do an Internet search for "image masking" and find at least two examples that demonstrate the technique of masking.

▶ Adventures in Design

These spreads contain client assignments showing readers how to approach a design project using the tools and design concepts taught in the book.

ABOUT THE AUTHORS

Annesa Hartman holds a master's degree in Teaching with Internet Technologies, focusing her atte ntion on instructional design for online technologies, and Web and graphic design concepts and programs. She is an Instructional Designer for Landmark College's Institute for Research and Training in Putney, Vt., where she designs and develops online courses for educators. For over 10 years she has taught computer graphic courses and is a freelance graphic designer with clients from around the world. She is the author of *Exploring Photoshop CS2, Exploring Illustrator CS2, Exploring Illustrator CS3,* and *Producing Interactive Television*. When she is not pushing pixels, she is performing in community theater and teaching yoga classes.

Ken Sholar holds a bachelor's degree in art from CSU Stanislaus. He is a lab manager at the MAGIC Lab, a computer lab dedicated to the advancement of art and technology, at Modesto Junior College (MJC), Calif. He has created online courseware for the Computer Graphics department at MJC and is also the author of *Exploring Illustrator CS3*. When not in cyberspace, he enjoys reading, creating art and wandering aimlessly in the Sierra Nevada foothills.

ACKNOWLEDGMENTS

Annesa Hartman:

It seems a dream that this book is now in its third edition and in full color. And not unlike any momentous task, it just would not have happened without the help of my friends, colleagues, and students. I wish to give special thanks to Ken Sholar, who with all energy, enthusiasm and creative talent took on the challenge of co-authoring this edition with me. Many, many thanks to all those who contributed content for the book's lessons, visual examples and "Adventures in Design," including Max Ruse, Geoff Burgess, Karen Kamenetzky, Bruce and Linda Lord, Terry Hartman, Darrel Anderson, Joel Hagen, Michael Dwyer, Glen Mitsui, Joe Summerhays, Natascha Roeoesli, Tim Warnock, Dave Garcez, Jeffrey Moring, and Brian Sinclair. Thanks always to Terry and Charmaine for keeping my spirits up during the depths of the writing process. And, finally much love to Dave Marx.

For their patient persistence (if there is such a thing), I also thank the staff at Thomson Delmar Learning. What a comfort to know that you are out there in full force promoting the Design Exploration series and making this experience worthwhile. Last, I would like to send a warm thank you to my mother, Carolyn Murov, whose photographic talent supplied many of the images found in the pages of this book.

Ken Sholar:

I want to thank Annesa Hartman for giving me the opportunity to participate in this literary journey. I also would like to thank Thomson Delmar Learning for its support and countless hours in bringing this book to fruition. I wish to give special thanks to those teachers that have guided and brought me here to this point in my life: Jim Griffin, Paul Pronoitis, Joel Hagen, Terry Hartman, and Richard Savini. And most of all, I want to thank my family, friends and loved ones for all their emotional support: my parents, Denise E. Yu, the Hartman family, the Tip Tankard crew, and the students, staff and faculty of the Computer Graphics and Computer Science departments at Modesto Junior College.

Thomson Delmar Learning and the authors would also like to thank Toni Toland for ensuring the technical accuracy of this text.

QUESTIONS AND FEEDBACK

Thomson Delmar Learning and the authors welcome your questions and feedback. If you have suggestions you think others would benefit from, please let us know and we will try to include them in the next edition.

To send us your questions and/or feedback, contact the publisher at:

Thomson Delmar Learning
Executive Woods
5 Maxwell Drive
Clifton Park, NY 12065
Attn: Media Arts & Design Team 800-998-7498

Or Annesa Hartman at:

Landmark College
Instructional and Graphic Designer
P.O. Box 820
River Road South
Putney, VT 05346
ahartman@landmark.edu

Or Ken Sholar at:

Modesto Junior College
435 College Ave.
Modesto, CA 95350
sholark@mjc.edu

Master Bedroom

| a discovery tour |

charting your course

We hope you have brushed up on your "ta-das," because you are in for a Harry Houdini of an experience—a venture into the digital wizardry of Adobe Photoshop. If there is only one program you should know as a graphic artist, Photoshop is it. And, if we begin to sound a bit highfalutin about its prospects, well, it is because we are. You can say Photoshop is the pinnacle (the Big Daddy) of all computer graphic programs, proven to handle in numerous ways just about any type of graphic image. In this chapter you will get hands-on practice with Photoshop itself and experience a first taste of its illusionary talents. Depending on your learning style, you can choose to "do" the lesson, "read" the lesson, or both. The trick is to get you started on the experience of Photoshop and then show you what makes it so magical.

goals

In this chapter you will:

- **Get excited about Photoshop**

- **Fix a bad photo and optimize it for the Web**

- **Explore some of Photoshop's tools and features**

- **Discover the purpose of Photoshop**

A MAGIC TOUR

No matter what kind of multimedia project you might be up against, Photoshop more often than not is going to play a pivotal role in the creation process. Think of it as the Swiss Army Knife of the digital imaging world. It will come to your rescue when the lighting for those wedding pictures is less than perfect—to remove the unwanted blemish on the bride's cheek or superimpose the indisposed from the family portrait. Take for instance the photograph shown on the left in Figure 1–1, which was taken by a point-and-shoot camera. The film was digitized on a CD and was later handed to us to put on the Web. To tell you the truth, the photo quality was dreadful. However, with our bag full of tricks (Photoshop), a wave of our magic wand (computer mouse), and $50 added to our client's invoice, we produced what looked like the real thing—a room in a fine country inn, not a room in a rundown shack. OK, so maybe the differences in the two photos are not that extreme, but our point is that with a little magic, and about 15 minutes of your time, you can make a "ho-hum" image look "oh-wow" and download it fast from the Web.

figure |1–1|

The original photo of a room in a country inn (left), and a 15-minute makeover version using Photoshop (right).

Lesson: The 15-Minute Photo Makeover

It is said that a magician never reveals her tricks, until now. In this lesson you will learn how we fixed up the country inn photo (see Figure 1–1) and made it Web ready. We will not get into too many specifics about the program just yet—there is plenty of that to come. However, you will learn enough secrets to get the idea that Photoshop is not just hocus-pocus.

Importing and Cropping the Photo

1. Open the Photoshop program. (A trial version is available for download at *http://www.adobe.com/products/photoshop*.) Install the program onto your hard drive.

2. Choose File > Open from the menu bar, and on your local hard drive browse for the Exploring PhotoshopCS3 **lessons/chap01_lessons/assets** folder. Open the file **masterbed.tif**.

> Note: As mentioned in the Preface, to save your work, you must make a copy of the chapter lessons to your local hard drive and select files from that location.

3. Press Shift-Tab to hide unnecessary window panels (at least for the time being). Visible should be your imported image of **masterbed.tif**, the toolbox to the left of the interface, and the tool Options bar and menu bar located at the top. See Figure 1–2.

figure |1–2|

The Photoshop interface (Mac).

4. From the menu bar at the top of the screen, choose View > Fit on Screen to enlarge the photo to the Photoshop window size.

5. Select Photoshop > Preferences > Units & Rulers (Mac), or Edit > Preferences > Units & Rulers (Windows), from the menu bar.

6. In the Preferences dialog box, set the Rulers units to "pixels" and click OK. See Figure 1–3. (If your rulers are not showing, select View > Rulers (Command/Ctrl R).)

figure 1–3

Set the Rulers units to pixels.

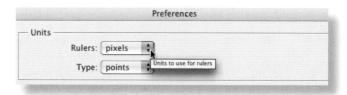

figure 1–4

Select the Crop tool in the toolbox.

7. Select the Crop tool in the toolbox. See Figure 1–4. With the Crop tool you can extract unnecessary or unflattering parts from an image.

8. In the tool Options bar found along the top of your image, just under the menu bar, type in the following parameters for the Crop tool. After entering a value, you may press the Tab key to move the cursor to the next field (see Figure 1–5).

- *Width:* 550 pixels
- *Height:* 350 pixels
- *Resolution:* 72 pixels/inch

figure 1–5

Enter parameters for the Crop tool in the Options bar.

9. From the upper, left corner of the image, click and drag with the Crop tool to the lower, right corner of the image. Select the entire image except for an unwanted section along the right edge. See Figure 1–6. If you feel the crop was not done right, press ESC and try again.

figure 1–6

Crop the image.

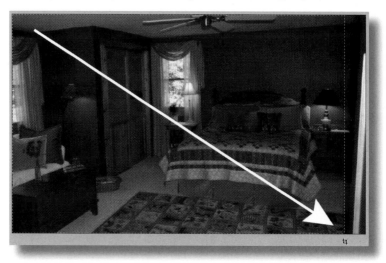

10. Click on the Crop tool icon in the tool-box to bring up the Crop dialog box. See Figure 1–7. Select the Crop option to execute the crop. (Alternatively, you can double-click inside the selected area or press Return (Mac) or Enter (Windows) to execute the crop.)

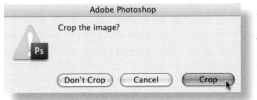

figure | 1–7 |

Execute the crop action.

> **Note:** Argh! What if you make a mistake? From the menu bar, select Window > History to open the History panel, if it is not already opened. Each step you perform in Photoshop is recorded in the History panel (up to 20 states by default). To go back a step, click on the state above the step you just made. For instance, from the Crop state, click up to the Open state to revert the file. See Figure 1–8. You can also press Command-Z (Mac) or Ctrl-Z (Windows) to undo your last step.

11. Choose View > Actual Pixels to see the final cropped image.

12. Choose File > Save As. Make sure you are set to save in your **chap01_lessons** folder (copied from the text's CD) when the Save As menu pops up. For Format, choose Photoshop (top of the list). Your filename should read **masterbed.psd** (the native file format for Photoshop).

figure | 1–8 |

The History panel—a life saver!

Fixing the Color

1. You have probably noticed that the color of this image is too red. That can be fixed in one easy step: choose Image > Adjustments > Auto Color. Ta-da!

2. To lighten the image, choose Image > Adjustments > Levels. The Levels histogram comes up. This determines the lights and darks (brightness and contrast) in an image. You will learn more about levels in later chapters. Right now, move the white arrow (on the right, lower side of the graph) inward until you get 200 in the Input Levels right box. Click OK. See Figure 1–9.

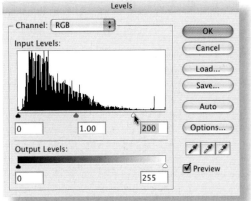

figure | 1–9 |

Adjust the photograph's brightness and contrast using Levels.

> **Note:** You may have noticed the Brightness/Contrast choice found under Image > Adjustments. We chose not to use this, as Levels gives us more control over our image.

figure | 1–10 |

The photo is located on one layer; the default layer called "Background."

Creating a Shadow and Border Effect

1. Choose Window > Layers to open the Layers panel. Layers organize information in Photoshop. Right now we only have one layer—our photo. See Figure 1–10.

2. In the Layers palette, double-click on the Background layer that contains the photo. The New Layer dialog box comes up. Type in **master bedroom** and click OK. (This renames the Background layer and unlocks it for editing.)

figure | 1–11 |

Increase the canvas size.

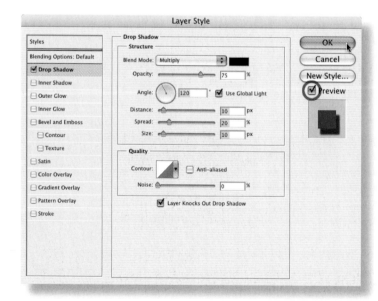

3. From the menu bar, choose Image > Canvas Size. For Width, type in **590** (pixels), and for Height, type in **390** (pixels). This will increase each side of the canvas by 20 pixels. On a side note, the Anchor box allows you to position where the current image will be on the new canvas. Let us keep it in the center for now. Click OK. See Figure 1–11.

4. From the menu bar, choose Layer > Layer Style > Drop Shadow. Select Preview on the right side of the Layer Style window, so you can view the changes you make in the dialog box directly on the document. Enter the following parameters and remember to use the Tab key to move among them quickly (see Figure 1–12):
   - *Angle:* 120 degrees
   - *Distance:* 10 pixels
   - *Spread:* 20%
   - *Size:* 10 pixels

5. Click OK.

> **Note:** In the Layers panel, notice the small "fx" icon next to the layer name. This indicates that there are effects (i.e., the drop shadow) on the image. To edit the effects, simply double-click on the "fx" icon to open the Layer Style dialog box.

figure | 1–12 |

Create a drop shadow.

6. Now, let us select just the photo and not the background, which can be tricky. In the Layers panel, place the cursor over the layer thumbnail (the small image in the layer). A pointer hand icon will appear. Press Command (Mac) or Ctrl (Windows) and click on the thumbnail. The photo (the object in the selected layer) will be selected in the document. This is indicated by a series of moving, dashed lines around the edge of the photo, also known as "marching ants." See Figure 1–13.

figure |1–13|

Marching ants indicate a selected area.

7. From the menu bar, choose Edit > Stroke. Enter the following parameters (see Figure 1–14):

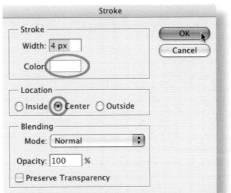

figure |1–14|

The Stroke options box.

- *Width:* 4 pixels
- *Color:* Click on the color box to open the Color Picker and choose white.
- *Location:* Center

> **Note:** If Edit > Stroke is dimmed and therefore unavailable, be sure the **master bedroom** layer is highlighted in the Layers panel.

8. Click OK.

9. Choose Select > Deselect to view the white border you just created around the photo. If you see a checkered background, you can remove this to better see your image by going to Photoshop > Preferences > Transparency & Gamut (Mac) or Edit > Preferences > Transparency & Gamut (Windows) and change the Grid Size to None.

10. Save your file.

> **Note:** If you receive a Maximize Compatibility Photoshop Format options dialog box, keep the option selected to ensure compatibility of this file with previous versions of Photoshop.

Creating a Title Effect

1. Select the Horizontal Type tool in the toolbox. See Figure 1–15.

2. In the Options bar, set the font type to Arial or Verdana, depending on what is available on your computer. Set the font size to 24 points. For color, click the color box in the options toolbox (see Figure 1–16) to open the Color Picker.

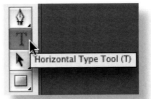

figure |1–15|

The Horizontal Type tool.

figure |1–16|

Change the font and font size, and set the text color.

figure |1–17|

The Eyedropper tool takes a sampling of color from the photograph.

3. Move the Color Picker dialog box to the right side of the screen, so you can see your image. With the Color Picker open, notice that your cursor changes to an eyedropper when you move it over the photo area. See Figure 1–17.

4. Move the Eyedropper tool over a light-brown area of the closet door frame in the photo and click to take a sample of the color (see Figure 1–17). The color is recorded in the Color Picker. Click OK to close the Color Picker.

5. With the Horizontal Type tool, click in the upper, left corner of the document. A blinking cursor will appear. Type in **Master Bedroom**.

6. Choose Layer > Layer Style > Outer Glow. Leave the default setting for the outer glow (unless you want to play on your own!) and click OK. See Figure 1–18.

figure |1–18|

The final, glowing title.

figure |1–19|

The Move tool.

7. Select the Move tool in the toolbox (see Figure 1–19). Place the Move tool over the text and click and drag it to a position of your liking on the photograph.

8. Save your file. You are almost there.

Optimizing the Image for the Web

1. OK, one last detail. Let us prepare this photograph so it can be used on the Web. We need to do two things: make it smaller in file size (compress it), so it will download quickly for those of us with slow Internet connections, and save it in JPEG format, which is a file format the Web can display (you will learn more about that in Chapter 11). For now, choose File > Save for Web & Devices. The document opens up in a new window.

2. Select the 2-Up option (see Figure 1–20). On the left side is your original image. On the right is the image you will compress for the Web. By having them side-by-side, you can compare the quality of the Web image with the original as you adjust the compression settings.

figure | 1–20 |

Select the 2-Up option in the Save For Web window.

3. In the Optimize panel, set the image quality to JPEG Low, next to the word **Preset** (see Figure 1–21). Note how the quality of the image on the right deteriorates compared to the image on the left. Look closely at the title text in particular.

figure | 1–21 |

The Optimize panel properly prepares the image for Web publication.

Note: If you are having difficulty seeing parts of an image, use the Hand tool on the left side of the window to navigate the image view right, left, up, or down.

4. Now, set the quality to JPEG High. Much better. We know you are wondering why you should ever use the JPEG Low setting. Well, look at the box with numbers right below the two images. You will note the lower the setting, the smaller the number, allowing for a faster download (more on this in Chapter 11).

5. Take a look at the estimated download time of the right-hand image at the bottom of the image's window. See Figure 1–22.

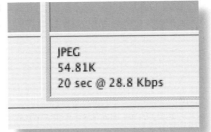

figure | 1–22 |

View the size and estimated download time of the Web-formatted image.

6. Click Save and save the **masterbed.jpg** file in your **lessons** folder—Photoshop automatically adds the jpg extension for you. The image is now ready to be placed on a Web page. See the completed image, shown in Figure 1–23.

figure | 1–23 |

The completed photograph—it is magic!

7. Select File > Save to save the final Photoshop (**.psd**) file. You did it!

PHOTOSHOP—IN BRIEF

As you have probably surmised by its name, fixing up photos is the essence of what Photoshop can do; what it was originally intended to do since its beginning in 1987 with the brothers Thomas Knoll and John Knoll and in 1990 when Adobe first licensed the product. Now Photoshop and its immense toolset have grown to be a vital part of any magician's repertoire—something you will begin to discover in the lessons of this book. No animator, illustrator, game developer, scientist, multimedia developer, or Web designer could survive without Photoshop. It has a way with working with one of the main ingredients of digital image construction—pixels. These are the tiny picture elements that, when placed together in a grid, make all the images we see on a computer screen. Chapter 3 gets into greater detail about pixels, among other important graphic essentials. For now, if we were to sum up what Photoshop does best in four simple bullet points, here is what you would get:

- Manipulates photographs and other digital imagery, such as select, cut, paste, clone, colorize, compress, erase, transform, and mask, and adds special effects
- Composites, layers, and blends photographs and images
- Draws and paints
- Converts photographs and imagery into different formats for different purposes, such as for use on the Web, for video, to print, and to import into other programs

SUMMARY

Photoshop is the "must know" of all computer graphic software packages. For the successful graphic artist, it is as vital a prop as are a deck of cards and a white rabbit to a magician. In this chapter you discovered one of Photoshop's greatest and most used secrets: how it can fix a badly exposed photograph and make it Web presentable. From here, there is only more magic to come.

in review

1. What does the command Shift-Tab do?

2. What is so great about the History panel?

3. In general, what are levels in Photoshop?

4. What are layers? How are they useful?

5. What are "marching ants"?

6. Name at least three uses for Photoshop.

exploring on your own

1. Visit the Photoshop area of the Adobe site at *http://www.adobe.com/products/photoshop/main.html*.

2. The programmers of software packages such as Photoshop love to play tricks and hide fun, little surprises within the programs they create. These surprises are called "Easter eggs," and you can find them in Photoshop if you know where to look and what to do.

   Here is how to find the infamous magician Merlin. In Photoshop, go to Window > Layers (if not already open). Hold down Option/Alt and click on the small arrow with three lines in the upper, right corner of the Layers window to open the layer options. Choose Palette Options in the drop-down menu. Merlin lives!

Tyrone

©2007 Carolyn Murov

| the staging area |

charting your course

If you were at a carnival, Chapter 1 would be the enticing gyp sy beckoning you into the tent of digital enchantment. It was only a teaser, offering a small taste of what Photoshop has to offer. In this chapter you will pull back the curtain, step inside the tent, adjust your eyes to the darkness, and become a part of the performance rather than remain a spectator. Here, you take center stage—where all the action happens—and explore the workspace and navigational features of the program.

goals

In this chapter you will:

- **Get comfortable with the Photoshop interface**
- **Set and delete preferences**
- **Navigate the workspace**

STAGING

Before you produce your first Photoshop masterpiece, it helps to get acquainted with the program's interface, or work area, and set it up to your desired specifications. In theater, this process is called staging. First, you will get familiar with such props as the document area, tool-box, menu bar, panels, and workspace. Second, you will practice using the navigational tools, avoiding any chance of getting lost among the bright lights of your virtual stage.

Lesson 1: Interface Highlights

Learn your way around in this lesson.

Identifying Props

1. Open Photoshop.

> **Note:** If a dialog box comes up asking if you would like to customize your color settings, choose No.

2. Choose File > New from menu bar. Enter the following information (see Figure 2–1):

- *Name:* Type **myfile**
- *Preset size:* Choose Default Photoshop Size
- *Color Mode:* Choose RGB Color, 8 bit
- *Background Contents:* Choose White

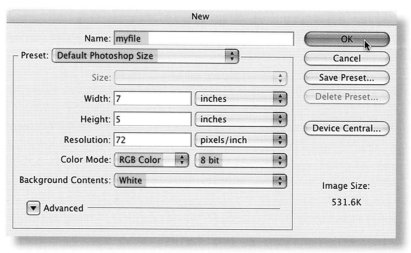

figure | 2–1 |

New Document options box.

3. The Photoshop interface may look different depending on whether you are a Macintosh or a Windows user. The main props, however, are the same. Compare your Photoshop interface with Figure 2–2 (Mac) and Figure 2–3 (Windows), and note where the various parts of the program are located.

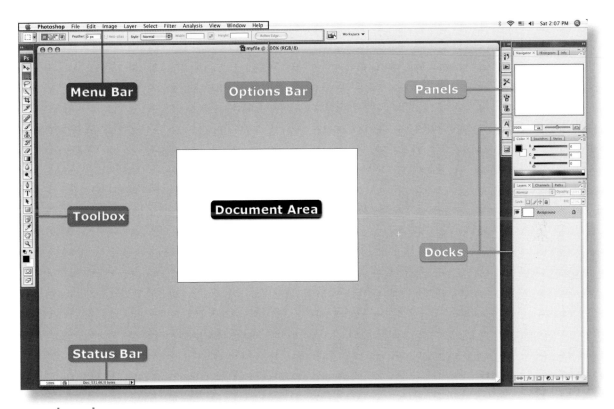

figure | 2–2 |

The Photoshop interface (Mac).

- *Document area:* When you created a new file in step 2, you specified properties for a document area. This is the blank area in the center of the interface where you do all of your work (consider this your canvas or stage). At the top of the document area is a document title bar, which provides information about the document, such as its name, current magnification, color mode, and bit depth. It is likely you will have many document windows open at the same time. To see which is which, simply look at the document title bars. See Figure 2–4. Each image you open or create in Photoshop will have different information in its document title bar. To see what images are open, go to Window in the menu bar. The open images are shown at the bottom of the list with a check mark next to the current document. To bring a file up front in the document area, simply click on its filename in the list.

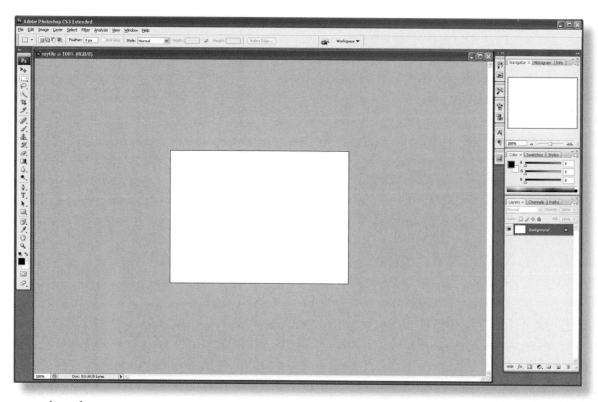

figure |2-3|

The Photoshop interface (Windows).

- *Menu bar:* Along the top of the interface is the menu bar, which contains all of the commands to perform certain tasks: File, Edit, Image, Layer, Select, Filter, View, Window, and Help. In CS3 Extended, there is an Analysis

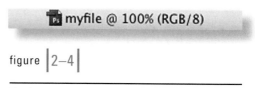

figure |2-4|

The document title bar shows specific information about an open document.

menu command as well. The commands are categorized so you can find them easily (so do not bother memorizing them all!). For example, if you want to open a panel window, go to Window and a list of options will pop up. To make global adjustments to an image, go to Image. To edit, go to Edit. You get the idea.

- *Tools Panel/Toolbox:* Located by default to the left of the work area is the toolbox. This is where you choose the tools you need to select, edit, modify, and create your Photoshop masterpiece (see Figure 2-5 for tool names and shortcut keys). In CS3, the toolbox is displayed in a long, single column. If you wish to use the double-column toolbox from prior versions of Photoshop, click on the light gray double arrow at the

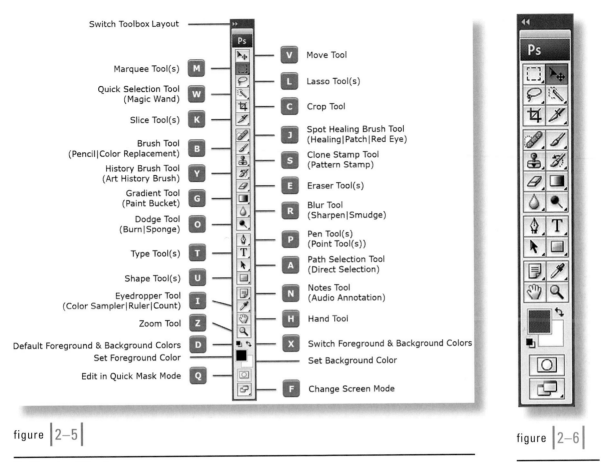

Switch Toolbox Layout

Marquee Tool(s) — M
Quick Selection Tool — W
(Magic Wand)
Slice Tool(s) — K
Brush Tool — B
(Pencil|Color Replacement)
History Brush Tool — Y
(Art History Brush)
Gradient Tool — G
(Paint Bucket)
Dodge Tool — O
(Burn|Sponge)
Type Tool(s) — T
Shape Tool(s) — U
Eyedropper Tool — I
(Color Sampler|Ruler|Count)
Zoom Tool — Z
Default Foreground & Background Colors — D
Set Foreground Color
Edit in Quick Mask Mode — Q

V — Move Tool
L — Lasso Tool(s)
C — Crop Tool
J — Spot Healing Brush Tool
(Healing|Patch|Red Eye)
S — Clone Stamp Tool
(Pattern Stamp)
E — Eraser Tool(s)
R — Blur Tool
(Sharpen|Smudge)
P — Pen Tool(s)
(Point Tool(s))
A — Path Selection Tool
(Direct Selection)
N — Notes Tool
(Audio Annotation)
H — Hand Tool
X — Switch Foreground & Background Colors
Set Background Color
F — Change Screen Mode

figure | 2–5 |

The Photoshop CS3 toolbox

figure | 2–6 |

The classic toolbox.

top of the toolbox. This will toggle between the new toolbox (see Figure 2-5) and the classic toolbox (see Figure 2-6). Tool icons with a black arrow in the corner contain hidden, related tools. With your cursor, click and hold down on a tool's icon to reveal the other tool choices (see Figure 2–7). You will be using the toolbox a lot, so always keep it handy. If you close it by mistake you can reopen it from the Window menu. You will learn about most of the tools in the next chapters, but if you are the curious type and cannot wait, choose Help > Photoshop Help on the menu bar, select the section Workspace, and review Tools.

- *Options bar:* Most of the tools selected in the toolbox have options. These are displayed in the Options bar, located along the top of the Document window, below the menu bar. The Options bar is context sensitive, which means it displays different information depending on what tool is selected. Try it out: select some tools in the toolbox and watch the content change in the Options bar with each new selection.

- *Panels:* Panels (referred to as palettes in previous versions of Photoshop), usually located to the right of the work area, help you modify and monitor your images. By default, panels are tabbed together in like-minded groups that can, in turn, be placed in docks.

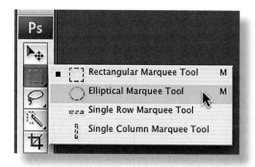

figure |2-7|

Reveal hidden tools in the toolbox.

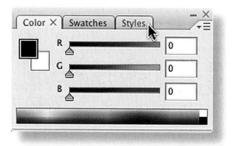

figure |2-8|

Panels grouped by similar topic. Select a tab to bring a panel forward.

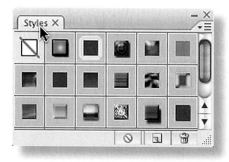

figure |2-9|

A panel can be separated from its group by clicking and dragging the title tab to a different area of the workspace.

However, you can separate them. Simply click on their title tabs and drag them to another area of the workspace. Of course, you can dock any panel back into a group by dragging its title bar over the desired panel group. See Figure 2–8 and Figure 2–9. If you want your panels out of the way, so you can better see your workspace, just hide them by pressing Shift-Tab. To bring them back, press Shift-Tab again. You can also close panels by selecting the Close button in the up per-right corner of any of the panel windows. To bring a panel back after you have closed it, go to Window on the menu bar and select the panel name.

- *Docks:* Photoshop CS3 offers a handy way to organize your favorite panels called docks. Docks are located on the right and/or left sides of the screen and can hold a single panel or groups of panels. Docks can be expanded or collapsed by clicking on the double arrows at the top of the dock. See Figure 2–10. To reorganize docks, drag the title tabs of any panel window into or on the border of a dock. On the right side of the Options bar, you will see a workspace button. If you click and hold down on the button, a drop-down list will appear with a list of preset workspaces to meet your image creation needs. A button placed to the left of the workspace button (between the workspace button and Options bar) provides access to the Adobe Bridge program, a stand-alone application for file browsing and management across Adobe's Creative Suite programs. Alternatively, get to the Bridge program by choosing File > Browse. Among many features, Bridge allows you to

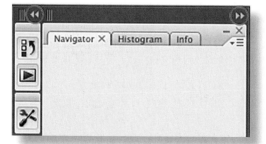

figure |2-10|

Quickly expand or collapse docks.

figure |2– 11|

The really cool Adobe Bridge. Find a file quickly and visually!

quickly browse for a file on your local hard drive, and what is really cool is that it provides a visual thumbnail of the files for easy selection. Check it out! See Figure 2–11.

- *Status bar:* The status bar is located at the bottom-left edge of the Document window. It shows you information about a document's size and dimensions, the current tool being used and its magnification level, and more. See Figure 2–12.

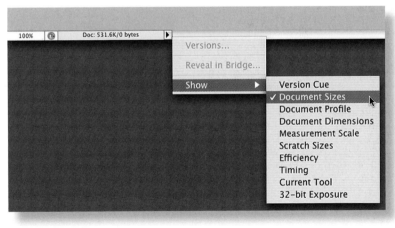

figure |2–12|

The status bar options.

If you click on the narrow bar to the left of the status bar options list, a visual comes up showing you the document size if it were to be printed on an 8.5-by-11-inch sheet. See Figure 2–13. We find this visual to be incredibly useful before we print a document

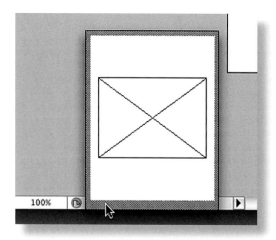

figure |2–13|

Document size if printed on 8.5-by-11-inch sheet.

figure |2–14|

Context menu for the Marquee tool. Right-click (Windows) or Ctrl-click (Mac) to get to the context menus.

because the document size you see on the screen is not necessarily the size it will be printed on paper. Photoshop can be pretty deceptive in this way. It has something to do with a thing called resolution, which you will learn about in later chapters.

- *Context menus:* Context menus appear when you right-click your mouse (Windows), or Ctrl-click (Mac). They are drop-down menus that give you quick access to various features of a tool you might be using. See Figure 2–14.

Marking the Stage

1. Place the cursor (do not click!) over the Rectangle tool in the toolbox. Note that a text equivalent of the tool name appears. This is called a tool tip. Next to the tool name there is also a shortcut key indicated. See Figure 2–15. (If your tool tips are not showing, you can turn them on using Photoshop > Preferences > Interface (Mac) or Edit > Preferences > Interface (Windows).)

2. Click and hold on the Rectangle tool to open other shape tool options. See Figure 2–16. Select the Ellipse tool.

3. Click on the Foreground color swatch in the toolbox to choose a color. See Figure 2–17.

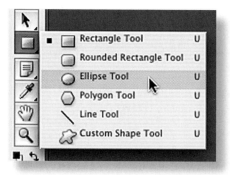

figure |2–16|

Click and hold on the Rectangle tool to reveal other shape options.

figure |2–15|

The tool tip for the Rectangle tool is revealed.

4. Select a color in the Color Picker and click OK. See Figure 2–18.

figure |2–17|

Set a foreground color.

5. Click and drag on the Document window to create an elliptical shape. Draw four or five shapes of different sizes. To create a perfect circle, hold down Shift as you click and drag to make the shape. See Figure 2–19.

> **Note:** If you want to undo something, use the History panel (Window > History, if it is not already open). Each step you perform in Photoshop is recorded in the History panel (up to 20 states by default). To go back a step, click on the state above the step you just made.

Color Picker (Foreground Color)

new

current

OK

Cancel

Add To Swatches

Color Libraries

○ H: 0 °   ○ L: 47
○ S: 75 %   ○ a: 60
○ B: 80 %   ○ b: 39
○ R: 204   C: 14 %
○ G: 51   M: 94 %
○ B: 51   Y: 88 %
cc3333   K: 4 %

☐ Only Web Colors

figure |2–18|

Select a color from the Color Picker.

figure |2–19|

Create elliptical shapes.

6. Unless you are up for playing around some more with this file, we are done with marking up the stage. However, save the file for use in the next lesson. Choose File > Save As. For Format, choose Photoshop. Name the file **myfile.psd** and save it to your **lessons** folder.

> Note: You might be wondering, "What's the '.psd' at the end of my filename?" This is the native file extension for all Photoshop files. If you see a file with this extension on the end, you know it was created in Adobe Photoshop.

Lesson 2: Customize Your Experience

Photoshop is smart—it remembers what you like. Every time you open it and do things like drag panels into your dock, set ruler units, or change how your cursor displays, Photoshop saves these preferences in a Preferences file located on your local hard drive. This is great when you want to reopen the program on your computer and have everything exactly where you left it. Let us show you how this works.

> Note: You can also save the arrangement of your favorite workspaces—the setup of panels, menus, and keyboard shortcuts—to your liking (see No. 1 of the Exploring On Your Own section at the end of this chapter).

Setting Preferences

1. Open Photoshop.

2. Choose File > Open and find the file **myfile.psd**.

> Note: If you do not have **myfile.psd**, choose **chap2L2.psd** in the **chap02_lessons** folder.

3. Close every panel window (except for the toolbox and the Layers panel) by clicking on the Close icon in the title bar of each panel. See Figure 2–20. (Choose Window > Layers to open the Layers panel, if you closed it accidentally.)

figure |2–20|

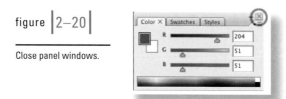

Close panel windows.

4. Select the layer called **Shape 1**.

5. In the Layers panel, click the black arrow with three horizontal lines in the upper-right corner of the window to open the panel's options. Choose Blending Options from the drop-down menu. See Figure 2–21.

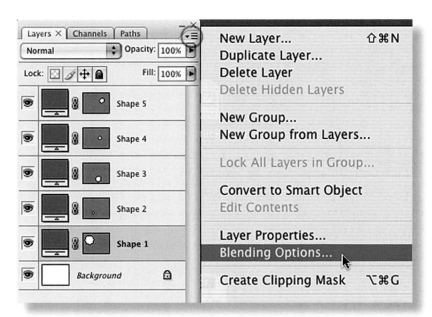

figure |2–21|

Options for the Layers panel.

6. In the Layer Style dialog box, choose the Drop Shadow and Bevel and Emboss style options. See Figure 2–22. Be sure Preview is selected in the dialog box, so you can see the styles applied automatically to the document. Click OK.

7. Select other layers (**Shape 2, Shape 3, Shape 4**, etc.) and apply other styles found in the Layer Styles dialog box. For example, choose the Outer Glow and Satin styles.

> Note: Yes, we know, the Layer Style dialog box can be overwhelming—no worries. We guarantee this will eventually be one of your favorite places to visit in Photoshop.

8. Without really knowing it, you have already been setting some file preferences. To set some more use the Preferences dialog box. Choose Photoshop > Preferences > Cursors (Mac) or Edit > Preferences > Cursors (Windows). Any change you make in this box is recorded in a preferences file for the next time you open the program. There are a lot of preference options. We will only tinker with a few. However, it is a good idea to look through all of them in case you want to make a change later.

9. Under the Cursors option, go to Other Cursors and select Precise. This changes the cursor of a selected tool from its standard icon to a more precise, crosshair indicator. See Figure 2–23. This crosshair indicates a precision cursor; that is, the center of the cursor is the exact spot where you will select, draw, or edit. This is much more accurate than an icon cursor. What if you like working with both cursors? Simple! Choose the Standard cursor in Other Cursors and use the Caps Lock key to toggle between the crosshair indicator and the regular cursor. For now though, let us keep it on Precise to show the advantage of Preferences.

figure |2–22|

Select style options.

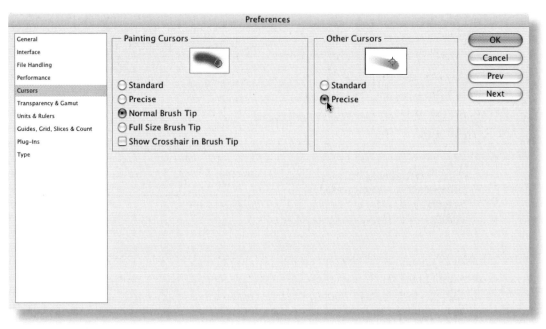

figure |2–23|

Change preferences in the Preferences dialog box.

10. Click OK to close the Preferences window.

11. Save your file as **myfile2.psd**.

12. Choose Photoshop > Quit Photoshop (Mac) or File > Exit (Windows) to shut down the program.

13. Reopen the program and your saved **myfile2.psd**. Note that your preferences have not changed. Precise cursors are still indicated in the Preferences dialog box, and the Layers panel is still open on your workspace.

Deleting Preferences

1. If you want to go back to Photoshop's default Preferences settings, first close Photoshop by choosing Photoshop > Quit Photoshop (Mac) or File > Exit (Windows).

2. Now, depending if you are on a Mac or a Windows computer, do one of the following:

- Press and hold Option-Command-Shift (Mac OS) or Alt-Control-Shift (Windows) immediately after launching Photoshop.

> **Note:** You must press the keys after Photoshop has started, but before the program actually opens. You will be prompted to delete the current settings file. See Figure 2–24.

Alternatively:

- In Windows, go to the **Documents and Settings\username\Application Data\Adobe\Adobe Photoshop CS3\ Adobe Photoshop CS3 Settings** folder. Delete the **Adobe Photoshop CS3 Prefs.psp** file.

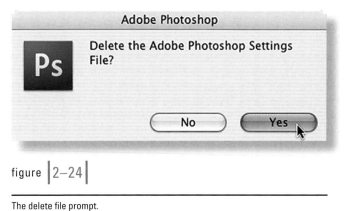

figure |2–24|

The delete file prompt.

> **Note:** Before deleting the preferences file, you might want to rename it and move it to the desktop as a safety copy.

- In Mac OS, go to the **Preferences** folder in the **System** folder (Mac OS 9.x) or **Library** folder under the username (Mac OS X), open the **Adobe Photoshop CS3 Settings** folder and place the **Adobe Photoshop CS3 Prefs.psp** file in the trash.

> **Note:** Before deleting the preferences file, you might want to rename it and move it to the desktop as a safety copy.

3. Once you have deleted the preferences file, reopen Photoshop to view the default setup. It will look something like that shown in Figure 2–25.

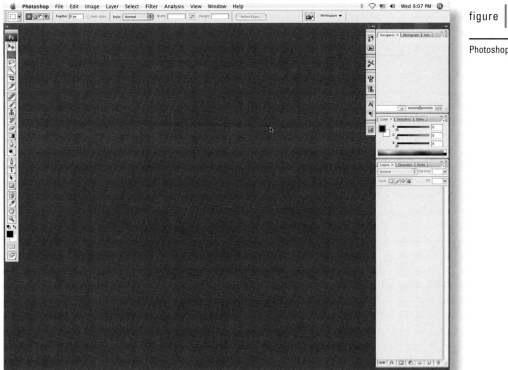

figure |2–25|

Photoshop with default setup.

SEEING IS BELIEVING

Have you ever been in the unfortunate situation where you paid $60 to see your favorite rock star in concert only to find yourself in the farthest row of the concert hall wishing you had a telescope in your back pocket? Well, you will be happy to know you will never have that problem working in Photoshop. No matter how many layers of objects you find yourself accumulating, there is a tool to help you see clearly where you are and what you are doing. In this next lesson, you will get up-close-and-personal with Photoshop's navigational features, such as the Hand and Zoom tools, the Navigator panel, and the screen and view modes.

Lesson 3: Navigational Features

Magnification Tools

1. In Photoshop, open the file **chap2L3.psd** in the **chap02_lessons** folder.

> **Note:** If you receive a dialog box stating, "Some text layers might need to be updated . . ." choose Update.

2. Choose View > Fit on Screen to magnify the image to fit in the window area. Note that the document title bar indicates the current magnification of the image. See Figure 2–26. This number varies depending on what view you have indicated for the document. For example, choose View > Print Size, which shows you the image size if it were to be printed (a number of factors influence how an image is viewed on screen, which will be covered in Chapter 3).

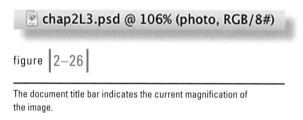

figure |2–26|

The document title bar indicates the current magnification of the image.

3. Choose View > Actual Pixels. This shows you the image size at 100% of the screen resolution (you will learn more about resolution in Chapter 3).

4. Select the Zoom tool in the toolbox. See Figure 2–27.

figure |2–27|

The Zoom tool.

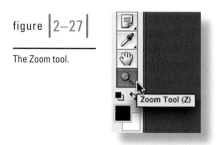

5. Click once with the Zoom tool over the image. It zooms in. Click again to zoom even closer.

6. Hold down Option (Mac) or Alt (Windows) to reverse the Zoom tool (note the minus sign in the Zoom tool cursor). Continue to hold down Option/Alt as you click once on the artwork to zoom back out. Click three more times to zoom out even further.

7. Let us zoom into a particular area of the photograph. With the Zoom tool selected, click and drag, from upper-left to lower-right, a rectangular shape over the copyright notice in the lower-left corner of the document. With this area marqueed, let go, and note how the area selected zooms in close. Whoa! See Figure 2–28.

figure |2–28|

Select an area to zoom close.

8. Select the Horizontal Type tool in the toolbox. Then click and drag over the text **2003** to select it (you will know when you can select type because the cursor changes from an I-beam with a box around it to a plain I-beam). Change the text to **2007**. See Figure 2–29.

figure |2–29|

Change the text.

9. Select the Hand tool in the toolbox (the tool right next to the Zoom tool in classic view, or just above it in single-column view). Click and drag with the Hand tool over the document, pushing it down until you see the **Tyrone** text at the top of the photo.

10. In the Layers panel, select the layer called **Tyrone**. Change the blending mode for the text from Normal to Color Burn. See Figure 2–30. Note that the text blends with the background colors of the photo.

> **Note:** There are a lot of different types of blending modes. Feel free to explore the others (such as Difference and Luminosity). Blending modes are used a lot, so this will not be the last time you get to play with them.

11. Be sure the Hand tool is selected in the toolbox. Note the options available for the Hand tool in the Options bar right below the menu bar. In the Options bar, select Fit Screen (alternatively, you can choose from the menu bar View > Fit on Screen, double-click on the Hand tool in the toolbox, or press Command 0 (Mac) or Ctrl 0 (Windows)). See Figure 2–31.

figure |2–30|

Located at the top of the Layers panel is the drop-down menu to change the blending modes of a layer.

figure |2–31|

The options bar for the Hand tool.

The Navigator Panel

1. The Navigator is another way to get a good view of your work. Choose Window > Navigator to open the Navigator panel (if it is not already open). Note in the panel window a small view of the image with a red border around it. See Figure 2–32.

figure |2–32|

The Navigator panel.

2. In the Navigator panel, slide the small arrow in the lower part of the window to the right to magnify the document or to the left to reduce it. Note that the red border adjusts in the viewing window to indicate what area is viewable in the document.

> Note: As an alternative to moving the slider to zoom in and out, you can click on the mountain-looking icons on each side of the slider. You can also type in a zoom percentage in the lower-left corner of the Navigator panel.

3. Magnify the image by sliding the arrow in the Navigator panel to the right. The red border area should grow smaller in the window.

4. Locate a specific area of the image by placing the cursor over the red border area in the Navigator panel (note that the cursor changes to the Hand tool). Now, click and drag the red border area.

Screen Modes

1. Choose View > Fit on Screen to see the complete image.

2. In the toolbox (lower part), click and hold down on the Change Screen Mode icon and select the Maximized Screen Mode option. See Figure 2–33.

3. Try Full Screen Mode with Menu bar.

4. Try Full Screen Mode.

5. Go back to Standard Screen Mode.

6. Close the file. You are done with this lesson.

figure |2–33|

There are four screen mode options located in the lower part of the toolbox. From top to bottom they are: Standard Screen Mode, Maximized Screen Mode, Full Screen Mode with Menu Bar, and Full Screen Mode (no menu bar).

SUMMARY

This chapter familiarized you with the Photoshop staging area—the workspace and navigational elements of the program. You also learned how to set your own preferences and, if necessary, delete them. Additionally, you got a first insight into how easy (dare we say "magical") it is to do such useful things as change your cursor icon, create a drop shadow behind a shape, and blend the colors of two layers.

in review

1. What does Shift-Tab do?

2. What does **.psd** at the end of a filename indicate?

3. What is Adobe Bridge? How is it useful?

4. What is the difference between View > Fit on Screen and View > Print Size?

5. What is a precise cursor? How can you change the cursor from Standard to Precise Mode?

6. What are two ways to reset your preferences to the default settings?

7. What is the purpose of the Navigator panel?

exploring on your own

1. There are many ways to customize your experience in Photoshop. Explore the various options for how your workspace could be set up by choosing Window > Workspace (or for some features the Workspace button on the Options bar). See Figure 2–34. Keep in mind, however, that you do not want to customize too much while you are doing the lessons in this book or things might get confusing; the lessons are based on the default arrangement of the workspace and keyboard shortcuts. Options include:

   - *Save/Delete Workspace:* Allows you to save (and delete later, if necessary) your favorite workspace setup (panels, menus and keyboard shortcuts) for quick access every time you use the program.

   - *Default Workspace:* Resets the Photoshop interface to its default arrangement.

   - *Keyboard Shortcuts & Menus:* Allows you to customize keyboard shortcuts for opening application menus, panels, and tools.

   - *Basic Workspace:* Minimizes the workspace area into the most basic, docked versions of the panels.

- *Legacy Workspace:* Resets the workspace to the previous version of Photoshop.

- *What's New in CS3:* When selected, new features of CS3 will be highlighted in blue on the menu bar. See Figure 2–35.

- Automation, Color and Tonal Correction, Painting and Retouching, Video and Film, and Web Design among others are pre-set workspaces designed for a specific task within the program. When selected, menu bar commands that are associated with the particular task are also color highlighted. For example, choose the Web Design workspace option (Window > Workspace > Web Design). Then, open, for example, the File menu and take note that commands such as Save for Web & Devices, Place, Import, Export, etc., are highlighted.

For more information on Workspaces in Photoshop, go to Help > Photoshop Help and in Contents, read the section Workspace > Workspace basics.

2. Create a new file. Use the Rectangle and Ellipse tools to make shapes. Fill each shape with a different color. Use the Zoom and/or Navigator panel to practice zooming in and out of the Document window. Move the file around with the Hand tool. Reset your preferences.

figure | 2–34 |

Customize your workspaces under Window>Workspace on the menu bar.

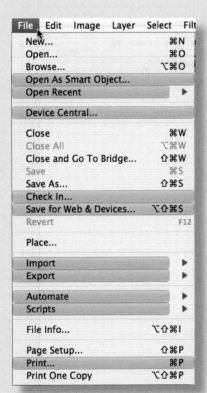

figure | 2–35 |

When the What's New in CS3 is selected, context specific menu items are color highlighted for certain workspaces.

| image essentials |

charting your course

Getting acquainted with the Photoshop staging area was the essence of Chapter 2. It allowed you to get comfortable in the space so the real show can begin. As you might already know, any well-trained artist has a background in the classics. If you are an actor, you study Shakespearean sonnets; a painter, Renaissance art; a musician, Mozart's symphonies; a dancer, ballet. The study of the classics not only provides some perspective from the past, but, more importantly, becomes a fundamental sounding board to grow creatively. Such a sounding board for a graphic artist would be an understanding of how computer graphics are generated, and that is what this chapter is about. Your classical training begins with a study of vectors and bitmaps; particularly bitmaps, since that is what Photoshop knows best. It also begins with other vital information, such as bit depth, resolution, and image formats. In addition, you will get more practice working with Photoshop's main ingredient: pixels.

goals

In this chapter you will:

- **Develop a firm grasp of the two types of digital images: vector and bitmap**
- **Discover the meaning of zeros and ones**
- **Master some tricks to make resolution your friend**
- **Learn about image formats and get an overview of common image format types**
- **Explore how images are created and edited using pixels**
- **Explore more tricks of the program with bitmaps and pixels in mind**

IMAGE CONSTRUCTION

No doubt you are eagerly waiting to get your hands on Photoshop again. However, it would not be right to send you on the next phase of the journey ill-equipped. It would be like sticking a light saber in your hand without guiding you in the art of "the Force"—you would survive a little while, probably create some really star-studded stuff, but eventually you will want finesse. Filters and effects only get you so far. The real advantage is to become one with the program—to know exactly what makes it tick. This applies not just to Photoshop but to any computer graphics program. Your training begins with an initial understanding of how images are constructed in the digital world. They come in two forms: bitmap (or raster) and vector.

The Brief on Bitmapped Images

Let us start by examining a basic black-and-white photograph. See Figure 3–1. To reproduce this image on paper is pretty straightforward: some black ink is deposited dot by dot on white paper. But how is this photo reproduced on a computer? Imagine this image is formed from a mosaic of tiles. However, instead of each tile being made of ceramic or glass, it is made of pixels—rectangular or square-shaped elements. When lined up side by side in a grid, these pixels form a complete image or pattern. See Figure 3–2. This grid of pixels is called a bitmap, and it is the manipulation of these types of images that is the heart of Photoshop.

figure | 3–1 |

A photograph reduced to black and white.

figure | 3–2 |

A photograph constructed from a grid of pixels.

Bit Depth

Two important concepts related to bitmaps are bit depth and image resolution. Let us start with bit depth. Going back to our black-and-white visual in Figure 3–1, how does the computer know to designate which part of the visual is black and which is white? Let us explain without getting too "techie." First, you must know that the brain of the computer knows only two numbers: zero and one. Yep, no deep math here—just zeros and ones. Amazingly, how the computer calculates different combinations (or strings) of zeros and ones produces every image, letter, and movement made on the computer. For instance, if you type **shazam** on your keyboard, the computer translates that word into its own language of zeros and ones—a string of data that looks something like 0111001101101010000110000101111010011000010110110100001101000001010.

Here is where it gets interesting. A single zero (0) or a single one (1) has a measurement called a "bit." Furthermore, a certain number of zeros and ones (bits) is represented in each pixel (tile) of a bitmapped image. (Are you still with us? Hang in there; it will soon be made clear.) This representation is an image's *bit depth*. In the instance of the black-and-white photo, a white pixel you see (or do not see) is translated as zero (off) in the computer brain and a black pixel is translated as one (on). Each pixel in this example is equal to one bit of color information, which can be either black or white.

Not surprisingly, a black-and-white image is sometimes referred to as a *one-bit image*. We will discuss the relationship of image color to bit depth in Chapter 5. For now, just remember that the larger an image's bit depth (accumulation of zeros and ones), the more variations of color it contains. See Figure 3–3. In general, a larger bit depth also produces an image with a larger file size.

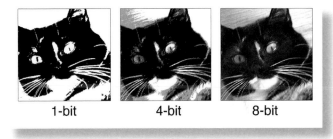

1-bit   4-bit   8-bit

figure |3–3|

The larger an image's bit depth, the more variations of color (for example, shades of gray) it contains.

Resolution

Resolution plays an important role in Photoshop, and the concept of resolution is going to crop up several times throughout this book. It is somewhat of an illusive term because it can be discussed in many different contexts, depending on how an image is being used. Ultimately, though, resolution works as a measurement for how much information a file contains. For our purposes right now, resolution is a way to describe the amount of pixels in an image, which results in what size an image might be when reproduced for print or the screen (i.e., the Web).

In Photoshop, an image with a resolution of 72 pixels per inch (ppi) and measuring 72 pixels in width and 72 pixels in length equals a 1-inch-by-1-inch image when set to a magnification of 100%. This makes an image with a total of 5,184 pixels. Huh? See Figure 3–4 for a visual.

Why 72? Well, that is the default screen resolution (the resolution set for viewing images on a screen) in Photoshop. If you do not believe us, go to Photoshop > Preferences > Units & Rulers

72ppi

72ppi

72 x 72 = 5,184

figure |3–4|

A 1-inch-by-1-inch image in Photoshop is set, by default, at a resolution of 72 ppi.

(Mac) or Edit > Preferences > Units & Rulers (Windows) and see for yourself (or see Figure 3–5). Do not mess around too much with this screen resolution setting. Keep it at 72 ppi. The number 72 also represents the average screen resolution of your monitor (newer monitors have a 96 ppi resolution). Also, 72 ppi is the resolution of Web images. This makes sense as Web images are viewed via a screen. (We know you are wondering, "Will my picture look better if I increase the screen resolution?" The answer is no. You are just squeezing more zeros and ones (bits) into the same area. The only thing you would be doing is making your file larger in size.)

figure | 3–5 |

The Preferences dialog box for setting screen resolution.

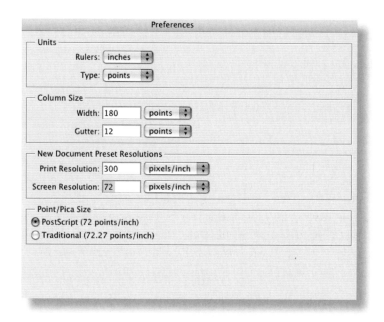

Now, by default, Photoshop views images at 100% based on the 72 ppi screen resolution. However, if you wanted to create an image that would print 1 inch by 1 inch, the resolution needed depends on the resolution of the output device (i.e., your printer). Let us say you wanted to create an image that needed to be 144 ppi. What would it look like in Photoshop if set to a screen resolution of 72 ppi? Well, let us find out:

1. Open Photoshop.

2. Choose File > New and enter the following information:
   - *Name:* res_72
   - *Preset:* Custom
   - *Width:* 1 inch
   - *Height:* 1 inch
   - *Resolution:* 72 pixels/inch
   - *Color Mode:* RGB Color, 8 bit
   - *Background Contents:* White

3. Click OK.

4. Choose View > Actual Pixels to ensure the document is at 100% magnification. You should see a blank document that is approximately 1 inch by 1. See Figure 3–6.

5. Keeping your **res_72** document open, choose File > New and enter the following information:

   - *Name:* res_144
   - *Preset:* Custom
   - *Width:* 1 inch
   - *Height:* 1 inch
   - *Resolution:* 144 pixels/inch
   - *Color Mode:* RGB Color, 8 bit
   - *Background Contents:* White

6. Click OK.

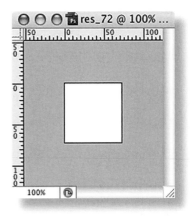

figure |3–6|

A 1-inch-by-1-inch document with a resolution of 72 ppi, 100% magnification, in Photoshop.

7. Choose View > Actual Pixels to ensure the document is at 100% magnification. You should see a blank document, but compared to the first document (**res_72**), it is visually four times the size. See Figure 3–7. Even though its dimensions were set to 1 inch by 1 inch like **res_72**, it appears bigger because you are viewing it at the default 72 ppi screen resolution (remember that setting in the Photoshop preferences?). To show all the pixels for **res_144** set at 144 ppi (a total of 20,736 pixels) at a screen resolution of 72, the document must visually expand its size, precisely four times the size of **res_72**.

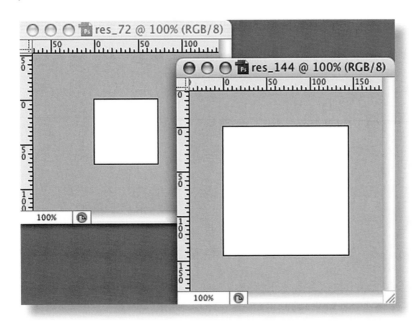

figure |3–7|

Compare the size of a 72-ppi document to a 144-ppi document at 100% magnification.

8. There is more. When the file **res_144** gets to its final output source—a printer, which in this case requires an image of 144 ppi—it will print at the intended 1-inch-by-1-inch size. Choose View > Print Size to see this calculation.

> **Note:** One more thing to be aware of is the file size of each of the documents created. File res_144 is four times bigger than res_72. See Figure 3–7 and note the document file size in the status bar at the bottom of each window: 61K versus 15K.

We totally understand if you are still unsure about the concept of resolution. Perhaps you even feel the urge to slam this book shut. Before you do, however, bookmark this page—you will probably want to refer to it again. If it is any comfort, this whole resolution idea really begins to sink in when you find yourself in an actual predicament (or two or three) using the program. Until such a predicament arrives, you will get plenty of practice with resolution throughout the lessons in this book.

The Brief on Vector Graphics

As you have discovered, when dealing with bitmap images, an image's resolution and pixel dimensions are interdependent. Adjusting the amount of pixels in a bitmap image affects its resolution, not to mention its visual quality, and vice versa. There is no way around it, unless you are working in vectors. Vectors are another way of constructing digital images. As part of our classical training, it is important we discuss vectors, but only briefly. Photoshop does have some vector support (which comes in handy when you need some flexibility with free-form drawing or when importing vector-based graphics created in other programs, such as Adobe Illustrator), but, as you know, it is not the heart of the program (bitmaps are!).

Vector graphics are made up of points and lines that describe an object's outline or shape. See Figure 3–8. Instead of being composed of a grid of square pixels (see Figure 3–2), a vector image is drawn based on mathematical calculations of X and Y coordinates. This means vectors are resolution independent: they can be scaled large (billboard size) or small (postage stamp size) and printed to any output device without loss of detail or clarity. If so, why not use vectors for all digital images? We hate to break it to you, but there is no one-stop shop. Vector graphics are great for a certain type of image design and for free-form drawing, including bold and illustrative types of graphics (i.e., logos and text treatments that can be easily scaled while retaining crisp lines and solid colors). On the flip side, bitmaps are a great way to represent continuous-tone images, such as photographs or digital paintings that have subtle gradations of color and shading.

figure |3–8|

Anatomy of a vector
graphic from
full-shade view to
outline view.

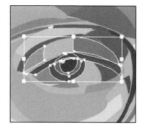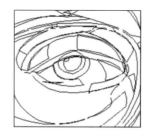

Seeing All Sides

Now that you have got an idea of the differences between bitmap and vector graphics, we must confess it is not all black and white. With the inundation of so many kinds of computer graphic software programs and variations thereof, you might find yourself sifting through a lot of digitized gray matter. Programs such as Adobe Photoshop, Adobe Fireworks, and GIMP are designed to work specifically with bitmap-constructed images. Adobe Illustrator, Adobe Flash, and CorelDRAW are designed to work with vector-based graphics. However, most programs, to some extent, have the ability to import and translate both vector and bitmap graphics. At first this convergence of image types might seem confusing, but once you understand how digital images are constructed, your work as a graphic artist becomes more productive.

Before moving on, you should know there are different image formats for different types of images. A format is described by an extension at the end of the filename, as in **image.jpg** or **mywork.tiff**. An image's format identifies whether it is composed of bitmaps or vectors. It also determines an image's file size and visual quality. There are many kinds of image file formats, depending on where you are going to use the image (i.e., print or Web, or exporting into another program).

Most graphic programs support the use of the following:

Bitmap-only Formats

- *BMP:* Limited bitmap file format not suitable for Web or prepress
- *GIF:* Compressed format mainly used for Internet graphics with solid colors and crisp lines
- *JPEG:* Compressed format used for Internet graphics, particularly photographs
- *PNG:* Versatile, bitmap-compressed format used mainly for Internet graphics
- *TIFF:* Uncompressed format for saving bitmapped images (although in Photoshop there are options for some compression capability with LZW being the best choice for compression with no loss in quality); most popular for artwork going to print

Vector and Bitmap-based Formats

- *EPS:* Flexible file format that can contain both bitmap and vector data; most vector images are saved in this format
- *PICT:* Used on Macintosh computers and can contain both vector and bitmap data
- *SWF:* The Macromedia Flash output format; a common vector-based graphics file format for the creation of scalable, compact graphics for the Web and hand-held devices
- *SVG (Scalable Vector Graphics):* Emerging XML-based vector format for the creation of scalable, compact graphics for the Web and hand-held devices

Importing and Exporting

In Photoshop, you can import (place) images and files saved in many types of formats. To import files into Photoshop and to view a list of the readable documents it supports, choose File > Place to place a file inside a currently open file or File > Open (All Readable Documents or All Formats) to open a file in a separate window.

You can also export (save) your Photoshop work into different formats depending on where it will go next in the design process—printed, published to the Web, or imported into another program. To export a file, choose File > Save As and select the format type you want to export.

PIXELS: THE MAIN INGREDIENT

Photoshop manipulates pixels like a sculptor molds clay. Pixels are the main ingredient from which all images are formed in the program. Just as a sculptor has numerous implements to mold his vision, the tools in Photoshop's toolbox are designed to shape pixels. For example, the Magic Wand tool selects them, the Crop tool deletes them, the Smudge tool smudges them, and the Clone Stamp tool duplicates them. You get the idea.

Lesson: Playing with Pixels

The purpose of this next lesson is to show you that no matter what mysterious tricks we get into in the upcoming chapters, the underlying truth is always the same: Photoshop is just a playground for pixels. See Figure 3–9.

figure | 3–9 |

The lesson before and after playing with pixels.

Lightening and Darkening Pixels

1. In Photoshop, choose File > Open. Open the file **chap3L1.psd** in the **chap03_lessons** folder.

2. Save a copy of this file in your **lessons** folder: choose File > Save As and name your file **chap3LI_yourname.psd**.

3. From the menu bar, choose Image > Adjustments > Auto Levels to have Photoshop automatically adjust the brightness and contrast (light- and dark-colored pixels) of the image. Ah, already much better.

Deleting and Transforming Pixels

1. With your **chap3L1_yourname.psd** file open, choose File > Open and open the file **tile.tif** located in the **chap03_lessons/assets** folder. In the next step you are going to move this tile pattern onto the **chap3L1_yourname.psd** file.

2. Select the Move tool in the toolbox. See Figure 3–10.

figure |3–10|

Select the Move tool in the toolbox.

3. Click and drag the selected tile pattern on top of the **chap3LI_yourname. psd** file, and then let go of the mouse button. A copy of the image will appear on the file. See Figure 3–11. Right on!

figure |3–11|

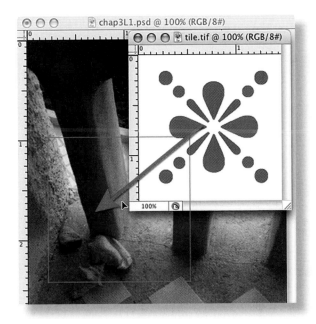

With the Move tool, drag the selected tile pattern over the main image to make a copy.

4. Close the **tile.tif** file.

5. Now, get rid of the white pixels around the tile pattern. Select the Magic Wand tool in the toolbox. See Figure 3–12.

figure |3–12|

Select the Magic Wand tool in the toolbox.

6. With the Magic Wand tool, click over a white section of the tile pattern. All white areas of the image are selected. Press Delete or choose Edit > Clear. Ta-da! No more white pixels. The Magic Wand really is magic.

7. Choose Select > Deselect (Apple/Command-D on the Mac or Ctrl-D on Windows). The marching ants are removed.

figure |3–13|

Rename the layer.

8. Select Window > Layers to open the Layers panel (if it is not already open).

9. Double-click on the text **Layer 1** and rename it **tile pattern**. See Figure 3–13.

10. Be sure the tile pattern layer is highlighted. Choose Edit > Free Transform. In the Options bar below the menu bar, enter the following (see Figure 3–14):

- *Width (W):* 32.0%
- *Height (H):* 32.0%
- *Set rotation:* 55.0 degrees

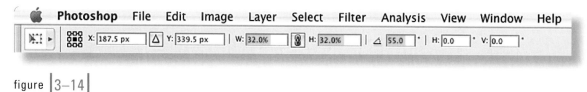

figure | 3–14 |

Scale and rotate pixels by entering exact increments in the Options bar for the Free Transform command.

> **Note:** As an alternative to entering exact scaling and rotation numbers in the Options bar, you can scale and rotate the transform box that surrounds the selected image. See Figure 3–15 and Figure 3–16.

figure | 3–15 |

Scale interactively by clicking and dragging on a corner of the Free Transform box.

figure | 3–16 |

Rotate interactively by clicking and dragging right above a corner of the Free Transform box. Note the rotation icon.

11. Select the Move tool in the toolbox. A dialog box will come up asking if you want to apply the transformation. Click Apply. (Double-clicking on the transformed image or hitting Return or Enter will work as well.)

12. Move the tile pattern over one of the floor tiles in the photograph. See Figure 3–17.

13. Choose File > Save and save your work.

> **Note:** If the Maximize Compatibility Options box appears, keep the default option selected.

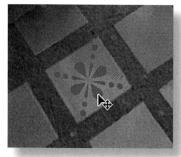

figure | 3–17 |

Move the tile pattern over a tile in the photograph.

Altering, Blending, and Duplicating Pixels

1. In the Layers panel, be sure the **tile pattern** layer is highlighted.

2. Choose Filter > Texture > Craquelure from the menu bar.

3. Adjust the Crack Spacing to 10, Crack Depth to 2, and Crack Brightness to 10. See Figure 3–18.

4. Click OK to apply the effect on the tile pattern.

5. Ctrl-click (Mac) or right-click (Windows) on the **tile pattern** layer. Select Blending Options from the pop-up menu. See Figure 3–19.

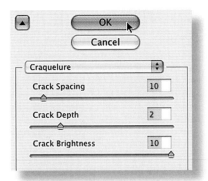

figure |3–18|

Adjust options for the Craquelure texture.

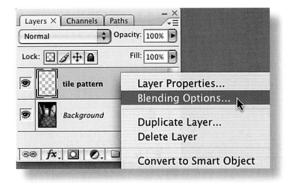

figure |3–19|

Select Blending Options.

6. In the Layer Style dialog box, check and then highlight (by selecting the name) the Bevel and Emboss style. The Bevel and Emboss options will appear to the right of the dialog box.

7. Be sure the Preview option is selected so you can see the Bevel and Emboss options directly applied to the pixels of the tile pattern. See Figure 3–20.

For Structure:

- *Style:* Pillow Emboss
- *Technique:* Smooth
- *Depth:* 1
- *Size:* 3
- *Soften:* 10

For Shading:

- *Angle:* 120
- *Altitude:* 50
- *Highlight Mode, Opacity:* 75
- *Shadow Mode, Opacity:* 75

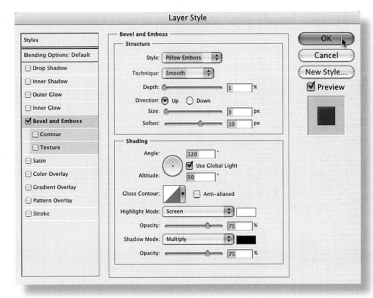

figure |3–20|

Select options for Bevel and Emboss.

8. Click OK to apply the effect.
To further blend the tile pattern into the photograph, be sure the **tile pattern** layer is highlighted. In the Layers panel, select Multiply for the blending mode and 60% Opacity. See Figure 3–21.

9. Select the Move tool in the toolbox.

figure |3–21|

Use a blending mode and opacity to further blend the tile pattern pixels with the photograph's pixels.

10. Place the cursor over the tile pattern, hold down Option (Mac) or Alt (Windows), and then click and drag to make a duplicate of the pattern with all of its effects. Move the duplicate over another tile in the photograph.

11. Create several more duplicates and place them over other tiles in the photograph. For reference, see the completed image in Figure 3–9.

> **Note:** Each time you create a duplicate tile pattern, it creates a new layer for that tile object in the Layers panel. To move an individual tile pattern, select that tile pattern's layer in the Layers panel. To delete a tile pattern, highlight its layer and click on the Trash Can icon in the lower-right corner of the Layers panel. If you find yourself trying to move an element of your image and it is not cooperating, check the Layers panel and make sure the correct layer is selected. Even the pros come across this problem, so do not be embarrassed if this happens.

12. Save the file with the new changes.

Hiding and Revealing Pixels

1. Let us open another file to add to your scene. Choose File > Open and open the file **ocean.tif** in the **chap03_lessons/assets** folder.

2. Select the Move tool in the toolbox. Place the cursor over the ocean photo and drag a copy of it to your **chap3L1_yourname** file.

3. Close **ocean.tif**.

4. Position the photo in the top area of the file.

5. Choose Select > Load Selection from the menu bar.

6. In the Load Selection dialog box, select **Channel: arches** (See Figure 3-22). Click OK.

figure |3–22|

Select a Channel in the Load Selections box.

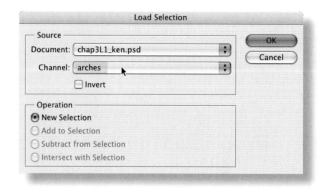

7. A selection (marked by marching ants) is indicated on the file. This selection was pre-made and saved for purposes of this lesson. You will learn how to make your own saved selections in Chapter 8.

8. Choose Layer > Layer Mask > Reveal Selection in the menu bar. Amazing! The selection reveals the ocean scene, masking out all other pixels. The photo has taken on a whole new perspective—much more inviting, we think.

9. Save your file. You are done playing with pixels (at least temporarily).

SUMMARY

This chapter was heavy duty! It was a big bite into the nitty-gritty of bitmap and vector graphics, bit depth, resolution, and image formats, not to mention an opportunity to practice playing with pixels. Like studying the classics in any field, however, it was important to get this fundamental information out of the way, so you can more easily, productively, and creatively progress to the next level of Photoshop know-how.

in review

1. Briefly describe the differences between bitmap and vector graphics.

2. What are bits? Why is a black-and-white image considered a one-bit image?

3. How does resolution affect a bitmap image's dimensions?

4. Bitmap images are most common for what type of images? Why?

5. Text and logo treatments are created best as what type of graphic? Why?

6. What is an image file format?

7. What is the main ingredient in Photoshop? Name five ways you altered this ingredient in the lesson.

exploring on your own

1. In Photoshop, go to Help > Photoshop Help. Under Contents, choose the topic "Opening and importing Images" and read the sections "Photoshop images," "Image size and resolution," "Creating, opening and importing Images," and "Placing files."

2. Play with blending other tile patterns and background images in the **chap3L1.psd** file. Some sample patterns and background images for your use are located in the **chap03_lessons/ samples** folder. You can also bring in your own tile patterns and background photos. For example, what would the image look like with an outer-space or underwater scene revealed through the arches?

Explorer pages

DARREL ANDERSON

"No matter what medium you work in . . . let the medium inform the process. Tap into that part of the brain that is able to recognize imagery. Don't preconceive too much, and allow the inspiration to occur to you and appear before you in the work."

 Learn more about this artist via podcast at *http://www.designexploration.com/podcasts*.

Digital Illustration: *leapLight*. © 2007 Darrel Anderson, Braid Media Arts

About Darrel Anderson

Darrel Anderson has been creating and inventing professionally for over 30 years. His early love of science was diverted into the visual arts as a teenager. He originally pursued drawing as a means of visualizing ideas and inventions.

Darrel and several of his friends started their art careers straight out of high school. They were "group taught"—taking on any and all art jobs, relying on collaboration and determination—the learn-as-you-go school. Underground Comics (under their own everyman studios label) and Science Fiction/Fantasy illustration were their primary fields.

In the early 1980s an illustration job landed an Atari 800 on Darrel's desk—this inevitably lead to a intertwining of art and science in his creative pursuits. Since then he has traced the common thread of imaging through printmaking, tool building (software), animation and illustration.

Darrel co-founded Braid Media Arts with Rick Berry. Braid is a group of creative collaborators with ongoing projects in the arts and sciences. Darrel designed and built their first Web site in 1995.

His diverse works include:

- Illustration of fiction by William Gibson, Arthur C. Clark, Ray Bradbury, and Stephen King;
- Magazine illustration for *Antic*, *MacWorld*, *Computer Graphics World*, and *WIRED*;
- Online illustrations for the SCi-FI Channel; CGI for the TriStar/Sony film *Johnny Mnemonic*;
- Creation of GroBoto, an intuitive, playful 3D graphics program built specifically for artists and designers who are not versed in the technical aspects of digital 3D.

"It's nice to mix it up . . . that's what I would say about tools for success. . . . And to be a good collaborator . . . it's one of the great ways to learn."

Darrel taught 3D graphics for the California state universities' Summer Arts Program, and has been a guest speaker at Tufts University, the Digital Burgess Conference, and several Contact, Cultures of the Imagination Conferences.

About the Work of Darrel Anderson

Darrel's notes on *winterWreathe* illustration:

"Although I use digital 3D tools extensively in my work, I have a bit of a love/hate relationship with them. I prefer work that is evocative rather than descriptive—and 3D usually has too much of the latter. Regardless of medium or tool, I use an exploratory approach—using the medium as a tool for seeing. The work is found in the process, rather than planned and executed. I find digital tools very well suited to this process—allowing infinite variety and flexibility. The ability to play with new combinations techniques—often with no preconception of their end effect—gives unmatched creative freedom and breadth.

"Because of this approach, I rarely use the same set of techniques twice—and often don't quite remember how I arrived at the final result . . . but here are a few nuts and bolts I do remember about *winterWreathe*.

"For this image I started with a 3D model created in GroBoto. I created several Photoshop layers with shifted and/or distorted versions of the alpha channel (provided by the 3D rendering) as layer masks. This clipping and overlaying provided energy and abstraction—breaking away from the photo-real rendering. Another image (just something of mine chosen at random), was added as a color layer. Some Dodge & Burn (often utilizing layer masks) and little blending work with a feathery brush and the Smudge Tool, helped pull everything together and provide a painterly feel."

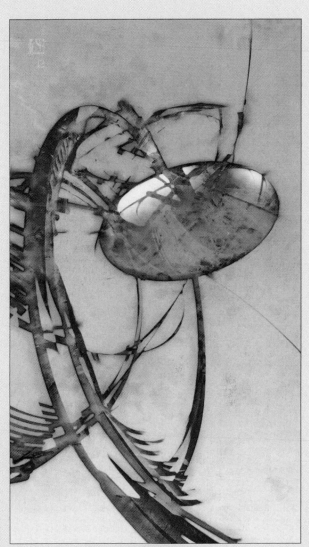

Digital Illustration: *winterWreathe*.
© 2007 Darrel Anderson, Braid Media Arts

Digital Illustration: *clockSpring*.
© 2007 Darrel Anderson, Braid Media Arts

Digital Illustration: *copperVine*.
© 2007 Darrel Anderson, Braid Media Arts

Joel Hagen

Joel Hagen, a collaborator with Darrel Anderson and computer graphics instructor, has his own style of abstract creation using Photoshop.

Wetware by Joel Hagen. Compliments of Joel Hagen.

Ice Ram by Joel Hagen. Compliments of Joel Hagen.

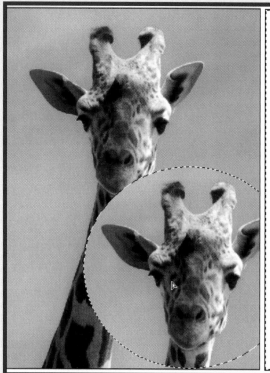

| selecting and transforming |

charting your course

After reading the Chapter 3, it is clear Photoshop knows pixels. And so will you, starting with this chapter. Using Photoshop's versatile and varied selection tools (such as the Marquee, Lasso, and Magic Wand tools) and transform commands (such as Scale, Rotate, and Skew), you get up-close-and-personal with selecting and transforming individual squares of color.

goals

In this chapter you will:

- **Get versatile with Photoshop's Selection and Transform tools**
- **Practice building a composite image**

ABOUT SELECTING AND TRANSFORMING

Selecting and transforming pixels work hand in hand. You select an area of your Photoshop image and then move, scale, or rotate it in some way (or add a fill or effect to it, which will be addressed in later chapters). Learning to select and transform pixels is a critical step in your study of Photoshop.

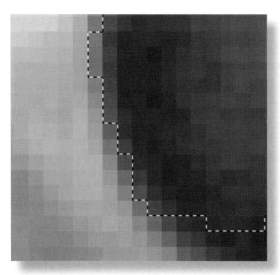

figure | 4–1 |

A selection is indicated by a dashed line known as "marching ants."

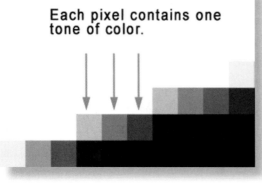

figure | 4–2 |

Each pixel is its own tone of color. Photoshop selects pixels based on their color range, or a tolerance.

How Do Selections Work?

When you select something on your Photoshop document—that is, when the marching ants appear (see Figure 4–1)—what exactly are you selecting and how do you control these selections? When you examine pixels closely, you see that each pixel produced is its own shade of color. The computer can select pixels based on these shades or tones (see Figure 4–2). For example, the Magic Wand tool knows what pixels to grab onto by where you apply it to an image and what you have determined is its color tolerance. Tolerance defines how similar in color a pixel must be to be selected, ranging from 0 to 255 (you will learn more about the 0-to-255 range in Chapter 5). Feathering of selections is similar to tolerance. This type of selection determines how much transparency is created in each pixel.

The selection accuracy is also controlled by the frequency and/or proximity of pixels in a given area. For example, a Lasso tool controls what pixels it snaps onto not only by the contrast of colors from pixel to pixel (edge contrast) but also by the number of pixels within the tool's positioned area. The accuracy settings for the selection tools are always found in the selected tool's Options bar. See Figure 4–3 on the next page.

All that being said, the concern here is not what feature of what tool does what (that is next), but to know that the big picture is this: Selections and their accuracy are determined by the color settings and location of pixels within a given area.

Overview of Selection Tools

Before you start playing with selection tools in the next lesson, here is an idea of what each tool does and why one tool might be better suited for particular selections than another.

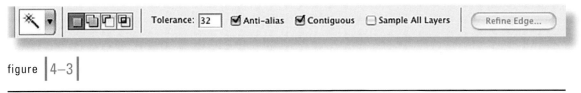

figure |4–3|

Options available in the Magic Wand tool's Options bar.

Select Menu

The quick and easy way to select all items on a layer is to choose the layer from the Layers panel and then, from the menu bar, choose Select > All (Command-A for Mac or Ctrl-A for Windows). From the menu bar you can also choose to deselect all items on a layer, reselect them, or invert the selection.

Marquee Tools

A marquee is a permanent canopy or bulletin board that projects over the entrance of a building, like those seen over Broadway theaters. They highlight, usually in bright, neon colors, the performance and performers of the evening. In Photoshop, the Marquee tools are used to highlight (select) an area as a shape, such as a rectangle, ellipse, or row or column of pixels. See Figure 4–4. The Marquee tools are the most convenient way to select areas of an image. However, because the selections are defined within a specific shape, the tools are not designed to select odd areas of pixels. For instance, if we wanted to select the eye of the giraffe in Figure 4–5 with minimal effort, we would use the Elliptical Marquee tool. If we wanted to select an area of the giraffe's neck to create a pattern or tile effect from it, we would use the Rectangular Marquee tool. See Figure 4–6 on the next page. If we wanted to select one of the irregular spots on the giraffe, we would use another tool, such as a Lasso tool.

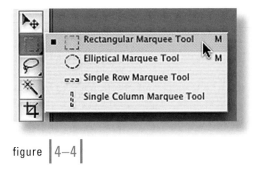

figure |4–4|

The Marquee tools available in the toolbox.

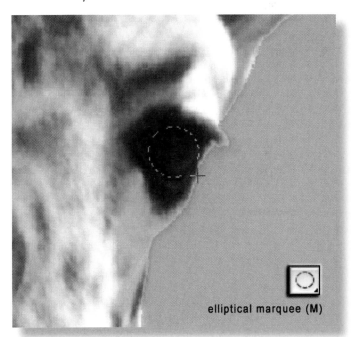

elliptical marquee (M)

figure |4–5|

Select circular areas with the Elliptical Marquee tool.

There are three styles of selecting you can choose in the Marquee tool's Options bar:

- *Normal:* In Normal style, you select the specific Marquee tool you want and then click and drag the tool over the area of the document you want to select. To constrain the shape proportionally, hold down Shift as you drag with the tool. When you let go of the tool, the

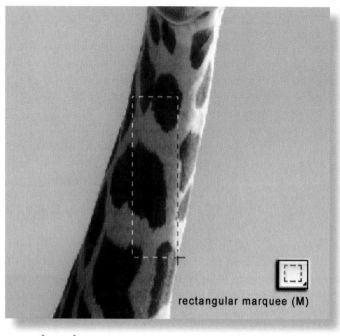

figure | 4–6 |

Select rectangular areas with the Rectangular Marquee tool.

figure | 4–7 |

The Normal Styles Options bar.

figure | 4–8 |

The Fixed Ratio Styles Options bar.

figure | 4–9 |

The Fixed Size Styles Options bar.

marching ants appear, indicating the selection. See Figure 4–7.

- *Fixed Ratio:* In this style, you can define a selection with a fixed height-to-width ratio. An example would be an image compatible for the NTSC TV format, which requires a 4-by-3 aspect ratio. See Figure 4–8.

- *Fixed Size:* If you already know exactly what size you want a selected area to be, you can enter it in the Fixed Size style of the Marquee tool's Options bar. Keep in mind that the number of pixels needed to create a 1-inch selection depends on the resolution of the image (this concept is covered in Chapter 3). See Figure 4–9.

Magic Wand

If you recall, we revealed the secret of the Magic Wand tool to you at the beginning of this lesson. This tool selects pixels based on a color range or color tolerance, which is set in the tool's Options bar. See Figure 4–10 on the next page. Enter a low value to select the few colors very similar to the pixel you click, or enter a higher value to select a broader range of colors. The pixels can be selected contiguously (sharing a boundary or touching each other) or non-contiguously.

For the giraffe on the left in Figure 4–11 on the next page, the Magic Wand tool's tolerance is set at 45 and is applied to the sky area around the giraffe. The range indicated is low enough that it selects the light pixels of the sky but not the darker pixels that define the giraffe. In the same figure, the giraffe on the right side has a tolerance set at 100—widening the range of color possibilities that can be selected. The Magic Wand tool is great for selecting odd areas of similar color in a photograph. See Figure 4–12 on the next page. To use the Magic Wand tool, choose the tool in the toolbox, set the Tolerance in the Options bar, and click on the area you want to sample for the selection.

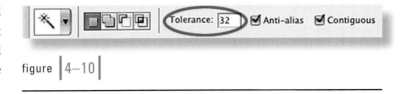

figure | 4–10 |

Select the Magic Wand tool in the toolbox to access its Tolerance settings in the Options bar.

Quick Selection Tool

If you are the type of person who loves to paint a selection out, then the Quick Selection tool might be the tool for you. This tool (new in CS3) lets you "paint" a selection that grows outward. The tool appears as a round-tip brush. As you click and drag it, it begins to create a selection around the areas you paint over.

Lasso Tools

Unless you are a surgeon or you can thread a needle with a steady hand, the Lasso tools can be tricky to master. It takes practice, but it is worth the effort when you want to select odd areas of an image, which might otherwise be impossible to do. There are three types of Lasso tools (see Figure 4–13 on the next page):

magic wand (W)

figure | 4–11 |

On the left, the color tolerance for the Magic Wand tool is set at 45 and is applied to the sky area of the image. On the right, the color tolerance is set at 100, expanding the selection area.

magic wand (W)

figure | 4–12 |

You can use the Magic Wand tool to select areas of similar color, such as the patch on the hide of the giraffe.

figure | 4–13 |

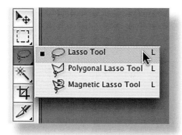

The Lasso tools in the toolbox.

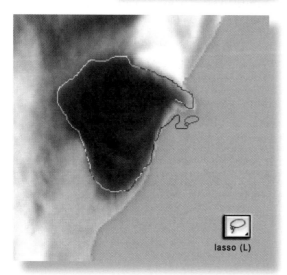

lasso (L)

figure | 4–14 |

Use of the Lasso tool.

- *Lasso:* This tool lets you draw selections with free-hand or straight-edged segments. See Figure 4–14. To create freehand segments, click and drag around an area. To create straight-edge segments, hold down Option/Alt, and click once at the beginning and once at the end. You can switch between both free-form and straight-edge modes as you draw—cool! To close (define) the selection, make sure you are at the beginning of your selection, and let go of the mouse button and Alt/Option.

- *Polygonal Lasso:* Like the Lasso tool, this tool lets you draw selections with freehand or straight-edge segments. To create freehand segments, hold down Option/Alt and drag over the area. To create straight-edge segments, click once on the spot where the segment should begin and then click at the end point. (Yes, the same commands do the opposite of the commands for the Lasso tool.) To close (define) the selection, double-click with the Polygonal Lasso pointer tool. See Figure 4–15 on the next page..

- *Magnetic Lasso:* Similar to the Magic Wand tool, the Magnetic Lasso tool is more or less attracted to pixels based on color and their proximity to one another. As you move along the edge of an object you want to select, the tool attaches to pixels with fastening points. The more fastening points, the more precise the selection border. If you draw free-form (click and then drag), the tool will automatically place fastening points based on the frequency you set in its Options bar. (To place fastening points wherever you want to, simply click with the tool.) The higher the frequency number set in the Options bar, the more fastening points are created, and therefore the more precise the selection border. You can also determine something called edge contrast, which defines the lasso's sensitivity to edges (contrasts in color) in the image. A lower percentage detects lower-contrast edges (i.e., a white pixel next to a light-gray pixel); a higher percentage detects edges that contrast

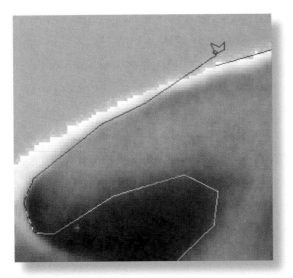

figure │4–15│

Use of the Polygonal Lasso tool.

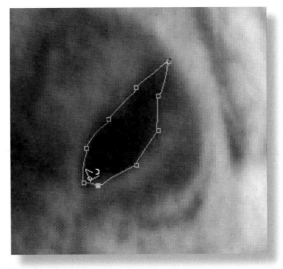

figure │4–16│

The Magnetic Lasso tool deposits fastening points to define the selection border. In this example, the frequency of fastening points is set to 80, quickly and more precisely selecting the intended area.

sharply with their surroundings (i.e., a dark-blue pixel next to a white pixel). Like the Polygonal Lasso tool, to close (define) the selection, double-click with the tool. See Figure 4–16.

Adding, Subtracting, and Refining Selection Areas

Inevitably your selections will not be perfect the first time. You might close and define the selection border and discover you missed some areas. You have two options here. You can redraw the selection, which is good practice but not always very efficient. Or, you can add to, subtract from, or intersect your selection area by choosing th ese options in the Selection tool's Options bar. See Figure 4–17. You can also add by selecting the Lasso, Magic Wand, or Marquee tool and holding down Shift as you draw over the areas you want to add. To subtract, choose a Selection

figure │4–17│

Add to, subtract from, or intersect your selection by choosing the option in the Options bar.

tool and hold down Option/Alt as you draw over the areas you want to remove from the selection. See Figure 4–18. In addition to modifying a selection, the Refine Edge button in the Options bar gives you the ability to refine the edges of a selection. See Figure 4-19. This is a great way to clean a selection's edge and how the selection looks against various backgrounds.

figure │4–18│

Hold down Shift to add to a selection. Hold down Option/Alt to subtract from a selection. Note the plus or minus icon next to the selection tool's pointer, depending on your choice of action.

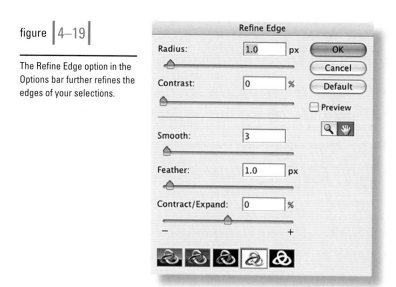

figure |4–19|

The Refine Edge option in the Options bar further refines the edges of your selections.

Selecting an Object on a Layer

When you begin to work with objects on multiple layers, often you will want to select items on a specific layer. In the lessons, there will be plenty of opportunities to practice this way of selecting, but in case you need to know right now, follow these three steps:

1. Choose Window > Layers to open the Layers panel (if not already open).

2. In the Layers panel, select the layer containing the item(s) you want to select. Be sure it is an active layer, not the Background layer.

> Note: To convert the Background layer to an active, editable layer, double-click on the Background layer thumbnail in the Layers panel and give it a new name.

3. Roll the pointer over the selected layer, and Ctrl-click (Windows) or Command-click (Mac) the layer's thumbnail. Note that the opaque items on that layer are selected in the document.

Quick Mask

Photoshop's Quick Mask selection feature can rock your world. It is complicated to get the gist of at first, but with time, it could become your favorite selection tool. See Figure 4–20. We will explain more about quick masks and let you practice masking in Chapter 8. For now, try to wrap your brain around the idea of making selections using a paintbrush (sized to your liking) and letting color differentiate what is fully and partially (semi-transparently) selected.

figure |4–20|

Get to Quick Mask Mode from the toolbox.

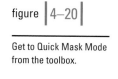

▶ **Don't Go There!**

Once you have an area selected, whatever you do next in the program—move, add a filter, paint, etc.—will be applied to that area only. On occasion, you might select something inadvertently (or forget it was selected) and then attempt to do something else, like paint on another layer. When this happens,

a warning circle comes up. See Figure 4–21. Do not freak out. Choose Select > Deselect from the menu bar to remove all selected areas (even those you cannot see), and then make sure the layer you want to modify is highlighted in the Layers panel.

figure | 4–21 |

Warning: You cannot do that! Deselect all and check to be sure you are on the layer you want to modify.

How Does Transforming Work?

Once you select something in Photoshop, you might want to transform it. This means moving, scaling, or rotating it. You can transform numerically—by entering an exact number(s) for the transformation in the Options bar. See Figure 4–22. Or, you can use the Free Transform command, which lets you interactively—and in one, continuous operation—transform (including rotate, scale and variations thereof, such as skew, distort, and set perspective) a selected item using selection handles and specific keyboard commands. See Figure 4–23.

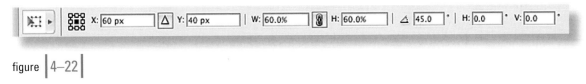

figure | 4–22 |

In a transform Options bar, you can numerically enter a transformation.

figure | 4–23 |

The Free Transform command lets you transform an object interactively and with keyboard commands by adjusting the bounding box handles.

Overview of Transform Tools

figure | 4–24 |

The Move tool in the toolbox.

Briefly, let us go over the Transform tools:

- *Move:* Since moving (translating) things is so much a part of Photoshop, the Move tool is probably the most-used tool in the program. See Figure 4–24.
- *Scale* and *Rotate:* To change the size of a selected object or to rotate it, choose Edit > Transform > Scale or Rotate. See Figure 4–25 and Figure 4–26.
- *Skew:* To slant an item vertically or horizontally, choose Edit > Transform > Skew.
- *Distort:* To stretch an item in all directions, choose Edit > Transform > Distort.
- *Perspective:* To apply one point perspective to an item (see Figure 4–27), choose Edit > Transform > Perspective.

> **Note:** When choosing Edit > Transform, you also have the options to rotate a selection 180 or 90 degrees, or to flip it horizontally (from left to right) or vertically (from top to bottom).

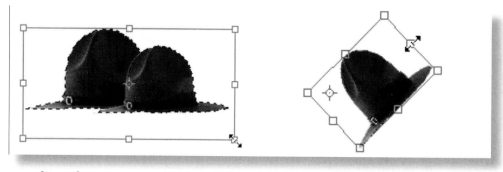

figure | 4–25 |

Scale proportionally by holding down Shift while dragging the scale handles on the corner of the selection. To scale disproportionately, drag the scale handles on the corner or sides of the free transform bounding area without holding Shift. Note that the hat on the right is also being rotated.

figure | 4–26 |

Position the pointer slightly outside a corner of the free transform bounding box to rotate the selection.

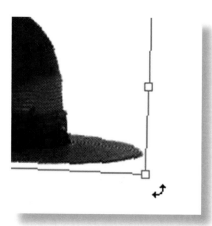

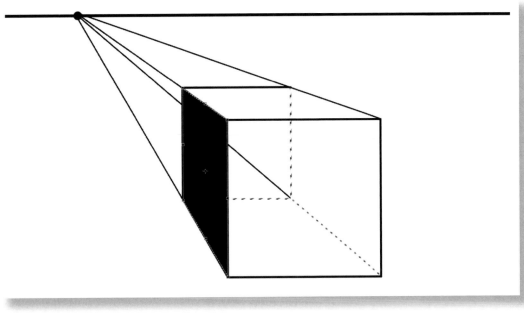

figure |4–27|

To create the illusion of a dimension, use a combination of the distort, skew, and perspective transformations.

More Options for Selections

You can do more with selections than just transform them. You can also copy, paste, delete, duplicate, paint, draw, adjust, or add an effect or filter to the selection. Most of these operations will become second nature as you work with the program, but let us go over them briefly.

- *Copy, Paste and Duplicate:* To copy and paste first make your selection, then choose Edit > Copy, go where you want to paste it, and choose Edit > Paste. If you paste it into the same document, it will create the copy on a new layer, and perhaps directly over the original selection. Use your Move tool if you need to move one object away from another. Like most programs, shortcut keys for copy are Command-C (Mac) and Ctrl-C (Windows); and for paste, Command-V (Mac) or Ctrl-V (Windows). To duplicate a selection on the same document first make a selection, choose the Move tool, and while rolling the pointer over the selection, hold down Option/Alt. A duplicate icon appears. See Figure 4–28. Click and drag to make the duplicate.

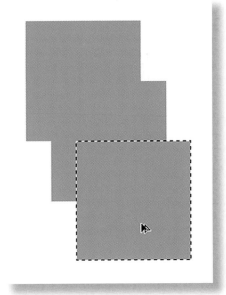

figure |4–28|

To duplicate, make a selection, choose the Move tool, hold down Alt/Option, and click and drag to make the duplication.

- *Delete:* To delete contents within a selection, press Delete on your keyboard or choose Edit > Clear. To remove the selection and paste it somewhere else, choose Edit >. See Figure 4–29.

figure | 4–29 |

On the left is a duplicate of the giraffe's head. On the right is the background selected and deleted.

- *Add Effect or Filter:* To adjust the color or add an effect or filter to a part of an image, select the layer and area you want to work on and then choose a filter from the Filter menu. Alternatively, you can invoke an image adjustment command (Image > Adjustments), such as Brightness/Contrast, Hue/Saturation, or Replace Color. You can also edit color fills and gradients. See Figure 4–30.

- *Paint, Draw, and Erase:* You can use the Brush, Pencil, and Erase tools within a selection—a convenient way to stay within the lines.

figure | 4–30 |

On the left the giraffe selection has been modified with the Plastic Wrap filter. On the right the background of the giraffe has been modified with a gradient and texture effect.

Lesson: Dressing Max

Finally, here is your chance to select and transform pixels. While dressing Max (see Figure 4–31) for school (the Photoshop way), you learn how to use the Marquee, Magic Wand, and Lasso tools. You will also learn to move, scale, and rotate objects, and to transfer and organize selected pixels from one file to another.

Setting Up the File

1. In Photoshop, choose File > Open. Open the file **chap4L1.psd** in the **chap04_lessons** folder.

2. Save a copy of this file in your **lessons** folder. Choose File > Save As, and name your file **chap4L1_yourname.psd**.

> **Note:** If you get a "Maximize compatibility" dialog box, keep the option checked and click OK.

figure | 4–31 |

Max before and after.

3. Choose View > Actual Pixels to see the document at 100% magnification. This is Max, a friend of Annesa's.

4. Choose Image > Image Size. Note that the image is set at 72 pixels per inch (ppi)—a good resolution if you want to use this image on the Web or for screen display. Close the dialog box.

5. Choose Window > Layers (if not already open) to view the three layers currently in the file. Each clothing item you bring into the file will have its own layer.

Selecting and Translating from One Document to Another

1. Choose File > Open and browse for **chap04_lessons/assets/hat.tif**. Click Open.

2. View the Layers panel. Note that the hat is located on a background layer. The Background layer is the default layer of any new Photoshop file. All other layers go above the Background layer, and you cannot change the stacking order, blending mode, or opacity of it. It is not necessary, however, to have a Background layer. Actually, we prefer to convert the Background layer into a regular layer, where we can create transparent content, move it anywhere in the Layers panel, and change its blending mode. To convert the Background layer of the hat image, double-click on the Background layer and enter a new layer name (such as **hat**) in the New Layer dialog box. See Figure 4–32.

3. Now, select the Magic Wand tool in the toolbox. See Figure 4–33. In the tool's Options bar, set the Tolerance to 10.

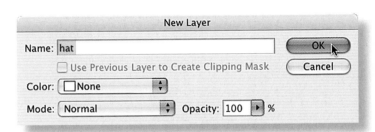

figure | 4–32 |

Change the Background layer to a regular layer, so you have more options.

4. Click on the white background of the hat image to select it. Press Delete to remove the background pixels. The grid image you see behind the hat indicates that area is transparent. The grid will not be saved when you convert the image into another format other than Photoshop (.psd) or when you print it. See Figure 4–34. You can change the grid size and colors in Preferences > Transparency & Gamut (Mac) or Edit > Preferences > Transparency & Gamut (Windows).

5. Choose Select > Inverse from the menu bar to select the hat area (the part you want!) rather than the background.

6. Position the **chap4L1_yourname** document (Max) and the **hat** document side by side on the screen. Select the **hat** document.

7. Select the Move tool in the toolbox. Move the pointer over the hat image and note the pointer has a scissors icon next to it. The scissors indicates that you can move the hat by dragging it. Click and drag the hat to the **chap4L1_yourname** document (Max). Let go of the mouse to deposit a copy on the file—hey, that is sweet! See Figure 4–35.

8. Close the **hat.tif** file. Do not save it; you are done with it.

Transforming the Hat

1. First, note in the Layers panel that the hat has been placed on a new layer at the top of the stack. Double-click on the layer title (**Layer 1**) and rename it **hat**. It is always good to keep your layers labeled intuitively. You never know when you are going to need to find something again.

2. On the Max document, it is obvious the hat is too big to fit on his head. If you do not believe us, be sure the **hat** layer is selected in the Layers panel, select the Move tool, and then move the hat so it is positioned over Max's head—huge! See Figure 4-36.

3. With the **hat** layer selected, choose Edit > Free Transform. Click and drag inward on a corner of the transform bounding box to scale the hat to fit Max's head. To do this uniformly, hold down Shift as you drag. If you make a mistake—no worries—Edit > Undo or reverse your steps in the History panel.

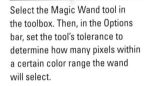

figure | 4–33 |

Select the Magic Wand tool in the toolbox. Then, in the Options bar, set the tool's tolerance to determine how many pixels within a certain color range the wand will select.

figure | 4–34 |

The transparent areas of a layer are indicated by a grid pattern.

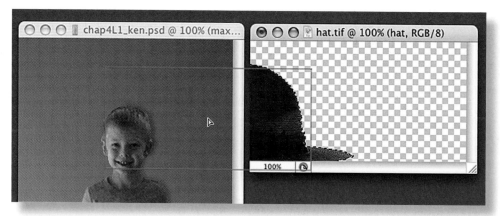

figure |4–35|

With the Move tool, drag the selection from one file to another to make a copy of it.

4. To position the hat, click near the center of the image—but not right on center, because that would move the object's registration point—and drag the hat to the desired location. If the hat seems to be jumping around his head, go to View > Snap on the menu bar and make sure it is unchecked.

5. To rotate the hat, position the pointer slightly outside a corner of the free transform bounding box. An icon with two curved arrows will appear. Click and drag to execute the rotation. See Figure 4–37.

6. To complete the transformation, do one of the following: click on the check-mark button in the Options bar, hit Return or Enter, or double-click on the hat. If you do not want to commit to the transformation, choose the warning circle button in the Options bar or hit Esc. See Figure 4–38.

7. Save your file.

figure |4–36|

The huge hat!

Adding Another Clothing Item

1. Choose **chap04_lessons/assets**. Open the **pants.tif** file.

2. Be sure the **pants** document is selected (click on it to bring it forward).

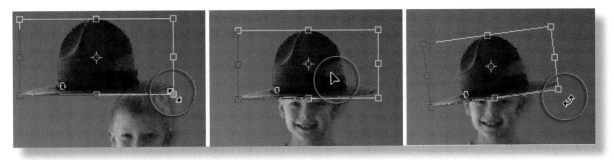

figure | 4–37 |

Three transformations occur to fit the hat on Max's head: scale, move, and rotate.

3. In the Layers panel, double-click on the Background layer to change it to a regular layer. Name it **pants**.

4. Select the white background pixels with the Magic Wand tool.

5. Hit Delete to remove the pixels.

6. Choose Select > Inverse to get just the pants.

7. With the Move tool, click on the pants and drag a copy of them to the **Max** document.

8. Close the **pants** file. No need to save changes.

9. On the **Max** file, rename **Layer 1** to **pants**.

10. Select the pants layer and choose Edit > Transform > Scale. In the Options bar resize the pants numerically by typing in 65 (%) for both the Width and the Height. See Figure 4–39.

11. Position the pants to fit on Max. Double-click on the selection to execute the transformation.

12. Note the stray, white pixels around the edge of the pants. To clean them up, select the **pants** layer, choose Layer > Matting > Defringe. For the Defringe Width, enter **4** (pixels). Click OK. Ahh, much nicer.

13. Save your file.

figure | 4–38 |

Complete the transformation by clicking the check mark on the Options bar.

figure | 4–39 |

Resize the pants numerically.

Adding to and Marqueeing a Selection

1. Choose File > Open and open the file **boots.tif** in **chap04_lessons/assets**.

2. Be sure the **boots** document is selected (click on it to bring it forward).

3. In the Layers panel, double-click on the Background layer to change it to a regular layer. Name it **boots**.

4. On the document, select the white background pixels with the Magic Wand tool.

5. Hit Delete to remove the pixels. Look closely. There are still some white areas that need to be removed within the loops of the boots. These white areas are enclosed by the red pixels of the boot and therefore were not detected by the Magic Wand tool.

6. Zoom in on the boot's loop on the far left-hand side of the document. See Figure 4–40.

7. Select the Lasso tool and draw around the white pixels in the center of the boot's loops. See Figure 4–41 and Figure 4–42). Close the circle shape and let go of the mouse to see the marching ants selection. This takes a steady hand, so if you find yourself selecting everything but the white pixels, choose Edit > Undo Lasso and try again.

8. OK, let us add to this selection. It will take some coordination on your part, so be patient. Select the Hand tool and move the document to the left until you see the next boot loop. Or, alternatively use the Navigation panel (Window>Navigator).

9. Select the Lasso tool and position the pointer over the white pixels in the center of the boot's loop. Hold down Shift and note that a plus (+) icon appears next to the Lasso pointer. Keep holding down Shift and draw around the white pixels within the boot loop. See Figure 4–43. Close the shape, let go of the mouse to see the marching ants selection. See Figure 4–44.

10. Keep adding to the selection. With the Hand tool, move the Document window to the left until you see the last boot loop on the right.

11. Select the Lasso tool and position your pointer over the white pixels in the center of the boot's loop. Hold down Shift and draw around the white pixels within the boot loop. Close the shape.

12. The white areas within each boot loop are selected. Hit Delete to remove the unwanted pixels.

13. Choose View > Actual Pixels to view the boots at 100% magnification.

figure | 4–40|

With the Zoom tool, marquee the area you want to see close up.

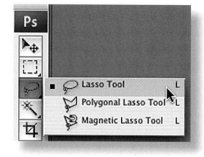

figure | 4–41|

Select the Lasso tool.

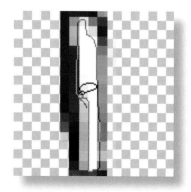

figure | 4–42|

With the Lasso tool, draw around the white pixels within the boot loop.

figure | 4–43 |

Hold down Shift to add to a selection.

figure | 4–44 |

Close the shape to define the selection.

14. To move the boots to Max's feet, position the **boot** document and **Max** document side by side on the screen. Select the Rectangular Marquee tool in the toolbox. See Figure 4–45.

15. Marquee around the boot on the left. See Figure 4–46. With the Move tool, click and drag a copy of the boot to the **Max** document. Position the boot over his right foot.

16. Select the other boot, and move a copy of it to Max's left foot.

17. Close **boots.tif** without saving it; you will not need it again.

18. In the Layers panel, rename **Layer 1** to **right_boot**, and **Layer 2** to **left_boot**.

19. Select the **right_boot** layer, and then choose Layer > Matting > Defringe. Type in 4 (pixels). Do the same thing for the **left_boot** layer.

20. Move the **pants** layer above the **boot** layers. See Figure 4–47. Position the boots, if necessary, to appear behind the pants.

21. Save the file.

figure | 4–45 |

Select the Rectangular Marquee tool.

figure | 4–46 |

Marquee around a boot and move it to another document.

Selecting a Textured Background

1. Open **shirt_blazer.tif** in the **chap04_lessons/assets** folder.

2. With the Lasso tool, draw a cursory selection around the blazer. Be sure to include the shirt and tie in the selection. See Figure 4–48.

3. With the Move tool, click and drag a copy of the blazer selection to the **Max** file.

4. In the Layers panel, rename the new layer **blazer** and move it above the other layers.

5. With the **blazer** layer is selected, choose the Magic Wand tool.

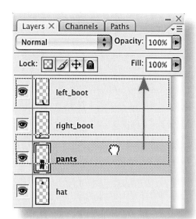

figure | 4–47 |

Rearrange the stacking order of layers by clicking and dragging a layer between two others.

6. In the Options bar for the Magic Wand tool, enter 40 for the Tolerance. Then click the green textured area to select it. Note that not all parts of the textured background have been selected.

7. Change the Magic Wand tool's Tolerance to 65 and reselect the textured background. Do you get more or all of the background pixels? Play with the tolerance until you get the green pixels selected. You might also need to add or subtract from your selection if some of the green pixels are not contiguous, or try selecting an area with the Contiguous option deselected in the Magic Wand tool's Options bar.

8. Press Delete on the keyboard to remove the selected background pixels.

9. Position and/or transform the blazer to fit Max. See Figure 4–49.

10. If you'd like more practice, on your own add the flowered shirt image to fit Max. (You might want to turn the visibility off on the **blazer** layer while doing this.)

11. Save the file. Max is dressed and ready to head off to school.

figure | 4–48 |

Cursorily select the blazer with the Lasso tool.

figure | 4–49 |

The stages of selecting a blazer for Max (steps 6 through 9).

SUMMARY

As you have learned, selecting and transforming objects is the most fundamental procedure you need to do in Photoshop. Identifying the best tools for the task makes these actions easier and more efficient to execute, letting you move on to more miraculous creations in the program.

in review

1. Describe how the color Tolerance setting works.

2. Name at least two ways to get better selection accuracy.

3. What selection tool is the least efficient in selecting irregular areas of an image?

4. What does the Contiguous option do when you are using the Magic Wand tool?

5. What shortcut key command lets you make straight-edge segment selections with the Lasso tool and freehand segments with the Polygonal Lasso tool?

6. Using any selection tool, what shortcut key command lets you add to a selection? Subtract from a selection?

7. One way to transform objects is numerically. What other way can you think of?

8. Describe what the Background layer is. How is it different from a regular layer?

exploring on your own

1. In Photoshop, go to Help > Photoshop Help. Under Contents, read the sections "Selecting" and "Retouching and Transforming" (no need to get into the retouching parts of this section, which is covered in Chapter 6). Also, refer to the section on Keyboard shortcuts > Default keyboard shortcuts > Keys for selecting and moving objects.

2. To complement Max, select and bring a copy of Mina the kitty (**chap04_lessons/assets/mina.tif**) into the **chap4L1 file** you created. For an example, see the "after" picture of Max—in Figure 4–31—to see how we placed Mina, or the **chap4L1_final.psd** in the **chap04_lessons** folder. We removed the unwanted background pixels, scaled her, flipped her horizontally (Edit > Transform > Flip Horizontal), rotated her, "defringed" her (Layer > Matting > Defringe), and added a drop shadow (Layer > Layer Style > Drop Shadow).

Explorer pages

TIM WARNOCK

Sunset Boulevard. Tim Warnock, Matte Painter/Concept Artist

Farewell. Tim Warnock, Matte Painter/Concept Artist

About Tim Warnock

Tim Warnock has been working as an artist for 12 years. In that time he has done a number of different things but digital tools, specifically Photoshop, have always been central to what he does. Working as a matte painter and concept artist he had the opportunity to be a part of films such as *Silent Hill*, *Babel*, and *The Number 23*.

Tim's post-secondary education began in the Graphic Design program at St. Lawrence College in Cornwall Ontario. After completing his studies there he went on to the Illustration program at Dawson College in Montreal Quebec. In addition to his college education he has taken 3D and matte painting training at the NAD Center in Montreal. To see more of his work, visit *http://www.thenextside.com*.

"Focus on fundamentals, perspective, color, lighting, scale—and all of those things. What you see as a mistake with a lot of young artists is they neglect those things. They might have really good 3D skills with texture and lighting, but the composition is terrible. Study the masters and even current artists who are highly regarded. When you master the fundamentals it's just a matter of learning the tools. You can then be given anything and create something that's solid."

 Learn more about this artist via podcast at *http://www.designexploration.com/podcasts.*

About the Work of Tim Warnock

Tim shares his work process: "Whenever I sit down to create a painting research is always the first thing that I do. This could involve searching for images online or going out and shooting reference material. I have a Canon Rebel XTi that takes 10MP images. As much as I can I like to use my own images because the resolution and color depth is greater than most of what I can find online.

"Once I'm satisfied with the research material I've gathered I set to working out my composition. This is accomplished with loose sketches in Photoshop. During this stage I will often begin playing with different photos to see what might work. This 'blocking in' stage is where the perspective, color pallet and composition gets worked out.

"From this point I make decisions about how the detail is to be achieved. Some things can be painted. Some things will require photographic material. Some things will require 3D elements. For *Desert Ruin* I had done a lot of research on Egypt for another project. I had come across so many interesting things that I was inspired to do this piece. Following the process above I combine many images to create one seamless image. This is where an understanding of perspective and color is critical. Special care is given to color values to create depth and ensure that everything is sitting in the same space. These color changes are made by using QuickMask to isolate sections of the image and then color corrected with tools like Curves or ColorBalance. I like to choose one image to be my main reference for lighting and values and refer to it often to ensure I'm headed in the right direction. Paint work is mainly done with standard Photoshop brushes, but I do occasionally create custom brushes for things like leaves and grass.

"The final application of the painting is a 2.5D matte painting incorporating a crane camera move that starts fairly low to the ground and finishes with this composition. To do this the painting is constructed on layers in Photoshop and then mapped onto rudimentary geometry in XSI (3D software) using camera projections. The end result is fairly realistic parallax and perspective shifts that couldn't be easily accomplished with a 2D compositing approach."

Desert Ruin. Tim Warnock, Matte Painter/Concept Artist

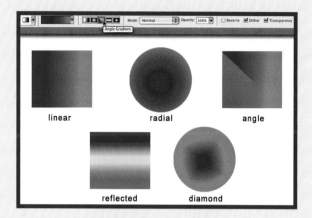

linear   radial   angle

reflected   diamond

| working with color |

charting your course

In Chapter 4 you selected and transformed pixels. Now you get to change the color of pixels. This chapter covers some fundamental concepts of color, such as how color is reproduced, color modes, and a hands-on study with color models that will pique your interest as a designer. We will also get into some important aspects of color specifically related to Photoshop, such as tips for managing color, dealing with channels, and using the color application tools.

goals

In this chapter you will:

- **Understand the concept of a color gamut**
- **Get acquainted with color models**
- **Know what color mode to use**
- **Apply color to pixels**
- **Explore the color features and tools**
- **Make gradients**
- **Study, hands-on, the use of color models and tonal value**

OPTICAL MIXING

Step away from your computer for a moment and find a painting somewhere. It could be the watercolor your child did or the acrylic piece you picked up at the local art auction. Look very closely at the painting. Examine how the brush strokes blend, how the mixing of pigment produces varied effects and transitions of color. When a color is blended with white, it produces a lighter version (tint) of the color, and when blended with black, a darker version (shade) of the color. This method of blending—mixing paint to produce colors—is different from how a computer produces color. In digital image-making, each individual color produced is contained in its own pixel area. See Figure 5–1. The effect of colors blending, like what is occurring in a traditional painting, is only an illusion manifested by our eyes, often referred to as optical mixing.

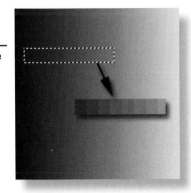

figure | 5–1 |

The image looks like a smooth gradient of color, but when we zoom in close to a selection, we see that each pixel contains its own shade of color.

Optical mixing is found in traditional painting and drawing and is often known as pointillism. Pointillism is a method of painting or illustration in which tiny dots (or shapes) of color are combined in such precision that, when viewed from a certain distance, the pattern forms a complete picture. Post-impressionist painter Georges Seurat (1859 to 1891) codified the technique of pointillism. Whereas other artists were blending paint colors on their canvases, he was creating the same effect by applying pigment in small dabs or points of pure color.

From *Understanding Art* (seventh edition), by Lois Fichner-Rathus, "Upon close inspection, the painting [Seurat's] appears to be a collection of dots of vibrant hues—complementary colors abutting one another, primary colors placed side by side. These hues intensify or blend to form yet another color in the eye of the viewer who beholds the canvas from a distance."

Chuck Close, a modern painter and photographer, uses this type of illusionary picture-making. He combines detailed pattern shapes into famous portraits. The method of creating patterns by sewing colored patches together in quilting is also a form of optical mixing. In what other ways might you think images are formed optically? See Figure 5–2.

figure | 5–2 |

A Sunday Afternoon on the Island of La Grande Jatte, by Georges Seurat. Using a technique called pointillism, Seurat painted this picture with thousands of dots of color.

When we look closely at a digital image, each pixel is one shade of color. When we view it from a distance, it appears to be a completely blended image. Digital images produce form through optical mixing. One technique that encourages this illusion is antialiasing. Antialiasing smoothes the jagged edges of a digital image by softening the color transition— with gradations of color or shades of gray—between edge pixels and background pixels. In other words, it makes an object that is composed of square pixels appear rounded, smoothed, or curved, not "pixelated." See Figure 5–3.

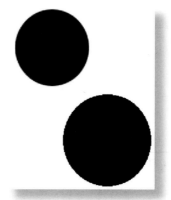

figure | 5–3 |

Image with and without antialiasing. The top circle has antialiasing applied and appears smoother. The bottom circle does not have antialiasing and appears "pixilated."

SPECTRAL ILLUSION

OK, we learned our eyes have an uncanny way of optically mixing colors to form recognizable images. Now, discover that our eyes view different colors depending on where we are and under what conditions we are looking. Every device that has the capability to reproduce color, such as a computer screen, a printer, or a TV, has its own color range (or limit), which is defined as its color space or gamut. For example, although today's monitors can view millions of colors, what we see on a computer screen is not all the colors available in our universe. In fact, our human color device—our eyes—can view many more colors than can any type of digitized screen or printer device.

Take a good look at Figure 5–4. The chart indicates the visual (human), computer screen (RGB), and print (CMYK) color gamuts. (You will learn about RGB and CMYK in the next section.) Notice the marked areas indicating the gamuts. All of the gamuts overlap; each is able to view some similar color shades. However, the print (CMYK) gamut, indicated by the smallest gamut area, has the least amount of viewable color possibilities.

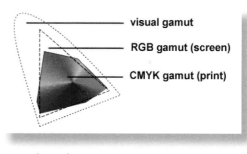

— visual gamut

— RGB gamut (screen)

— CMYK gamut (print)

figure | 5–4 |

The visual, screen, and print gamuts.

So, when you pick a color for your digital image in Photoshop—which, by default, uses the RGB screen gamut— and print it, you might find that color to be different from the one you picked. Most likely, the color you picked in Photoshop is not available in the printer's gamut. It gets even more particular. For example, a CRT monitor and a LCD monitor will show the same color blue differently, as will a PC monitor versus a Macintosh monitor. No doubt this predicament is very frustrating, but once you understand why it happens there are many ways to achieve the result you want (this is what is referred to as "Keeping colors consistent" in the Photoshop Help file—Help > Photoshop Help > Contents). In fact, that is just another of Photoshop's many talents: the ability to simulate for users what colors will eventually look like once they are reproduced from different devices. We cannot cover all the ways in this chapter, but we will get you started with some explanation of color models and modes and provide you with some additional reading in the "Exploring on Your Own" section.

CHOOSING A COLOR MODEL

A color model is a system for describing color. You use color models when choosing, creating, and controlling colors in your digital images. All color models use numeric values to represent the visible spectrum of color. For instance, the truest red color on a screen is indicated as 255 Red, 0 Green, 0 Blue (or 255,0,0). There are many different color models, but in computer graphics and specifically in Photoshop, we will look at the following: Grayscale, RGB, HSB, CMYK, and Lab.

Grayscale

The Grayscale color model is used to select tints of black ranging in brightness from 0% (white) to 100% (black). When you convert color images into grayscale in Photoshop the luminosity (tonal level) of each color in the artwork becomes a representation of a shade of gray (you get a taste of this in the lesson). To select colors in grayscale, choose Window > Color (if not already open) and from the panel's Options menu, choose the Grayscale Slider. See Figure 5–5.

figure 5–5

The Color panel with the Grayscale model selected.

RGB

The RGB model represents the primary colors of visible light: red, green, and blue (RGB). The mixing of red, green, and blue light in various proportions and intensities produces a wide range of colors in our visual spectrum. RGB color is also referred to as additive color. When R, G, and B lights are combined, equally they create white, which is what you see when all light is reflected back to the eye. (The absence of colored light is black—what you get when you wander down a cave without a flashlight.) When R, G, and B overlap, they create cyan, magenta, and yellow. See Figure 5–6. Devices that reproduce color with light are using the RGB color model. Examples are your TV, the miniscule screen on your PDA, and, of course, your computer monitor.

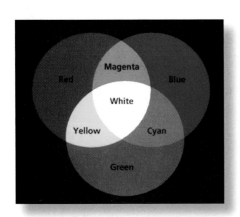

figure 5–6

The RGB color model.

Each component (red, green, or blue) in the RGB color model is labeled a value ranging from 0 to 255. This means you can have a total of 256 shades of red, 256 shades of green, and 256 shades of blue, and any combination thereof (a lot of colors!). For example, the most intense red color is represented as 255 (R), 0 (G), 0 (B), and a shade of deep purple is represented as 137 (R), 95 (G), 137 (B). See Figure 5–7.

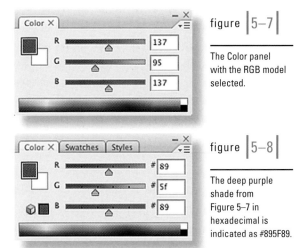

figure |5–7|

The Color panel with the RGB model selected.

Photoshop also includes the Web Color model, a modified RGB model that indicates a spectrum of colors most appropriate for use on the Web. The color components in the Web Color space are measured using hexadecimal, a number/letter system used to represent colors. For example, the same shade of deep purple from Figure 5–7 in hexadecimal is indicated as #895F89. See Figure 5–8.

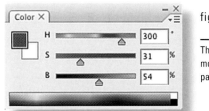

figure |5–8|

The deep purple shade from Figure 5–7 in hexadecimal is indicated as #895F89.

HSB

Color can also be defined as levels of HSB—hue, saturation, and brightness. Hue identifies a main color property or name, such as "blue" or "orange." It is measured by a percentage from 0 to 360 degrees, as if picking colors from a standard color wheel. (See the Exploring On Your Own section of this chapter for color wheel examples.) Saturation is the strength or purity of color. It is measured as an amount of gray in proportion to the hue, ranging from 0% (gray) to 100% (fully saturated). Brightness is the relative lightness or darkness of a hue, measured as a percentage from 0% (black) to 100% (white). See Figure 5–9.

figure |5–9|

The HSB color model in the Color panel.

CMYK

In contrast to the RGB color model, which reproduces color based on light, the CMYK model reproduces color based on pigment or ink. The colors of CMYK—cyan (C), magenta (M), yellow (Y), and black (K, or Key)—are called subtractive, because when you add these pigments to a white page or canvas, they subtract or absorb some of the light, leaving what is left over to reflect back to your eyes. When the colors overlap, interestingly, they produce red, green, and blue (RGB). See Figure 5–10.

The "black" part of the CMYK color model is a bit illusive. To print a true black color on white, a higher percentage of cyan is mixed with magenta and yellow; it is not really an equal amount of each color as the Figure 5–10 diagram might lead you to believe. An equal mixing would actually result in muddy brown, not black, because of the absorption that occurs when ink hits paper. This is why black ink is used in addition to the subtractive primaries cyan, magenta, and yellow in four-color printing.

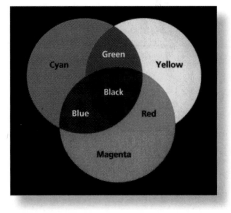

figure |5–10|

The CMYK color model.

figure |5–11|

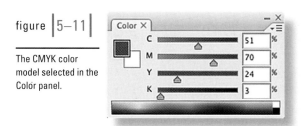

The CMYK color model selected in the Color panel.

Each color component of the CMYK model is represented by a percentage ranging from 0% to 100%. To produce a shade of mauve-colored paint, for example, you mix 51% cyan, 70% magenta, 24% yellow, and 3% black. See Figure 5–11. In the print industry, this combining of the CMYK colors is called four-color process (or full-color printing). The individual colors produced by the mixing of any of these four colors are appropriately identified as process colors. In addition to process colors, another color type used in printing is spot colors. These are special colors composed of premixed inks that require their own printing plate other than the ones used for four-color processing. You will run into process and spot color types as you work with colors in Photoshop, but do not worry about them right now. Preparing an image for a professional print job can easily become an advanced topic beyond the scope of this book. A good start is to know that if your Photoshop graphic is going to go to print, you should choose colors in the CMYK model.

Lab

Specifically in Photoshop, color can also be defined as Lab, based on the human perception of color—the colors seen by a person with normal vision. The primary color components of Lab include lightness (or L) and two chromatic components: *a* for green and red and *b* for blue and yellow. See Figure 5–12. Interestingly, Lab color is not often used by the average Photoshop user. However, it plays a vital role behind the scenes. Lab describes color by how it looks to the human eye rather than through the lens (limited color range) of a particular device (a monitor, digital camera, or desktop printer). That is why Lab is considered a device-independent color model, which makes it a great color mode for Photoshop

figure |5–12|

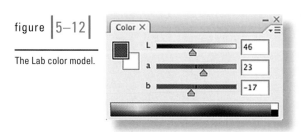

The Lab color model.

to use when it needs to convert colors based on a user's specified color management system. You could think of it as the color system used to adjust colors between color systems. If we just lost you here, do not worry. It is good to know Lab exists, but it is not necessary to completely comprehend in the initial stages of your Photoshop study.

GETTING IN THE MODE

Although you can select colors from various color models, ultimately you will want to set up your Photoshop image to a specific color mode or working space depending on the artwork's intended purpose. A color mode determines how your artwork will be output, either for display on screen (RGB) or for print (CMYK). When you create a new document in Photoshop, you must specify the color mode. You can do this when you first create the document or by switching modes while working on the document. See Figure 5–13. The main color modes are Bitmap, Grayscale, RGB Color, CMYK Color, and Lab Color.

Photoshop also includes specialized modes (such as Duotone, Multichannel, and Indexed Color) that you can delve into on your own. You can change between the CMYK and RGB Color modes at any time by choosing Image > Mode on the menu bar. There are a couple of reasons you might want to change color mode: (1) you want to use one of Photoshop's tools or filters, which can only be applied when the document is in RGB Color mode; and (2) you change your mind about where you want to output your artwork. Be aware that moving

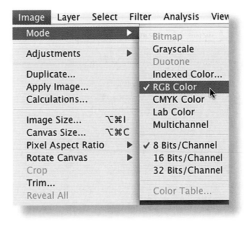

figure |5–13|

Set the color mode of a document.

between modes can cause significant shifts in the colors you see on the screen, and it can degrade the color accuracy of the image if you move between modes too many times.

Why all this color mode business? Well, remember, when it comes to color reproduction, what you see is not necessarily what you are going to get from print to screen and screen to print, but it does not hurt to try every means possible to get it close. Setting the proper color mode is one of those means—you specify the mode when you first make the document (File > New) or while working on the document (Image > Mode).

APPLYING COLOR

Applying color in Photoshop starts out easy enough. First choose the color you want, and then apply it to a selected area with a command or tool. The hard part comes in trying to decide what color you want. There are, of course, numerous "theoretical ways" in which to pick colors that work well together. One suggestion is to use a standard color wheel to identify complementary colors; colors that are opposite each other on the color wheel, such as blue and orange. (For an example color wheel and more information on color wheels, see the "Exploring On Your Own" section at the end of this chapter.) The use of color models or wheels to mix and choose a color can help to identify color based on a numeric numbering system, but for the inquisitive-minded artist, it might be just as well to play with colors until you see something you like—just remember that the color you see on the screen might not visually reproduce exactly as the same color to another medium, such as on a piece of paper.

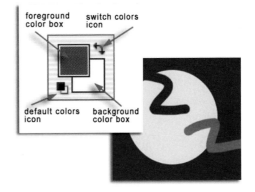

In Photoshop, you choose colors for either a foreground or background. The foreground color is used to paint, fill, and stroke selections, while the background color is used to make gradient fills and fill in the erased areas of an image. See Figure 5–14.

figure |5–14|

The upper image indicates options for the foreground and background selection area of the toolbox. The lower image shows how erasing an image reveals the background color (black).

figure 5–15

figure 5–15

Select the Paint Bucket tool to fill in selections.

Color is applied using the Paint Bucket tool or a drawing or brush tool, or by choosing Edit > Fill or Stroke. See Figure 5–15. You can also take a sample of an existing color within an image with the Eyedropper tool. See Figure 5–16.

figure 5–16

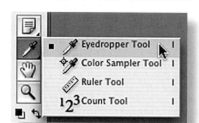

Select the Eyedropper tool and take a sample of color from an image.

You can choose colors in the Color panel, the Color Picker (accessed by clicking the foreground or background color selection box in the toolbox), or the Swatches panel. You can also create graduated blends of color using the Gradient tool. Each of these color selection options is described in the sections that follow.

The Color Panel

The Color panel (see Figure 5–17) allows you to choose various color models in which to work and to switch between choosing and adjusting colors on either the foreground or background of a selected object.

figure 5–17

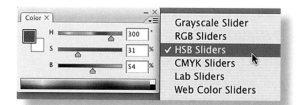

Go to Window > Color (if not already open) to open the Color panel.

The Color Picker and Color Libraries

The Color Picker (see Figure 5–18) is a sophisticated version of the Color panel, offering the option to view, select, and adjust colors from a number of color models in one window. It can be a little overwhelming, so we will break it down for you in the following figures.

figure 5–18

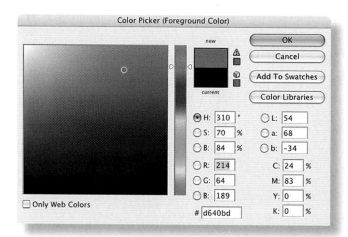

Full view of the Color Picker.

At the top of the window, the Color Picker title appears followed by the words *Foreground Color* or *Background Color* to make you aware of the color being changed (refer to Figure 5–18). You choose your colors on the left side of the Color Picker. See Figure 5–19. The spectrum bar on the right is where you pick the hue, such as red, blue, or green. The large box to the left allows you to adjust the hue's saturation (moving horizontally) and brightness (moving vertically).

figure |5–19|

The left side of the Color Picker is for choosing colors.

The area shown in Figure 5–20 is where you preview the colors you are selecting in the Color Picker. Your current color selections are updated automatically in the top area of the box, while the lower part indicates the original color on a selected object. Next to the color indicator are gamut warnings. Gamut warnings pop up when you have chosen a color that is outside either the Web-safe (the 3D box icon) or the CMYK (alert triangle icon) gamut. When you click on the 3D box icon, the color shifts to the closest Web-safe color. Similarly, when you click on the alert triangle, the color shifts to the closest CMYK (print) color. This is a really handy feature!

figure |5–20|

In the Color Picker, there is an area to preview a color you have chosen above the color that is already applied to the object.

On the right side of the Color Picker (see Figure 5–21), you can adjust colors numerically in any of the four color models: HSB, RGB, CMYK, and Lab. The hexadecimal color code (#) for selected colors is provided for artwork intended for Web pages.

By choosing the Color Libraries button on the Color Picker, a whole new world of color possibilities emerges. This area (see Figure 5–22) lets you choose predefined color libraries, equivalent to those in printed swatch books, such as PANTONE or TRUMATCH.

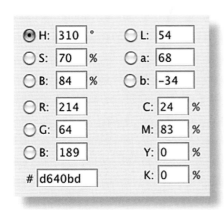

figure |5–21|

Adjust colors numerically on the right side of the Color Picker.

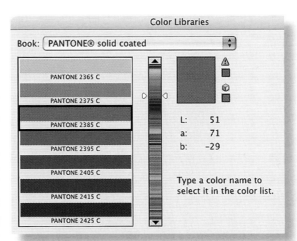

figure |5–22|

Color Libraries area of the Color Picker.

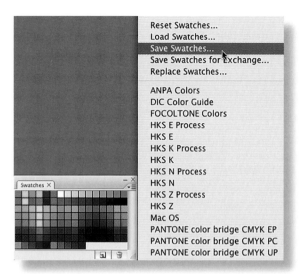

figure |5-23|

The Swatches panel.

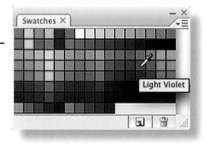

figure |5-24|

Click on a swatch to use that color in your image.

The Swatches Panel

After you spend long hours picking out your favorite colors, it is good to know you can save them in the Swatches panel. See Figure 5–23. To apply your saved colors to selected objects, click on your saved swatches in the Swatches panel window. See Figure 5–24. You can make swatch libraries to reuse in other documents or use one of the many already provided for you. The Swatches panel will not only save and load your specific color selections, but also will load other custom color libraries.

The Gradient Tool and Gradient Panel

Gradients are graduated color blends. They are useful to create smooth transitions of color on an object or across multiple objects, giving them a more dimensional look. Gradients come in several varieties, including linear, radial, angle, reflected, and diamond, which you can choose from the Gradient tools Options bar. See Figure 5–25. Gradients are created in the Gradient Editor (see Figure 5–26) and then applied with the Gradient tool (see Figure 5–27) in the toolbox. To get to the Editor, select the Gradient tool in the toolbox, and then click inside the gradient sample area in the Options bar to open the Editor and edit the gradient (refer to Figure 5–26 for steps).

figure |5-25|

Gradient Options bar and examples of the different gradient blends.

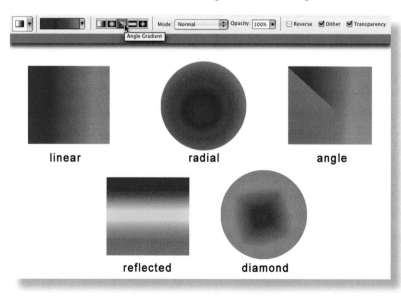

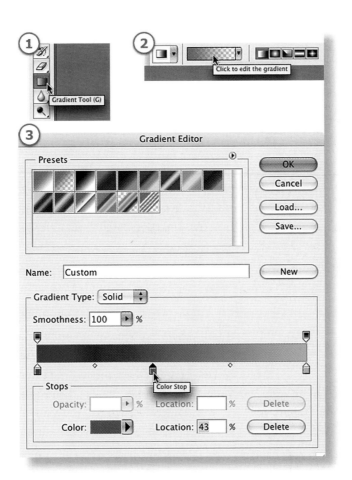

figure | 5–26 |

To modify or create new gradients, use the Gradient Editor.

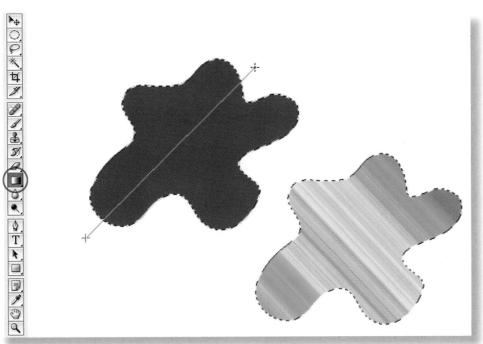

figure | 5–27 |

Gradient tool.

Solid gradients are the most common Gradient Type to choose in the Gradient Editor, but you can also have fun with Noise gradients, a more random blending of color with variable roughness. Expect to spend a lot of time in the Editor making and saving new gradients. You will get some practice in the next lesson.

ADJUSTING COLOR

A big part of dealing with color in Photoshop is adjusting color that is already in an image. There are a multitude of image adjustment options (Image > Adjustments) that can absorb your time and creativity—including options to change the tonal quality of a photograph (highlights, shadows, and mid-tones) and a photograph's hue and saturation levels. You will get exclusively into adjusting color in Chapter 6. However, let us explain the importance of channels and bit depth.

About Channels and Bit Depth

We cannot skip the concept of channels and the effect of bit depth when working with color in Photoshop. Inevitably, you will run into both. When you really start getting into the mysteries of color correction and manipulation, channels will provide the necessary clues to reach the result you want. Channels are grayscale images that store information about each primary color of a color model. For example, the RGB model contains a red channel, a green channel, a blue channel, and a composite channel (which is all three channels put together and what you normally see when you view the image). To view the channels available in any document, choose Window > Channels, if not already open. See Figure 5–28.

figure 5–28

The Channels panel.

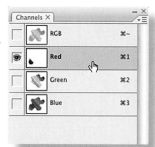

Each channel can be edited separately, giving you full control over specific ranges of color in the image. For example, if your photograph is too red, you can lesson the amount of red in the image with the Channel Mixer (Image > Adjustments > Channel Mixer). See Figure 5–29. You can also create additional channels, such as a spot color to be used in the printing process or an alpha channel, which stores a specific selection or mask (this will be covered in Chapter 8).

The more channels in an image, the larger the image file size, which is where bit depth comes in again. Remember, in Chapter 3, we mentioned that the larger an image's bit depth (accumulation of zeros and ones), the more variations of color an image can contain. Moreover, the more variations, the larger the image file size. All of this bit depth information is stored in channels. A black-and-white image, also called a one-bit image

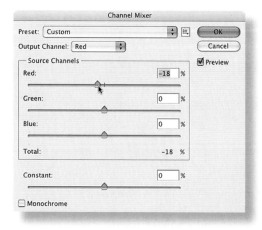

figure 5–29

Adjust the red pixels in the image using the Channel Mixer.

or bitmap, has one channel and a bit depth of 1, with the possibility of holding only two colors—black and white. See Figure 5–30. The same image saved in CMYK color, which has four channels and more room to store colors, has a file size of 351.1K—heavy! See Figure 5–31.

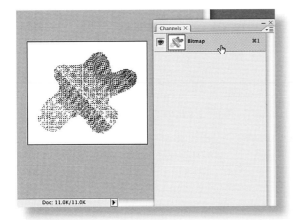

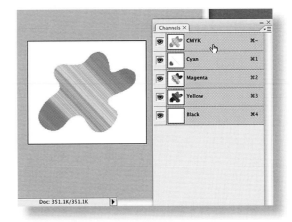

figure | 5–30 |

figure | 5–31 |

A one-bit image (or bitmap) has one channel, which supports a bit depth of two colors, black and white. Note the file size of the image in the lower-left corner: 11K.

An image saved in the CMYK Color mode has four channels and more room to store colors. Note its file size: 351.6K.

There actually is method to this madness, but we are only going to take you so far as to understand that bit depth, channels, and color models are all interrelated:

- Bitmap images have one channel, and contain 1 bit of color (black and white).
- Grayscale images have one channel that contains 8 bits of color, which can produce 256 different shades of gray.
- RGB images have three channels of color that contain 8 bits of color per channel, which can produce 256 shades of each of the colors red, green, and blue. (Remember that each bit contains two possible values: 0 or 1. To calculate the total possible amount of shades, take 2 to the 8th power (8 bits): $2 \times 2 \times 2 \times 2 \times 2 \times 2 \times 2 \times 2 = 256$ shades. To calculate the total amount of colors in RGB, take 256 shades to the 3rd power (red, green and blue): $256 \times 256 \times 256 = 16.7$ million colors.)
- CMYK images have four channels of color that contain 8 bits of color per channel, which can produce 256 shades of each of the colors cyan, magenta, yellow, and black.

> Note: Living in the "more is better" world that we seem to be in, Photoshop also offers the capability of creating images containing 16 bits (65 thousand shades per color channel) or 32 bits (four billion shades per color channel) of color per channel—expanding the amount of color variations that can be stored in the image. Why so much? The need is specific depending on the area of computer graphics. For instance, in the realm of digital photography, photographers use HDR to pull out details and nuances in their photos that may be invisible to the naked eye. What is HDR? HDR, aka high-dynamic range, is a term often associated with 32-bit images. In contrast, 8-bit and 16-bit images are considered low-dynamic range. (Note that there are many fine details to what classifies a HDR and LDR image that go well beyond the scope of this book).

Lesson: Playing with Color Models

In this lesson, discover how to pair complementary colors, blend them with gradients, and adjust to grayscale. Refer to Figure 5–32.

figure |5–32|

Lesson example
shown in grayscale.

Setting Up the File

1. In Photoshop, choose File > Open. Open the file **chap5L1.psd** in the **chap05_lessons** folder.

> Note: If a dialog box comes up indicating "some layers might need to be updated . . ." choose "No."

2. Save a copy of this file in your **lessons** folder: choose File > Save As and name your file **chap5LI_yourname.psd**. This file contains a template and guides for you to build the color models lesson.

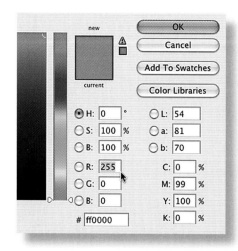

figure |5–33|

Select a true red in the Color Picker.

> Note: If you do not see the guidelines, choose View > Show > Guides. Also, make sure Snap is checked under View > Snap.

3. Open the Layers panel, if it is not already open, (Window > Layers). Select **Layer 1** and name it **red**.

Creating True Opposites

1. Click on the foreground color swatch in the toolbox to open the Color Picker.

2. In the RGB model settings area, enter **255** for red, **0** for green, and **0** for blue. Red 225 is the truest red color you can create on the screen. Click OK. See Figure 5–33.

3. Select the Rectangle tool in the toolbox. See Figure 5–34.

4. In the Options bar, select the Fill pixels option. See Figure 5–35.

5. In the Options bar, select the Geometry options pop-up to display the options for the Rectangle tool (the second down-pointing arrow from the left of the Options bar). In the Rectangle Options box, choose Fixed Size, and then for W, enter **.62 in.** and for H, enter **.66 in.** See Figure 5–36.

> **Note:** As an alternative to setting a fixed size for the rectangle, you can choose Unconstrained and draw the rectangle free-form using the guides and template as positioning markers.

6. Click on the down-pointing arrow of the Geometry options pop-up to close the window.

7. Place your cursor in the upper-left corner of the first rectangle shape indicated on the file. Then, click to place the fixed-size rectangle—click and drag down if you are creating an unconstrained rectangle. See Figure 5–37.

8. Select the Move tool, and place the pointer over the red rectangle you just created.

9. Hold down Option/Alt, and then click and drag to the right to make a copy of the rectangle. Place it right next to the first rectangle. Now, you have what appears to be a red rectangle.

> **Note:** As you drag the duplicate, also hold down Shift to constrain its horizontal positioning.

10. Note that when you make a duplicate it creates a new layer in the Layers panel (red copy). Rename this layer **cyan**.

11. With the **cyan** layer selected, choose Image > Adjustments > Invert to create the complement (invert or dyad) of the red color, which is cyan.

figure | 5–34 |

Select the Rectangle tool.

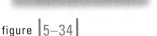

figure | 5–35 |

Select the Fill pixels option in the Rectangle tool's Options bar.

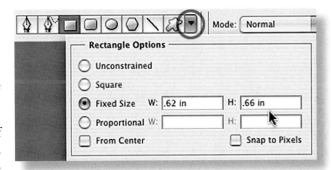

figure | 5–36 |

Set a fixed size for the rectangle in its Options bar.

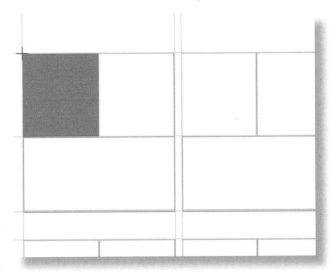

figure | 5–37 |

Place the rectangle on the document.

Note: In the Exploring On Your Own section of this chapter, visit the color wheels. Identify the red section in the wheel, and note the cyan section directly opposite it. Interestingly, the RGB and CMYK color models overlap in the color wheel to create a full spectrum of colors.

12. Create a new layer (Layer > New > Layer) and name it **green**.

13. Double-click on the foreground color box in the toolbox to open the Color Picker.

14. Click the foreground color at the bottom of the toolbox. In the RGB model settings area, enter **0** for red, **255** for green, and **0** for blue.

Note: You can also set this color using the Color panel (Window > Color).

15. Select the Rectangle tool in the toolbox.

16. Click on the upper-left corner of the boxed area next to the cyan rectangle to deposit a green rectangle, or drag a box approximately the same size as the others. See Figure 5–38.

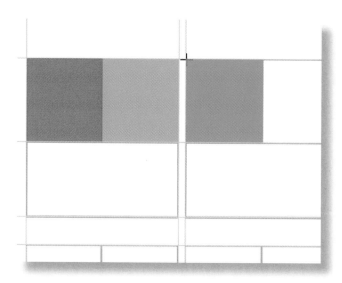

17. Select the Move tool, hold down Alt/Option, and create a duplicate of the green box right next to itself.

18. Rename the duplicate layer **magenta**, the complement (invert or dyad) of green.

19. Choose Image > Adjustments > Invert—or press Command-I (Mac) or CTRL-I (Windows)— to convert the color to magenta.

20. Click on the foreground color swatch in the toolbox to open the Color Picker.

21. In the RGB model settings area, enter **0** for red, **0** for green, and **255** for blue.

22. Create a new Layer and name it **blue**.

23. Create a blue rectangle in the boxed area next to the magenta rectangle.

24. Duplicate the rectangle using the Move tool.

25. Rename its layer **yellow**.

26. Invert the color. See Figure 5–39.

27. Save your file.

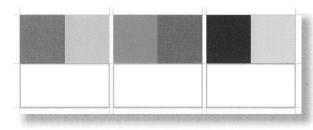

figure |5–39|

Lesson with inverted colors.

Creating a Gradient Between Two Complements

1. Select the Gradient tool in the toolbox. See Figure 5–40.

2. Click inside the gradient sample in the Options bar to open the Gradient Editor. See Figure 5–41.

3. Let us blend a custom gradient using the red and cyan complements. This will create all hues between the two, including chromatic gray in the center. Position the Gradient Editor so you can also see the red and cyan rectangles on the document.

figure |5–40|

Select the Gradient tool.

figure |5–41|

To open the Gradient Editor, click inside the gradient sample in the Options bar.

▶ Don't Go There!

Be sure to click inside the gradient sample area, not on the down-pointing arrow next to it. The options under the down-pointing arrow only give you the currently saved gradients, not the full Gradient Editor window.

---

4. In the Gradient Editor, select the color stop on the left-hand bottom side of the gradient ramp (it will highlight in black). See Figure 5–42.

5. Position the pointer over the red rectangle in your document and note that the pointer changes into an Eyedropper tool. Click on the red to take a sample of the color. The sample is automatically placed into the selected color stop of the gradient ramp. See Figure 5–43.

6. Select the color stop on the right-hand bottom side of the gradient ramp.

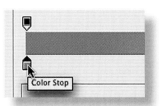

figure |5–42|

Select a color stop to apply a color to the gradient.

figure 5–43

Take a sample of color to apply to the selected color stop.

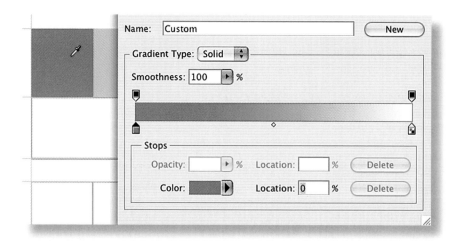

7. Take a sample of the cyan-colored rectangle in the document. The gradient between the two colors is created.

> **Note:** A wonderful thing you can do with gradients is change the opacity settings (levels of transparency) of any color in the gradient. In this example, we want the gradient color at full opacity, so be sure both opacity stops are set at 100%. See Figure 5–44. Also, for future reference, you might want to add more colors to your gradient. To do this, click in the lower part of the gradient ramp to create more color stops. See Figure 5–45. To remove color stops, click and drag them down and away from the ramp and, amazingly, they disappear.

figure 5–44

Set the opacity stops at 100%.

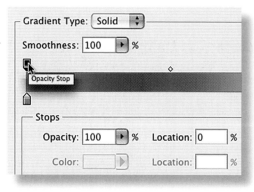

figure 5–45

Add color stops to create more color blends.

8. Select New to define (save) the gradient in the gradient sample area. Click OK to close the Gradient Editor.

9. OK, you have made the gradient, now let us apply it to the document. Create a new layer and name it **gradient1**.

10. Select the Rectangular Marquee tool in the toolbox—be sure it is the Marquee tool, not the Rectangle tool.

11. Select the rectangle area below the red and cyan boxed areas. Marching ants should appear, indicating the selection.

12. Select the Gradient tool in the toolbox.

13. Hold down Shift, click and drag the tool from left to right in the selected area, and then let go to apply the gradient. See Figure 5–46.

14. Create a new layer and name it **gradient2**.

15. Follow steps 1–14 to create and apply another new gradient using green and magenta under the green and magenta boxed areas.

16. Ditto for the blue and yellow area. See Figure 5–47.

17. Save your file.

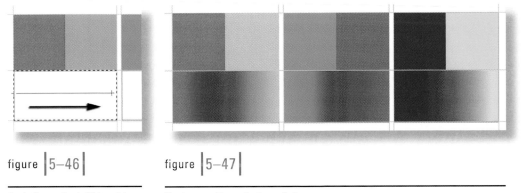

figure | 5–46 |

figure | 5–47 |

Apply the gradient. Click and drag with the tool from left to right.

The lesson with gradients applied.

Exploring Complementary Hues

1. Let us do a little experiment. First, choose View > Show > Guides to turn off the guides in the document and to get a better look at what you are doing.

2. In the Layers panel, select the top layer (**gradient3**), hold down Shift, and then click on the lower layer (red). This action selects all the layers between gradient3 and red. See Figure 5–48. Do not select the template layer set and Background layer.

3. In the Layers panel, click on the down arrow with three bars in the upper-right corner of the panel to open the drop-down options. Choose Merge Layers to combine the selected layers. See Figure 5–48. Rename the layer **top_color_set**. See Figure 5–49.

4. It is not a bad idea to save your file with a new name, preserving the original file with all layers intact—you never know when you might need access to those layers again. Choose File > Save As and save the file in your **lessons** folder as **chap5L1_ yourname_merge.psd**.

figure | 5–48 |

Merge linked layers.

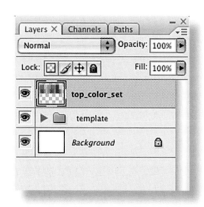

figure |5–49|

All the layers are merged and renamed.

figure |5–50|

Duplicate the color set layer.

5. Make a duplicate of the color set using the Option/Alt key and the Move tool. Place it in a new layer below the top color set layer. See Figure 5–50.

6. Rename the new layer **bottom_color_set**.

7. Select the **bottom_color_set** layer, and then choose Image > Adjustments > Hue/Saturation. Check that Preview is selected in the Hue/Saturation display, and that you can see your document. Move the Hue slider all the way to the right and watch how the colors change through all the complementary hues. Move the Hue slider all the way to the left and you get the same result. Set the Hue slider to 125 to see the intermediate complementary colors within the spectrum. These sets of colors are good starting points for creating colors that go well together.

8. While you are in the Hue/Saturation dialog, play with the Saturation and Lightness settings. Saturation increases or decreases the intensity (vibrancy) of the colors. Lightness lightens and darkens the colors. Click OK.

9. Save the file.

Go Grayscale

1. Every color in the spectrum has an equivalent gray tone. To identify the gray tones in the image, choose Image > Mode > Grayscale. Choose the Don't Flatten option to preserve the layers in the document. If the window pops up, click on the Discard button to discard the color in the image.

> Note: The variations of shades in the grayscale image. Once a file is converted to grayscale, it completely discards all color information. You can go back to RGB or CMYK mode at any time to add more color, but the parts originally converted to grayscale will remain that way. With this in mind, it is a good idea to keep a saved version of your file in full color before converting to grayscale.

2. Choose File > Save As and save a copy of this file as **chap5L1_yourname_gray.psd**. That is all for now.

SUMMARY

Now that you know how color performs in Photoshop—optical mixing, digital style—and how to apply it, hopefully your world is coming up rainbows (or, if anything spinning color wheels and spectrum arrays). There is a definite correlation between where color is reproduced and how it appears to us visually. Lucky for us, Photoshop has the distinctive capability to translate different modes of color, preparing our artwork for all types of output.

in review

1. Describe how optical mixing works.

2. What is antialiasing in digital imaging?

3. Define color space, or gamut. Name some devices that use gamuts.

4. What is the distinction between a color model and a color mode?

5. RGB is considered an additive color model, CMYK subtractive. Why?

6. Why is the Lab color model considered device-independent?

7. What are gamut warnings in Photoshop and where do you find them?

8. What kind of information is stored in channels?

9. What is a complementary color?

10. Where do you find and use color stops in Photoshop?

exploring on your own

1. Using a color wheel to choose colors that visually work well together can be very useful. See example color wheels in Figure 5–51 and Figure 5–52. To learn more about color wheels and color theory:

   - Color Matters: *http://www.colormatters.com/colortheory.html*

   - Download some color wheels from Tigercolor: *http://www.tigercolor.com/color-lab/color-wheel/color-wheels.htm*

- Use the Color Schemes Generator from Wellstyled.com to pick colors quickly: *http://wellstyled.com/tools/colorscheme2/index-en.html*

- Create your own color wheel using Photoshop: *http://www.good-tutorials.com/ tutorial/14492*

figure |5–51|

An example color wheel.

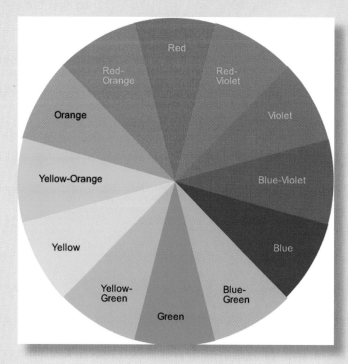

figure |5–52|

Another type of color wheel.

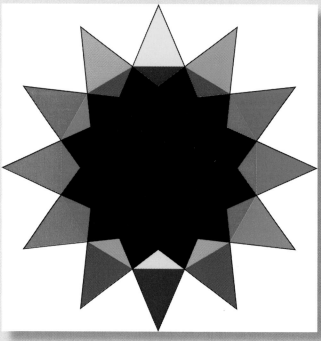

2. Go to the Photoshop Help (Help > Photoshop Help > Contents) and look up the topic "Color" and "Color management." You will find a lot of interesting information about how to best set up your work area and document, so you achieve consistency of color when you reproduce the image on different devices and platforms. You might find yourself ready to absorb some of it. You might wait to read other parts when you start feeling more comfortable with using the program.

3. Practice saving and loading a swatch library. The commands to do this are located in the Swatches panel drop-down options menu.

4. Create a Georges Seurat Pointillism effect in Photoshop. Open any photograph and choose Filter > Pixelate > Pointillize.

5. Create and publish your own color schemes using Adobe Labs dynamic color selector program at: *http://kuler.adobe.com/*

Explorer pages

NATASCHA ROEOESLI

About Natascha Roeoesli

Besides the fact her parents are photographers, Natascha has not had any specific art education. She did consider attending art school in Switzerland but felt it was not good enough even though she did make the acceptance test. Most of her knowledge comes from observing her surroundings. She loves to try to figure out why something works the way it does. Physics are an important part of understanding how colors work or how we see shapes and much more. Being self-educated is, in her opinion, a great advantage because it forces you to really understand what you are painting instead of learning theory by heart. "However, there are books" Natascha claims, "—like *Exploring Photoshop CS3* or theory books—that help you fill in the gaps you might not have elsewhere."

Natascha has worked for over two years for the game industry and, in addition, several fantasy authors and private clients.

To view more of her work, visit *http://www.tascha.ch/*.

Wax Dragon. Compliments of Natascha Roeoesli.
In the tutorials section of her Web site (*http://www.tascha.ch/*),
Natascha shares her techniques for creating such effects as the
silky fabric on the female character in *Wax Dragon*.

Can't Stand the Light.
Compliments of Natascha Roeoesli.

About Natascha's Work

In her own words Natascha shares her artistic process in the creation of *Can't Stand the Light*:

"*Can't Stand the Light* started as normal pencil sketch where I brainstormed a few compositions and character tryouts.

"Once I had the general idea I used Adobe Photoshop and my Wacom tablet to rough in some guidelines to work from using a hard-edged brush, which imitates a ball pen or ink pen.

"I am much more of a painter than a drawer and think more in shapes than lines. This is the reason I am normally not taking much time for sketches. The lines, however, help me to not make big anatomical mistakes and stay somewhat true to my initial idea.

"Once I do have the rough layout I copy this layer and hide it as a backup and create a new background layer, which I fill with the color I want to use for my ambient light (green for forest, blue for sky, and so on). The original sketch layer now gets painted on, starting with roughing in color using a brush with special settings, like 80% flow. This helps with not painting full opacity and lets the background color get mixed into everything I paint (most important: skin color). Switching the brushes during painting is also quite important.

"My paintings develop a lot while I work. They constantly change as I am trying out different hairdos or clothing combinations for my characters. Even the color scheme for this changed drastically during the process. Using Photoshop's amazing color adjustment tools I shifted the colors of the almost finished painting and then worked some more with the changed color scheme.

"Using the Color Picker is something I do almost without a break. Picking colors from my background and mixing them ever so slightly with the main objects (or the other way around) helps to unify the painting.

"I also use a lot of layers. Mainly to keep the background, foreground, and main objects separated from each other. In this case I was able to correct a compositional error and move the character slightly more to the right from where she started out. I did this to give more focus to the hand and more space to the left."

Summer. Compliments of Natascha Roeoesli.

| image correction |

charting your course

It is no surprise that Photoshop is used widely for correcting photographs. After all, it was the curiosity of brothers John and Thomas Knoll with darkroom photography and computer programming that brought Photoshop into existence and into the hands of consumers in 1990. Like any great inventor, John kept asking questions: How can the personal computer save photographs into other formats or adjust the contrast (lights and darks) in a photographic image? In all simplicity and complexity (depending on how you look at it), the answers are now at your fingertips in the form of Photoshop CS3.

This chapter presents fundamental techniques in the image-correction process. A photograph's tonal and color quality, not to mention its subject matter, is unique, and in so many ways is subject to the judgment of the artist. However, there are some general steps we can use as a springboard for understanding the image correction process. Let us take a look at them.

goals

In this chapter you will:

- **Experience six basic steps for image correction**
- **Learn how to use Levels to affect the brightness and contrast in an image**
- **Get familiar with the image retouching tools, such as Clone Stamp, Smudge, Dodge, and Sharpen**
- **Add an effect to a photograph**

SIX STEPS OF EN"LIGHT"ENMENT

So, you have a photograph and it needs correction. It is too dark, too light, the color is off, something is missing, and something has got to go. It is all so overwhelming that you wonder where to begin. When Annesa teaches students Photoshop's capabilities for image correction for the first time, she starts with six basic steps: import, resize, enhance, retouch, effect, and save. You might choose to use all of the steps or some of them, depending on the photograph. Let us review the steps with you and then you can explore them in the lesson.

Import

To get your photographic image into Photoshop, it must be in a digital format. You can get the image from a digital camera, scan it in, or download it from a CD or the internet. Try to get the highest-resolution image you possibly can. It is better to have more pixels to work with than fewer. You can also obtain images from a stock image distributor, such as Corbis, Comstock, or PictureQuest, but those kinds of images are usually already corrected and will not need much tonal adjustment. To import an image into Photoshop, choose File > Open and browse for the image on your system.

Resize

It is unlikely your image will be exactly the dimensions and/or orientation you desire for its final output. You might need to change its dimensional size and resolution, add more or less area to the overall canvas, or crop out unnecessary parts. Whatever you do, save a copy of the original image in case you want to use it again.

Image Dimensions, Resolution, and Mode

First you might want to check the image's resolution and size to be sure it contains enough pixels to complete the task you have chosen. For example, if you want the image to be printed on a fine magazine cover, you will want the resolution to be about 300 pixels per inch (ppi). If it is going to be printed in a newspaper, 150 ppi will suffice. For the Web or another digital environment, 72 ppi will work. (If you need to review the section on the relationship between resolution and the size of an image, see Chapter 3.) To adjust the size and resolution of an image, go to Image > Image Size.

You should check what color mode the image is in (Grayscale, RGB, CMYK) and set it to the mode you would like to work in (review color modes in Chapter 5). Be aware that you can do certain things in some modes and not in others. For example, if you change to Grayscale mode, all color will be discarded from the image—and will never return on that part of the image again. If you choose RGB, you can work with the many effects and filters in the program that are otherwise unavailable in other modes. Remember, when your image is almost complete, it is important to set the mode for its intended output. In general, use RGB for screen display, CMYK for print.

Canvas

It is possible you will want to add some more blank canvas area around the image, perhaps to include some text, a border, or other elements. To adjust the canvas size, choose Image > Canvas Size. See Figure 6–1 and Figure 6–2.

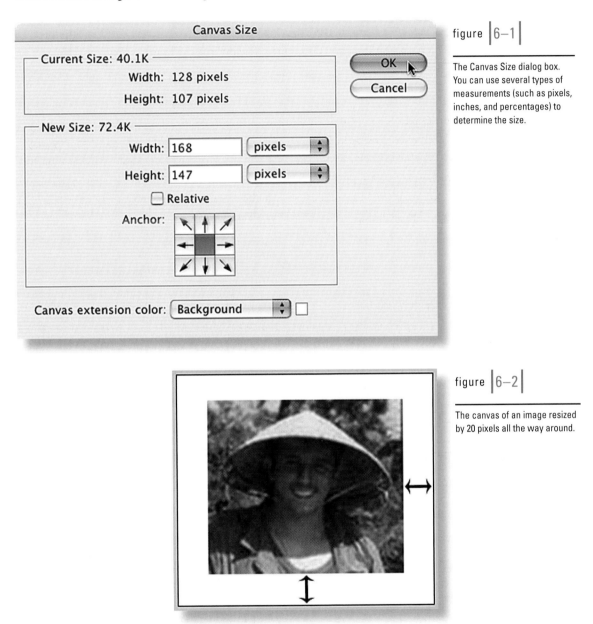

figure |6–1|

The Canvas Size dialog box. You can use several types of measurements (such as pixels, inches, and percentages) to determine the size.

figure |6–2|

The canvas of an image resized by 20 pixels all the way around.

Cropping

When the composition of your photograph is not right or it was not aligned properly during the scanning process, it is time to bring out the Crop tool. Reminiscent of a bout of spring cleaning, the Crop tool can put everything in its place and remove unwanted or unusable areas. To crop, select the Crop tool and click and drag over the area of the image you want to keep. Once the area is defined you can readjust or rotate the Crop selection more precisely before committing to the crop action. See Figure 6–3.

figure |6–3|

Specify and adjust a crop selection.

Enhance

Enhancing is where you begin to get into the heart of image correction, which includes adjustments to an image's tonal (brightness and contrast) levels and color balance. Under Image > Adjustments, you will find many commands that relate to tonal and color balance editing. See Figure 6–4. Photoshop features auto-correction commands for quick fixes to photographs (Auto Levels, Auto Contrast, Auto Color). However, if you want the ability for more precise correction to specific pixels and their tonal quality, learn to use the Levels, Curves, and Channel Mixer options. See Figure 6–5 and Figure 6–6 (on the next page).

Retouch

It can be a full-time job retouching photographs—fixing the very large or very minute blemishes. There definitely is a talent to retouching so it looks transparent to the viewer, but Photoshop makes it easier—quite painless, really—with such tools as the Clone Stamp, Healing Brush, Spot Healing Brush, Pattern Stamp, Patches, Red Eye, Smudge, Blur, and Sharpen tools. See Figure 6–7 and Figure 6–8 (on the next page).

Effect

Once the photograph is beautified the way you like it, you can consider adding something more, such as an effect, a text element, a frame or border, or a filter or color enhancement. See Figure 6–9 (on the next page).

Save

Hopefully, all along you save as you work on your image correcting, but final thought goes to output and creating copies of the work for its intended purpose. This might include saving the image in a compressed JPEG format for Web publication or in TIFF format to head to the printer or page layout program.

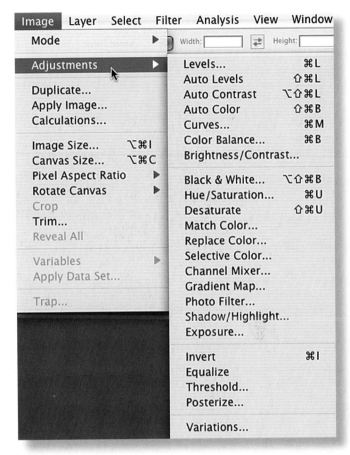

figure |6–4|

Options available for image enhancements.

figure |6–5|

An image before adjustments to its tonal range.

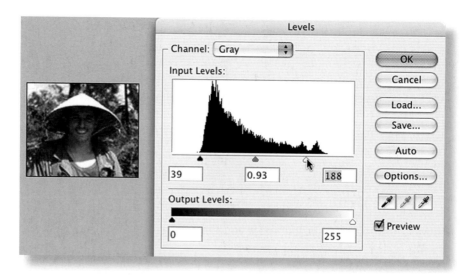

figure |6-6|

An image after adjustments to its tonal range. For more precise control over the shadows, mid-tones, and highlights of an image, adjust the histogram (graph of the total distribution of colored pixels in an image).

figure |6-7|

Use the Clone Stamp tool to take sampled areas of an image to use in place of unwanted areas.

figure |6-8|

The Dodge tool quickly lightens areas of an image.

figure |6-9|

Using feathering, a soft effect is added around the image.

Lesson: Correcting the Mike Photo

In this lesson you will experience the six basic steps of image correction, and then you will be on your way to correcting and enhancing your own photographs. See Figure 6–10.

Import

1. In Photoshop, choose File > Open. Open the file **chap6L1.psd** in the **chap06_lessons** folder.

2. Save a copy of this file in your **lessons** folder. Choose File > Save As and name it **chap6L1_yourname.psd**.

3. Choose View > Actual Pixels to see the document at 100% magnification. This is a photograph taken of Annesa's friend's brother, Mike, during the Vietnam War. You can see the photo is faded and worn. With this photo, let us go through the six image-correction steps. The first step, import, has already been completed.

Resize

1. The photograph is in RGB Color mode, but for simplicity—in this lesson—change it to Grayscale. Choose Image > Mode > Grayscale. A dialog box asks if you would like to discard all color information in the photo. Choose Discard, and rest assured that you have a backup copy of the color version.

figure |6–10|

The lesson before and after. Original photo compliments of Bruce and Linda Lord.

Note: Another option for making more precise adjustments to the black, whites and grays of an image is Image > Adjustments > Black & White. This adjustment leaves the image in RGB Color mode, yet it offers different photographic filters and color channel adjustment options to create the grayscale image. See Figure 6–11. For a review of channels, see the section on "Adjusting Color" in Chapter 5. For further study of color balance, you can explore the color version of the photo in the "Exploring on Your Own" section of this chapter.

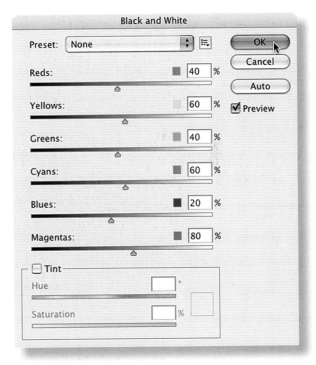

figure |6–11|

Make subtle adjustments to a grayscale image using the Black & White adjustment feature.

2. Choose Image > Image Size. The photo's resolution is currently set to 300 ppi. At this resolution, if the photo goes to print it will be approximately 2.7 by 2.3 inches. Uncheck the Resample Image option (see Figure 6–12) and enter **150** ppi for the Resolution. The overall print dimensions increase. For most print jobs 150 ppi is a good resolution—a higher resolution is needed for high-quality magazine covers and similar media, which you will learn about in Chapter 10. Click OK.

3. Choose View > Print Size to see the exact dimensions of the photograph if it were to be printed.

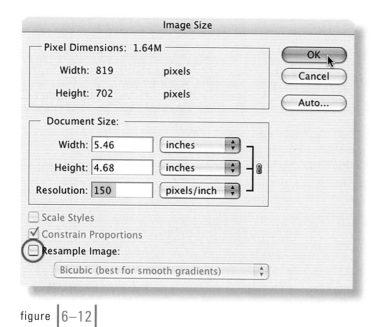

figure |6–12|

Always check the image size of your document, so you know what you are working with. Uncheck Resample Image if you want to change the resolution and keep the highest visual quality of the image.

Choose View > Actual Pixels to see the size of the image on screen—almost twice as big because the screen views at about 72 ppi. (If we just lost you here, review the section on resolution in Chapter 3.)

4. OK, you have set the image size, but as you can see the image is crooked on the canvas, which can happen in the scanning process when the image is not properly aligned on the scanning bed. Select the Crop tool in the toolbox (fifth tool down). Click and drag an area around the photograph inside the tattered black border. Use the Crop tool to scale and rotate the photograph, just as you would using Edit > Transform (see Figure 6–13), and then execute the crop (see Figure 6–14).

5. Save the file.

figure |6–13|

Using the transform handles, adjust the crop selection around the image.

Enhance

1. Now for the fun stuff. Choose Image > Adjustments > Auto Levels and note the automatic tonal correction made to the image. It is looking better already. Let us backtrack and try a different method—something with more control. Choose Edit > Undo Auto Levels.

2. Open the Layers panel. Choose Layer > New Adjustment Layer > Levels. Keep the **Levels 1** layer name and click OK. A histogram comes up. This is a graph that shows the distribution of shadows, mid-tones, and highlights in an image. The far-left marker at the bottom of the graph indicates the end range for the darkest (shadow) pixels in the image. The far-right marker indicates the end range for the lightest (highlight) pixels in the image. The marker in the middle adjusts all chromatic gray pixels in between. The higher the graph in a particular area, the more instances of that particular shade in the image. See Figure 6–15.

3. A quick way to find a good tonal balance in the image is to move the black (shadow) marker on the histogram inward until it aligns with the first vertical stretch of pixels in the histogram. Do the same with the white (highlight) marker. Note the changes occurring directly on the document. Adjust the mid-tones marker to the right or left to get a visual of how much control you have over the photo's brightness and contrast. Refer to Figure 6–15.

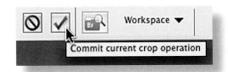

figure |6–14|

Choose the check mark on the Options bar to execute the crop.

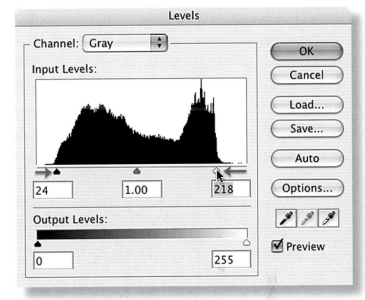

figure |6–15|

Adjust the levels by moving the shadow, mid-tone, and highlight markers. Be sure to preview the document as you make changes.

▶ Don't Go There!

A more direct way to get to the Levels option in Photoshop is to choose Image > Adjustments > Levels. However, this option applies your level changes directly on the selected image layer. To avoid committing right away to your tonal adjustments, use an adjustment layer (Layer > New Adjustment Layer), which places a layer above the original image and works like a temporary overlay. See Figure 6–16. If you do not like the adjustment or change your mind, delete the layer and the original image will remain intact.

4. Once you get the levels to your liking, click OK to close the dialog.

5. OK, let us add some color back into the image—a sepia tone. First change the image mode to RGB via Image > Mode > RGB Color. Select the Don't Merge option.

6. Be sure the **mike_photo** layer is highlighted, and then choose Image > Adjustments > Photo Filter. Select the Sepia filter from the drop-down menu. Try a Density setting of about 75%. What do you think? Feel free to try the other filters if sepia is not your color. See Figure 6–17.

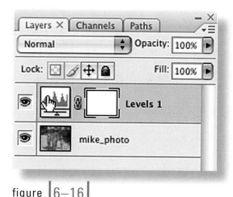

figure 6–16

A levels adjustment layer located above the image the layer is affecting. To edit the levels, double-click on the histogram thumbnail in the adjustment layer.

Note: Alternatively, you can colorize the image by choosing Image > Adjustments > Hue/Saturation, selecting the Colorize option, and setting the Hue, Saturation, and Lightness levels to your liking.

7. Let us work with the Sharpen feature. This next enhancement is optional, but it is sometimes necessary on images that have gone through a scanning process, which tends to overly blur some images. Sharpening is also a good idea when you want to bump up the readability of text in a photo. Select the **mike photo** layer, and then choose Filter > Sharpen > Sharpen and note the subtle clarity in the image. (If you did not catch this the first time, choose Edit > Undo Sharpen, zoom in closer to the image, redo the step to see the shift in image detail, and then zoom out to see that it is, indeed, an improvement.)

8. Save your work.

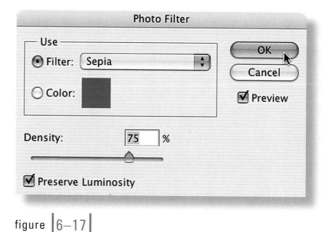

figure 6–17

Colorize the photograph with a photo filter.

Retouch

1. OK, on to some real magic. The Mike photo is well worn. Note the stains and scratches on the photo, particularly those on the left-hand side See Figure 6–18.

2. Change the pointer icon to a brush, so it will work more accurately: choose Photoshop > Preferences > Cursors (Mac) or Edit > Preferences > Cursors (Windows). Under Painting Cursors, choose Normal Brush Tip (if it is not already selected). Click OK.

3. Select the Clone Stamp tool in the toolbox. See Figure 6–19.

4. In the Options bar, click on the brush thumbnail to open the brush options. Click on the arrow to the right of the drop-down menu to open further options. Choose to view the brushes with Small Thumbnails. See Figure 6–20. The Clone Stamp tool takes a picture of an area of an image that can be brushed in elsewhere on the image. The brush size determines the size of the picture area. Choose the Soft Round 27-pixels brush.

5. Place the Clone Stamp tool over an unstained, lighter area on the left-hand side of the image. See Figure 6–21. Hold down Alt/Option and click to take a picture (sample) of that pixel area (zoom in if necessary).

figure |6–18|

The circled areas indicate scratches and stains in the photo.

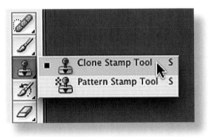

figure |6–19|

The Clone Stamp tool.

6. Position the pointer over one of the stained areas of the image, and click once to apply the saved picture over the stained area. Click and drag (brush) lightly over the stained area to blend it into the background pixels. See Figure 6–22. Note that when you click and drag over an area, a crosshair comes up. The crosshair indicates the area that is being copied by the brush in another

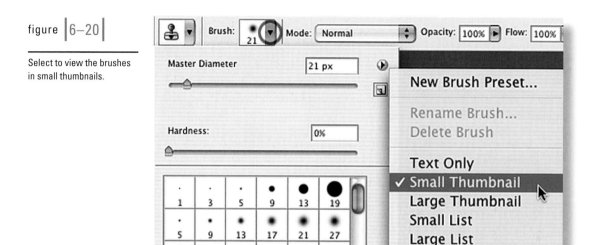

figure |6–20|

Select to view the brushes in small thumbnails.

area. Huh? Frankly, at first this relationship between the crosshair and the brush can be somewhat frustrating, but once you understand how the tool works, it does make sense. The first picture taken with the Clone Stamp tool (when you hold down Option/Alt) is applied to a new area when you click elsewhere on the image. This indicates the relative starting point of what the crosshair will continue to pick up as you click and drag (brush) over the area. See Figure 6–23.

7. On the menu bar, go to Window > Clone Source to open the Clone Source panel. See Figure 6–24. This panel lets you save samples in the upper five squares by clicking on one of

figure |6–21|

Position the Clone Stamp tool over an area, hold down Option/Alt, and click to take a picture (sample) of the pixels.

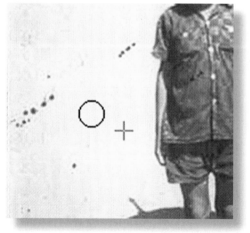

figure |6–22|

Blending the area into the background pixels.

them and setting a clone source (when you hold down Alt/Option) in the image. The first square already has a saved sample from our first attempt at cloning. Also, clicking on Show Overlay at the bottom of the panel will reveal a ghost image of the clone source (the crosshair) over the original image. This is a nifty tool once you are comfortable with cloning but, for now, let us leave it unchecked.

8. Continue to take samples of clean areas of the image and apply them to the stained or scratched areas. You might want to change your brush size, depending on the area size you are taking a sample of. To do this, Ctrl-click (Mac) or right-click (Windows) over the area you are working with, which brings up the brush options box. Once you have made your adjustments to the brush, press Enter to exit the menu. See Figure 6–25. Also, the bracket [] keys offer another quick way of changing brush sizes. The [key decreases the size of the brush while the] key increases it.

9. For another retouch tool that might do the trick, select the Smudge tool in the toolbox. See Figure 6–26.

10. Zoom in on the scratch on the boy's knee on the left side of the photo.

11. Gently blend the darker pixels of the boy's knee into the light scratched area. See Figure 6–27.

12. Zoom out to 100% magnification—to do this quickly, press Command/Ctrl. Note that Mike's face is dark under his hat. Zoom in on his face (Command/Ctrl + zooms in).

figure | 6–23 |

First picture applied to a new area. Note the crosshair on the boy's nose. The pixels in this area are being applied by the brush above and to the left.

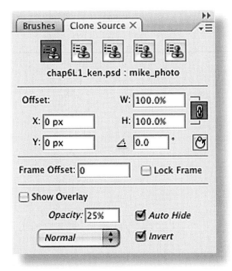

figure | 6–24 |

Options in the Clone Source panel.

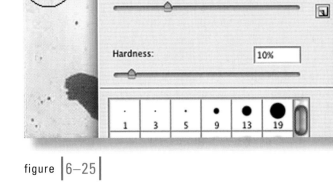

figure | 6–25 |

Adjust brush size with a right-click (Windows) or Ctrl-click (Mac) or using the bracket keys.

figure | 6–26 |

The Smudge tool is hiding under the Blur tool in the toolbox

figure | 6–27 |

Hiding blemishes with the Smudge tool.

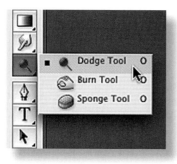

figure | 6–28 |

The Dodge tool in the toolbox.

13. Select the Dodge tool in the toolbox (see Figure 6–28) and in the Options bar set Exposure to 5%. In the Options bar, also adjust your brush size, if necessary (we chose 5 for the brush size—quite small).

14. Gently brush the Dodge tool over Mike's cheeks to lighten them slightly.

15. Zoom out to 100% magnification to see the subtle result. If you dodged too much, either undo actions in the History panel or use the Burn tool (under the Dodge tool in the toolbox) to redo the darker effect.

16. Using your newly found tools, retouch other areas of the photo.

17. Save your document.

Effect

1. With the Effect step you can add any sort of inspiration to a photo. For the Mike photo, let us make a frame. See the after version of Figure 6–10, for example.

2. In the menu bar, go to Layer > Flatten Image. This will unite the **Levels 1** layer and the **mike_photo** layer into one layer.

3. To create a clean, dark gray border, pick a dark gray as your foreground color. Next, go to Image > Canvas Size on the menu bar. Change the width to 610 pixels, height to 484 pixels, and choose Foreground in the Canvas extension color. See Figure 6–29.

4. Select the Elliptical Marquee tool in the toolbox. Position the cursor on Mike's belt buckle, hold down Shift and Option/ Alt, and then click and draw from the center a circle around the three figures. If you wish to move the selection, click inside the selection area and move it.

5. Choose Select > Inverse to inverse the selection area— marching ants should appear around the edges of the photo.

6. Choose Edit > Stroke, choose 4 pixels. See Figure 6–30.

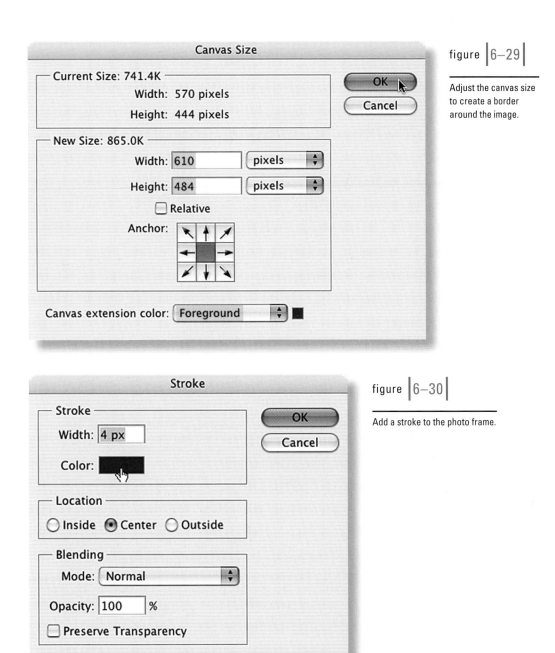

7. Choose Filter > Texture > Texturizer. The Photoshop Filter Gallery window appears with Texturizer options open. In the Texturizer menu, choose the Canvas option (see Figure 6–31) and set the Scaling and Relief to your liking. Click OK when completed.

> **Note:** You can preview the changes being made directly on your document without closing the Texturizer Photoshop Filter Gallery.

8. Choose Select > Deselect—Command-D (Mac), Ctrl-D (Windows).

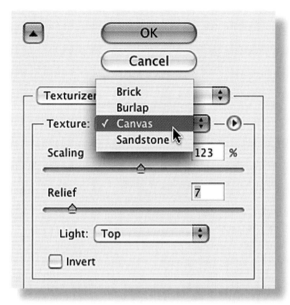

figure | 6–31 |

Add a texture to the selected frame area.

Save

1. Save a Photoshop version of your corrected image (maybe even two or three versions along the way). Choose File > Save As and save a final .psd version in your **lessons** folder.

2. Let us save two other versions for different output. For print, choose File > Save As and under Format, select TIFF. Click Save. In the TIFF Options box, select NONE for Image Compression, and select Discard Layers and Save a Copy for Layer Compression. (The Discard Layers and Save a Copy option will save a flattened copy of your image, but the image you are currently working on is still the "original.") See Figure 6–32.

3. And, one for the Web. Choose File > Save As, Format: JPEG. Set the Image Options Quality to 8, so there is some compression placed on the image, but not so much to ruin its quality.

> **Note:** You can also choose File > Save for Web & Devices to save in JPEG format. However, this opens up another big dialog box of choices you might not want to deal with right now. We will get into that in Chapter 11.

You are done with the image-correction process.

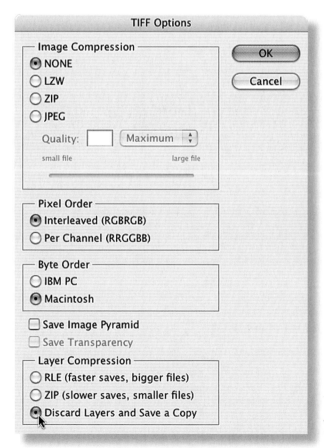

figure | 6–32 |

Select the TIFF options.

SUMMARY

A whole new world—blemish-free—has opened up to you in this chapter. Using the powerful image-correction tools and processes available in Photoshop, every photograph has the potential for perfection, even if it is not completely true in content.

in review

1. What are the six basic steps for image correction?

2. Why is checking the resolution setting of an imported photograph or image important?

3. Why might someone work in RGB Color mode over other modes?

4. What are you adjusting when moving the sliders in the Levels histogram?

5. What keyboard command must you press to take a pixel sample with the Clone Stamp tool?

6. When working with the retouching tools, why would viewing your cursor as Brush Size be helpful? Where do you go to make this setting?

7. What is the advantage of using an adjustment layer to make color or tonal corrections on an image?

8. Why would you save backup copies of the original photograph before retouching it?

exploring on your own

1. In the Photoshop Help files (Help > Photoshop Help), expand your knowledge of levels and discover the wonders of curves. See the sections on "Making color and tonal adjustment."

2. Explore color correction using a color version of the Mike photo. Using the Channel Mixer, remove the red overcast in the **chap6L1 file**. For information on using the Channel Mixer, consult the Help files.

3. As learned in the lesson, the Clone Stamp tool can correct imperfections or duplicate areas of an image by sampling pixels elsewhere on the image or from other images. There are three other photo retouching tools that work similarly to the Clone Stamp tool, but with slight variations in effect—Healing Brush, Spot Healing Brush, and Patch tool. See Figure 6–33.

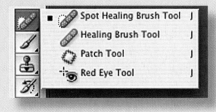

figure | 6–33 |

Other photo retouching tools to explore.

Executed like the Clone Stamp, the Healing Brush tool matches the texture, lighting, transparency, and shading of the sampled pixels—determined by the size of the brush you choose—to the pixels being healed. As a result, the repaired pixels blend seamlessly into the rest of the image. The Spot Healing Brush tool offers the same effect as the Healing Brush tool. However, there is no requirement to specify (take a snapshot of) a sample spot to apply elsewhere. The Spot Healing Brush tool automatically samples the pixels by Proximity Match (by what pixels surround the edge of the retouched area), or by Create Texture, using the pixels in the selection to create a texture in which to fix the area. Amazing, really! See Figure 6–34.

The Patch tool works just like the Healing tools, but instead of defining a retouch area with a chosen brush size, you draw a selection around the source or destination area you want to sample and then repair that selection from another area or pattern. See Figure 6–35.

To practice these tools, retouch the photo of a dilapidated shack in **chap06_lessons/samples/patch.jpg**.

figure | 6–34 |

1. Photo before retouching with the Spot Healing Brush.
2. Photo after correcting pixels with the Spot Healing Brush.

figure |6–35|

1. Photo before using the Patch tool.
2. Photo after using the Patch tool.

4. Found in the same area of the toolbox as the Healing and Patch tools, the Red Eye tool is worth a try. To quickly remove red eye from flash-photographed people, or the white and green reflections in flash photos of animals, select the Red Eye tool, and click on the unwanted area. For practice with this tool, use the **red_eye.jpg** in the **chap06_lessons/samples** folder.

5. Another tool to play with in the Photoshop toolbox is the Color Replacement tool. Using brush strokes, this tool simplifies replacing specific colors in your image. Select the tool (see Figure 6–36), choose a brush size in the Options bar, select a foreground color or take a sample of color (Alt/Option) in the image, then brush the color onto the area of the image you would like to modify.

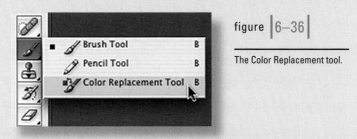

figure |6–36|

The Color Replacement tool.

Explorer pages

MICHAEL DWYER

"With design it's not a pure art . . . it's not self-expression totally. You are fulfilling a purpose for a client, which is business. You must blend the art and business together. And you have to have a thick skin to take criticism . . . even, if you know in your heart it's wrong. You have to educate your clients, but at some point you have to bend to their vision . . . adapt, compromise with the client and the design."

 Learn more about this artist via podcast at *http://www.designexploration.com/podcasts.*

About Michael Dwyer

Michael Dwyer studied fine art at SUNY Purchase and the School of the Museum of Fine Arts (Tufts) in Boston, Mass. On the road of sculpture and public art he took a detour to graphic design. During the last 12 years he has worked for large corporations and small studios, most notably YOE! Studio in Peekskill, N.Y. At YOE! he designed logos, packaging, ads, magazines, Web sites and animations for clients, such as the Discovery Channel, Pepperidge Farm, Golden Books, Mudd Jeans, Cartoon Network, and AOL.

Currently he is the creative director at EZ Marketing Group (EZMG) in Harrison, N.Y. EZMG's clients include the *New York Times*, Universal News, and Nuttin' But Stringz.

Michael teaches graphic design courses online for the Art Institute of Pittsburgh and Westwood College. In his spare time he produces short documentaries, including his most recent, *Mom and Pop Shop*.

To see more of his work, visit *http://www.crackanegg.com.*

Package design by Michael Dwyer.

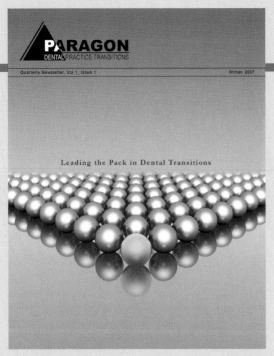

Newsletter cover for a dental practice transition company. Compliments of Michael Dwyer.

Print ad for a guitar magazine. Compliments of Michael Dwyer.

Poster design for Discovery Channel. Compliments of Michael Dwyer.

About the Work of Michael Dwyer

In his own words, Michael shares his experience working with the Discovery Channel:

"One of the most successful and fun clients I have had the opportunity to work with has been the Discovery Channel's 'Crocodile Hunter' program. When Discovery first approached the studio they had a very popular show and a logo, but that was about it as far as a brand or defined image of the show. I developed three possible 'looks' or directions that they could pursue. One approach emphasized the dangerous elements of the show, the second had a comic book/super hero feel, and the third focused on the environmental aspects of Steve Irwin's work, which is ultimately the direction they chose to develop.

"Once the basic direction had been chosen I worked with a team of designers and an illustrator to develop an entire style guide for the client. I prefer working in a collaborative environment where all the designers can feed off each other's ideas. An atmosphere of sharing makes the project seem more like play than actual work.

"A style guide typically includes logos, a color panel, fonts, type treatments, patterns, textures, and final art. The style guide allows other artists or third parties to create any variety of merchandise and still maintain a cohesive and coherent brand."

Going Nowhere

| drawing and painting |

7

charting your course

So far, we have spent a lot of time working with photographs in Photoshop—cropping, selecting, and transforming them, and altering tonal values and color. In this chapter, you get an introduction to the drawing and painting tools. These tools advance the possibilities of what you can do in Photoshop to another creative level. With little doubt, as you play with the Brush, Pencil, Pen, and Shape tools—not to mention path and type elements—you may get lost in what could be a complex amalgamation of colors and shapes. It is like looking into a kaleidoscope—where complex patterns and designs allure you into amazement.

If you were to take the kaleidoscope apart, however, you would find that how it produces this amazing eye candy is but an artifact of a simple design—a few reflective mirrors, some light, and a myriad of objects: confetti, beads, jewels, glass, and pressed flowers. The same goes for drawing and painting in Photoshop, except instead of spinning objects making these dazzling images, it is another type of back-lit object. Yes, you guessed it—pixels.

goals

In this chapter you will:

- **Master pixel painting with the Pencil and Brush tools**
- **Recognize how vectors serve as a temporary mold for more flexible and free-form drawing and offer cross-compatibility support between pixel-based and vector-based programs**
- **Make path, fill, and stroke geometric and free-form shapes**
- **Draw a nonrepresentational art piece**

DRAWING AND PAINTING

PIXELS—A CONTEMPORARY ART MEDIUM

With pixels, you can simulate art styles through the use of the Pencil and Brush tools (and filter effects, discussed later in this chapter). Want to paint with watercolors or an airbrush? Draw with charcoal or chalk? With a mouse or pressure-sensitive digitizing tablet, you can. In addition, you can paint other elements, such as textured grass, scattered leaves and flowers, swirls, and patterns using the brush libraries. And with custom brushes you can paint just about anything else. You can change brush sizes, opacity, blending modes, and flow attributes. (We fear if you are the doodling type, you will never get beyond this chapter!)

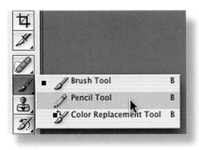

figure | 7–1 |

Pencil and Brush tools in the toolbox.

Using the Pencil and Brush Tools

The Pencil and Brush tools are found in the toolbox. See Figure 7–1. These tools let you paint with any foreground color you choose. In general, the Pencil tool creates hard-edged, freehand lines of color, and the Brush tool creates soft strokes of color. To compare and contrast the same styles used with both the Pencil and Brush tools, see Figure 7–2 and Figure 7–3.

We recommend that you set your cursor preferences to indicate the brush size you are using. To do this, go to Photoshop > Preferences

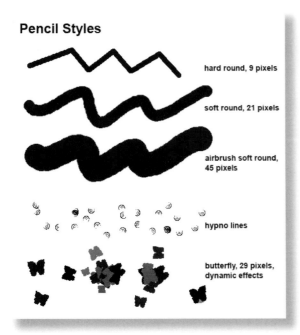

Pencil Styles

hard round, 9 pixels

soft round, 21 pixels

airbrush soft round, 45 pixels

hypno lines

butterfly, 29 pixels, dynamic effects

figure | 7–2 |

A small sampling of pencil styles and sizes.

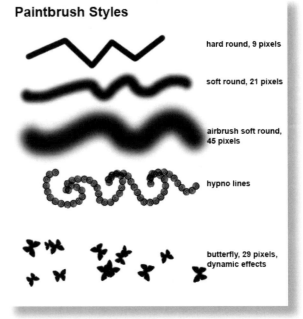

Paintbrush Styles

hard round, 9 pixels

soft round, 21 pixels

airbrush soft round, 45 pixels

hypno lines

butterfly, 29 pixels, dynamic effects

figure | 7–3 |

A small sampling of brush styles and sizes.

> Cursors (Mac) or Edit > Preferences > Cursors (Windows) and, under Painting Cursors, choose Normal Brush Tip. There are several places to make adjustments and add variations to your Pencil or Brush tool, for example, in the Options bar (see Figure 7–4), in the Brushes panel (Window > Brushes, Figure 7–5), and in the context menu when you Ctrl-click (Mac) or right-click (Windows) over an area with the tool. See Figure 7–6 on the next page.

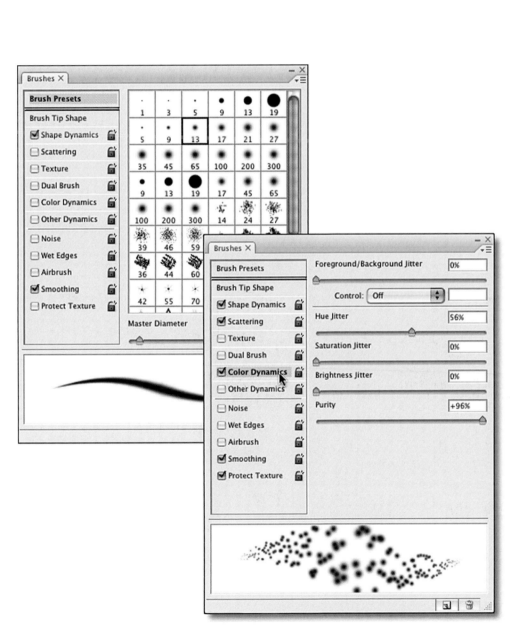

figure |7–4|

The Brush tool's Options bar (Pencil tool options are similar).

figure |7–5|

The Brushes panel (also used with the Pencil tool). On the left-hand side you can click on an effect name to bring up its properties (i.e., for Color Dynamics choose the Color Dynamics title). To apply the effect to your brush, check the box to the left of the effect's name.

figure | 7–6 |

Context menu for the Brush tool. As you paint, you can quickly change the tool's diameter, hardness, or style.

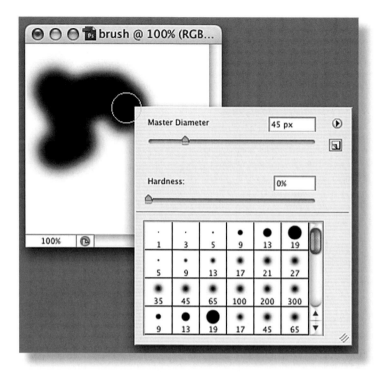

In the chapter lesson, you will get to practice with the Pencil and Brush tools, but that is still a few pages away and the temptation to start messing around with these tools is usually urgent. So, let us do it—pronto!

1. In Photoshop, choose File > New and create a document any size.

2. Check the preferences to make sure that under Cursors, the Normal Brush Tip painting cursor is selected.

3. Set a foreground color in the toolbox or the Color panel. This is the color you will draw with.

4. Select the Pencil tool in the toolbox. See Figure 7–1. In the Options bar, click on the second inverted arrow to open the Brush (also Pencil) Preset picker. Choose a pencil in the scrolling list. See Figure 7–7.

> **Note:** Alternatively, you can go to Window > Brushes and open the Brushes panel, which contains these options and more.

For future reference, in the Options bar you can also adjust the Pencil tool's blending modes and opacity. Hold off on exploring these options until you feel comfortable with the basic settings.

5. Place the cursor over your blank document and click and drag to start drawing.

> **Note:** To create straight lines, click down with the Pencil tool, hold down Shift, and then click down in another place on the document. (Do not click and drag, just click-click-click . . . while holding down Shift. If you do not hold it down you just make dots. Try it and see!)

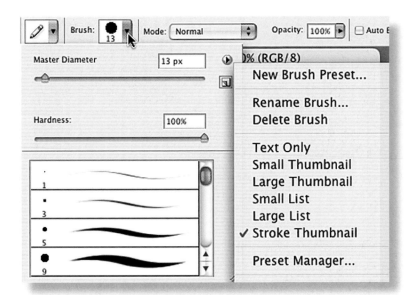

figure |7–7|

Open the Brush (also Pencil) Preset picker. Note that in the Options drop-down menu for the Preset picker, the view in this example is set to Stroke Thumbnail.

6. Draw to your heart's content, changing colors and pencil attributes.

7. To erase, use the Eraser tool. See Figure 7–8. Like the Pencil tool's diameter (size), the Eraser tool's diameter can be set in the Options bar. Remember that the bracket keys will increase or decrease the diameter of the selected drawing tool. Whatever background color you have chosen in the toolbox is the color the Eraser tool reveals. So, if your document started out with a white background, make sure white is set in the background color swatch of the toolbox to completely remove whatever you are erasing.

figure |7–8|

The Eraser tool. The color it reveals is determined by the background color.

Note: You can undo your strokes in the History panel.

8. Select the Brush tool in the toolbox.

9. Select a Brush Preset in the Brushes panel (Window > Brushes). For more options (not that you need them right now), click the arrow with three horizontal lines in the upper-right corner of the panel and, from the drop-down Options menu, choose another brush library from the list at the bottom (i.e., from Dry Media Brushes or Special Effect Brushes). To add the brush library to the current list of brushes in the Brushes panel, select Append when the dialog box comes up. See Figure 7–9.

figure |7–9|

Choose Append to add brushes to your existing brush style list.

Note: In the Brush panel's drop-down Options menu are settings for how you might like to view the brush styles in the Panel window. Such settings include Text Only, Small or Large Thumbnail, Small or Large List, or Stroke Thumbnail.

---

10. Paint with your chosen brush. Alter the brush options in the Options bar. Change the brush tip size and colors, and adjust the Flow setting. See Figure 7–10.

figure | 7–10 |

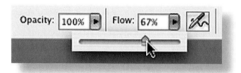

Adjust the Flow setting of the brush and see what effect this has when you paint.

11. Play with the adjustments in the Brushes panel; try Scattering, for example. Click on the Scattering option on the left-hand side of the panel (it highlights in blue and a check mark appears in its checkbox). Then adjust its settings in the options area to the right. See Figure 7–11. To remove Scattering from the brush, click on the checkbox to the left of the Scattering option.

figure | 7–11 |

Adjust settings for the Scattering effect in the Brushes panel.

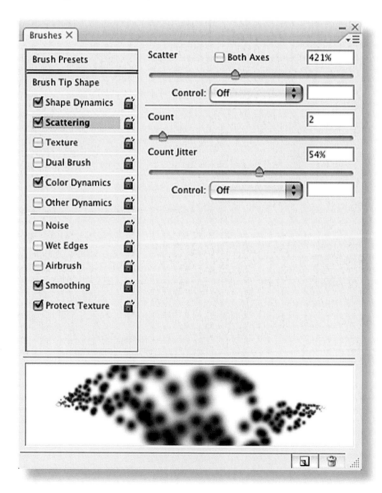

Making a Custom Brush

Photoshop has provided a plethora of brush styles, but inevitably, there will be a need for something more and different. This is where making custom brushes comes in handy. A sample selection from any image or photograph can be used as a custom brush. First, marquee the area of the image you would like to use as a brush (be sure the correct layer in the Layers panel is selected), choose Edit > Define Brush Preset, and give your brush a name.

The custom brush shows up in the Brush Presets list in the Brushes panel. See Figure 7–12 and Figure 7–13. You can also draw or paint a pattern or shape, select it, and then choose Edit > Define Brush Preset. See Figure 7–14.

figure | 7–12 |

Need a brush of zebra stripes? Make a selection of part of a zebra picture and save it as a custom brush.

figure |7–13|

The zebra brush is saved in the Brushes panel under Brush Presets.

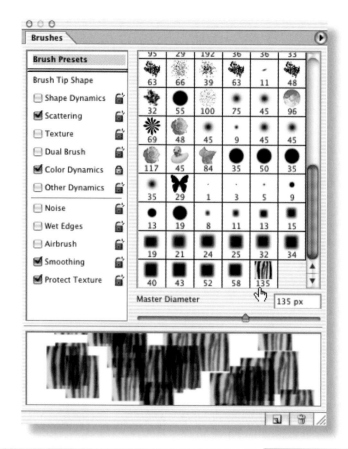

figure |7–14|

Draw your own shapes (i.e., hearts) and make them into custom brushes.

VECTORS—A GUEST APPEARANCE

We wish we could make it simple and tell you it is all black and white in regard to learning this program, but there are gray areas to tend to. Even though Photoshop is the pixel master, it can work with vectors on a minimal level—enough to use as a temporary solution for creating more flexibility in your drawing and for compatibility purposes when importing and exporting between programs. It is temporary in the sense that you can draw and make shapes using vector attributes, where no pixels are associated with the paths drawn, but that is only until the objects become rasterized (turned into pixels) with a fill or stroke color.

> Note: For a review of the differences between vectors and bitmaps, see Chapter 3.

In several places and processes within the program, vectors make a guest appearance, such as when you use the Pen tool and create paths, with vector masks, with type, and when you save in vector-supported file formats.

Paths

Paths are vector lines you draw in Photoshop. They are used to define areas of an image and make new shapes or selections. You make paths using the Pen tool (see next section) or Shape tools, or by converting a selection into a path. To see created paths, go to Window > Paths. See Figure 7–15.

Let us make some paths, so you can experience how they work.

1. Create a new document, and make it about 500 by 500 pixels in size.

2. Press Shift-Tab to hide unneeded panels, if necessary.

3. In the toolbox, set your foreground and background colors to their defaults (black foreground, white background) by pressing the D key.

4. Choose Window > Paths to open the Paths panel. Note that no paths are indicated in the panel—yet.

5. Select the Freeform Pen tool in the toolbox. See Figure 7–16.

> Note: The ways of the Pen tools are vast and somewhat complicated (see the next section). For now, using the Freeform Pen tool is a good way to start.

figure | 7–15 |

The Paths panel.

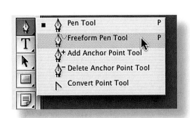

figure | 7–16 |

Select the Freeform Pen tool.

figure |7–17|

Choose the Paths shape option.

6. In the Options bar for the Freeform Pen tool, choose the Paths shape option, which is the second icon (the square with the Pen symbol in the middle). See Figure 7–17.

7. Click and drag the Freeform Pen tool on your blank canvas, making a circular, closed shape. To close a shape, approach the beginning of the path and an O-shape will appear near the tool. The shape is indicated as a work path in the Paths panel. See Figure 7–18. A work path is temporary. Unless you save it, it will be replaced when you draw another path.

figure |7–18|

A path is indicated as a temporary work path in the Paths panel.

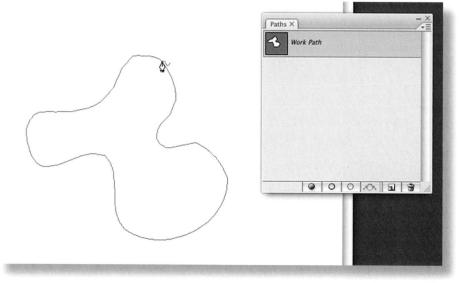

8. Before you save a path, first replace the work path with another path. Try this: Select the Rectangular Marquee tool (second tool in the toolbox). Click and drag on your canvas to define the rectangle. Right now, it is considered a selection (indicated by marching ants). In the Paths panel, click on the arrow with three lines in the upper-right corner to open its options, and then choose Make Work Path. See Figure 7–19. Set the Tolerance (smoothness) of the path to 2.0. Note in the Paths panel that the circular work path you made before has been replaced by a new, rectangular work path.

figure |7–19|

In the Paths panel, change a selection into a work path.

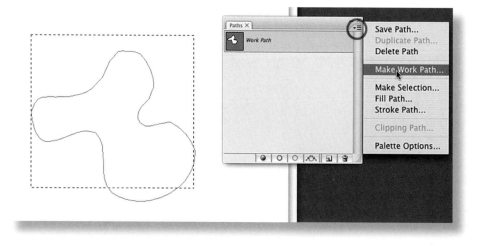

9. With a work path you can modify the path freely (using vectors) before committing to the final, bit-mapped version. Select the Direct Selection tool in the toolbox. This tool lets you select individual points on the path to modify it. See Figure 7–20. Click on a line of the rectangular work path to select it. Note the points on each corner (called anchor points). Click and drag one of the corner points to modify the rectangular shape into a triangular shape. See Figure 7–21. The work path is updated in the Paths panel.

10. From the Path panel's options (click on the arrow with three lines in upper-right corner), choose Save Path. Name it **mytriangle**.

11. Let us rasterize this shape; cast it in stone, so to speak. Choose Window > Layers. Double-click on the Background layer to release it to a regular layer.

figure | 7–20 |

Select the Direct Selection tool in the toolbox to select individual anchor points on a path.

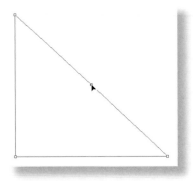

figure | 7–21 |

Move an anchor point to create a triangular shape out of a rectangular shape.

12. Go back to the Paths panel and select the **mytriangle** path. From the panel's options, choose Fill Path. See Figure 7–22. Click OK. A copy of the triangle path becomes a permanent bitmap object in the current layer—in other words, you cannot use the Direct Selection tool to select individual points on the filled shape. In the Paths panel, however, the **mytriangle** work path is still available for modification. See Figure 7–23.

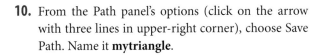

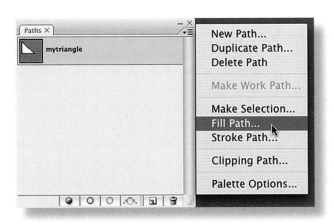

figure | 7–22 |

Make a work path a bitmapped object by filling the path.

figure | 7–23 |

A path becomes a bitmap object in the layers panel.

The Pen Tool

Ahh, the Pen tool, an instrument that either wreaks havoc or invokes joy, depending on your experience with it. We are not going to delve into the intricate workings of this tool in this book. It is an available option for drawing in Photoshop but, truthfully, it is best utilized in a vector-robust program, such as Adobe Illustrator. In fact, its use is so important in that program that we spend almost a complete chapter on the Pen tool in our book *Exploring Illustrator CS3*.

In brief, the Pen tool lets you draw straight and curved vector segments and paths, connected by anchor points. With each click of the tool, anchor points are deposited and can be selected and modified with the Direct Selection tool (what you experienced in the last section on Paths). Through direction lines and direction points (together called direction handles), anchor points define the position and curve attributes of each line segment. See Figure 7–24. Because it is so precise, the Pen tool is excellent for tracing around complex shapes. In the following steps, practice drawing straight and curved lines with the tool, first randomly to get a feel for it and then more precisely to trace images.

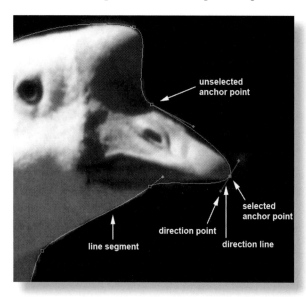

figure | 7–24 |

Anatomy of a path.

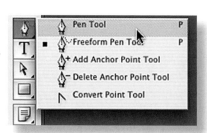

figure | 7–25 |

Select the Pen tool in the toolbox.

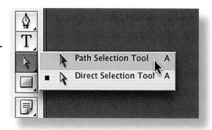

figure | 7–26 |

Select the Path Selection tool.

1. In Photoshop, choose File > New and make a new, blank document (any size).

2. Select the Pen tool in the toolbox. See Figure 7–25.

3. As if you are doodling on a piece of paper, randomly click to place anchor points on the document. To create straight-line segments, click the Pen tool and then pick it up and click somewhere else—keep clicking to make straight lines.

4. To end the path, Command-click (Mac) or Ctrl-click (Windows) anywhere away from all objects, or click on the first point of your path to close it.

5. To make curved lines, click and drag, keeping the mouse button pressed. Continue to click and drag to make curves. Fun, huh?

6. With no objective, continue to make straight and curved lines. Use the Direct Selection tool to select and modify individual anchor points. Use the Path Selection tool (see Figure 7–26) to select a complete path, so you can move it or delete it.

7. Now for more precision drawing. Open **pen_practice.psd** from the **chap07_lessons** folder.

8. Choose Window > Layers and make sure **drawing_layer** is highlighted. See Figure 7-27.

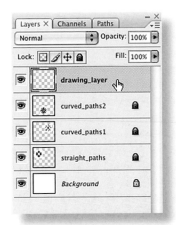

figure | 7–27 |

The drawing_layer selected.

9. Select the Pen tool in the toolbox.

10. In the Options bar for the Pen tool, choose the Paths shape option. See Figure 7–28.

11. Click once on a corner of one of the diamonds in the first shape. This action makes an anchor point. Click the next corner, then the next, and then close the shape by clicking on the first anchor point. See Figure 7–29. If you make a mistake (which is likely when you first attempt to use this tool), select the previous step in the History panel. If you are a perfectionist and want perfect, straight-line segments between anchor points, hold down Shift as you click down each point to constrain them to 45 degree angles.

figure | 7–28 |

Choose the Paths shape option in the Options bar.

12. Practice creating straight-line segments on the other three diamond shapes. Choose Window > Paths to view the work paths you have created.

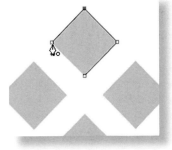

figure | 7–29 |

Each time you click with the Pen tool, you create an anchor point.

13. On the next tile shape (resembling a sunburst), click once with the Pen tool on a tip of one of the teardrop shapes, and then click and drag on the rounded head of the teardrop to create a curve. (With your finger still on the mouse you can continue to drag out to create a rounder curve and also move the direction handle up-down or in-out to make the line tangent with the tracing image.) See Figure 7–30. Click again—do not drag—on the anchor point at the bottom of the teardrop to close the shape. Continue tracing the other teardrop shapes, and the circle in the middle. For fun: Can you draw the circle in the middle using only two anchor points?

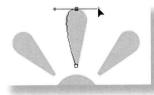

figure | 7–30 |

Create a curved-line segment by clicking and dragging with the Pen tool.

14. Continue your Pen practice on the flower shape.

15. Change your vector shapes into bitmapped shapes. First, choose a foreground color for the fill. Next, select the **Work Path** layer in the Paths panel. Click on the arrow with three lines in the upper-right corner of the Panel window, choose Fill Path, and click OK.

16. See **pen_practice_final.psd** in the **chap07_lessons** folder for a completed version of this exercise. View the work paths in the Paths panel. The paths were stroked with a brush style with color dynamics turned on. To apply the stroke, choose Stroke Path from the Paths panel's options menu or click on the shortcut at the bottom of the Panel window. See Figure 7–31.

figure |7–31|

To quickly apply a stroke to a work path, select the shortcut at the bottom of the Paths panel.

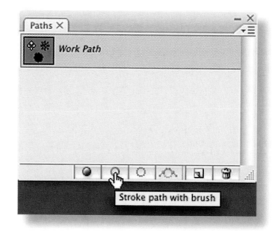

Vector Masks

Masks in Photoshop are a way to hide and reveal areas of an image. They are very useful in image editing and can create interesting effects (see Chapter 8). Since we are currently covering the modes of working with vectors, we want to mention vector masks.

Vectors produce graphics with clean, sharp edges (not pixelated). To take advantage of this attribute, Photoshop offers you the ability to create vector masks. On a layer, vector masks produce a sharp-edged shape that is useful when you want to add a design element with clean, defined edges or when you wish to export into a vector-based program, such as Adobe Illustrator. The vector mask is defined in the Layers and Paths panels. See Figure 7–32. Use the Pen or Shape tools (see later section in this chapter) to draw a work path, and then define its vector mask by choosing Layer > Vector Mask > Reveal All or Hide All.

figure |7–32|

A vector mask is defined in the Layers and Paths panels.

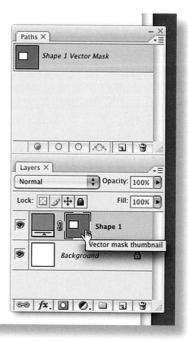

Type

Have you ever noticed that when you print a document of text in a word processing program, like Microsoft Word, that the text is very clean and crisp looking, and no matter what size you make it—12 pt or 60 pt—it always looks this way? On the other hand, when you print off a piece of clipart that was scaled really big on the document, it looks kind of blurry and pixelated. Why? Well, the type contains vector data that keep the letter shapes sharp looking and that can be scaled big or small because, as you discovered in Chapter 3, vectors are not dependent on resolution. Therefore, when type is printed on a printer that supports this vector data, it looks really good and is easily readable. In contrast, the clipart is constrained by its resolution (composed of bitmapped pixels) and must remain a particular size to preserve its crispness when printed.

In regard to type in Photoshop, it works very similar to how it is reproduced in a word processing program. When first created, it locates itself on its own layer. It also contains vector data, so you can easily modify it without worrying about how good it is going to look when printed. To apply type to a Photoshop document, select the Horizontal Type tool (see Figure 7–33), click within the document, and begin typing.

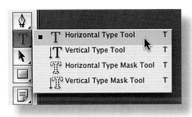

figure |7–33|

The Horizontal Type tool in the toolbox.

You can adjust a type's font, size, orientation, and color in the Options bar, similar to editing type in a word processing program. Alternatively, choose Window > Character and Window > Paragraph for more formatting choices. See Figure 7–34.

figure |7–34|

Format text in a Type tool's Options bar and Character panel.

▶ Don't Go There!

Although we have made the analogy of how type works in Photoshop to how it works in a word processing program, we do not recommend using Photoshop as a word processing program, even if you are going to create large bodies of text in an image or layout. For adding headlines and body copy, use a layout program, such as Adobe InDesign, Illustrator, or QuarkXPress. These programs support type characteristics much better. We highly recommend using type only as a design element in Photoshop.

Vector Compatibility

As presented in Chapter 3, some image formats support vector data, some do not. When you work in Photoshop's native format (PSD), any vector masks, work paths, and type you create is preserved in that temporary state until you decide to rasterize it—which you might need to do to add certain effects and filters to the object. When you go to save your work, however, you must decide whether you want to keep the vector data in the file. This depends on where it is headed. If you save a file in the EPS or PDF formats, the vector data is preserved (see Figure 7–35) when the file is opened in a vector-based program, such as Adobe InDesign or Illustrator. You can select and edit individual objects and the anchor points that define them.

If saved in a TIFF or JPEG format and opened in a vector-based program, the vector data is rasterized (flattened into pixels). See Figure 7–36 and Figure 7–37. The **chap07_lessons/samples** folder contains several saved versions of an image in different formats. If you have Adobe Illustrator, for instance, you can import these versions into the program and then select the image or image parts to see what vector attributes of the image have remained. You can also import each version into Photoshop and see what happens. Does the vector data remain intact or is everything rasterized?

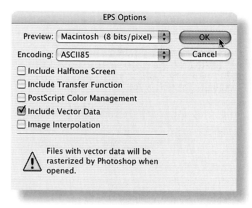

figure | 7–35 |

When saving in EPS, the vector data can be preserved (indicated by a check mark), but note the warning. It will not be preserved when reopened in Photoshop, only when opened in a fully vector-supported program, such as Adobe Illustrator.

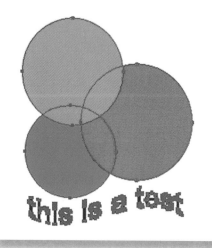

figure | 7–36 |

This EPS-formatted version of a file was saved in Photoshop and opened in Illustrator. When you click on the grouped item, you can see the editable, individual anchor points that comprise vector objects.

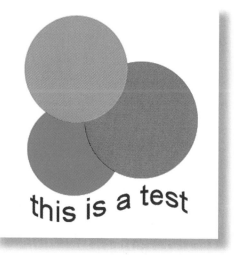

figure | 7–37 |

This JPEG-formatted version of a file was saved in Photoshop and opened in Illustrator. Because JPEG does not support vector data, when opened in Illustrator or Photoshop it is composed of bitmapped pixels only.

MAKING SHAPES

In almost any art class you learn how to draw geometric shapes, and in previous chapters you have made shapes. However, now that you have learned about the characteristics of drawing with vectors and bitmaps, you can better understand the shape-making tools and options. One way to make shapes quickly is to make a selection (i.e., draw with the Marquee or Lasso tools) and then fill or stroke the shape by choosing Edit > Fill (or Stroke). There is also a set of Shape tools (see Figure 7–38) that provide you with selections to choose from in the Options bar. See Figure 7–39. Such selections include the type of shape (shape layers or vector masks, paths, or fill pixels), the characteristics of each of which were covered in the last sections on drawing with vectors versus pixels. And depending on what shape type you choose, you also have the ability to add, subtract, exclude, and intersect shapes as well as add styles (pre-made effects).

figure | 7–38 |

The Shape tools available in the toolbox.

figure | 7–39 |

The Shape tool's Options bar.

Practice the following steps for some familiarity with the Shape tools.

1. Create a new file about 500 by 500 pixels in size. Make sure the background content is white.

2. Select the Rounded Rectangle tool in the toolbox. See Figure 7–38.

3. In the Options bar, select the Fill pixels style option. See Figure 7–40.

figure | 7–40 |

Select the Fill pixels option to make rasterized shapes.

> **Note:** In the Options bar, you can modify the geometric options for the selected shape by clicking on the second inverted arrow. See Figure 7–41.

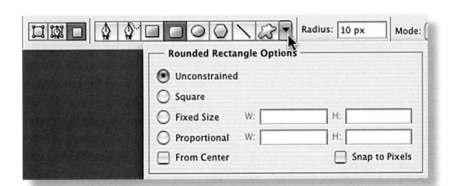

figure | 7–41 |

You can alter the geometric options for a selected shape in the Options bar.

4. Set a foreground color in the toolbox.

5. Click and draw a rounded rectangle on the blank canvas.

6. Open the Layers panel and note that the rectangle is a rasterized image on the Background layer.

7. Select the Paths style option in the Options bar. See Figure 7–42.

figure | 7–42 |

Select the Paths style option.

8. Select the Polygon tool.

9. Draw a polygon on the document. It is a temporary work path you can alter.

10. Open the Paths panel to see the work path.

11. Select the Shape layers style option in the Options bar. See Figure 7–43.

figure | 7–43 |

Select the Shape layers style option.

12. Choose a new foreground color.

13. Select the Custom Shape tool and, in the Shape Options drop-down menu, choose a custom shape. See Figure 7–44.

> **Note:** You can also make your own custom shapes to put in the menu. See the Photoshop Help files for details.

figure | 7–44 |

Select a custom shape.

14. Draw the shape on the document. Note in the Layers panel a new layer containing the shape and its vector mask.

15. Select Subtract from shape area in the Options bar, and then draw another custom shape overlapping the first custom shape you made. See Figure 7–45 and Figure 7–46. Explore the other shape modification options, such as for adding, intersecting, or excluding a shape from another.

figure | 7–45 |

Select Subtract from shape area in the Options bar.

figure | 7–46 |

The shape of one object subtracted from another.

16. Select a Style option from the Options bar. See Figure 7–47. The selected shape is updated with the style. Pretty slick, eh?

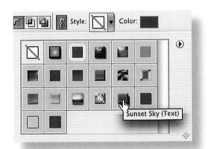

figure | 7–47 |

Select a shape style.

Lesson: Nonrepresentational Art Creation

You will be surprised to find that this lesson contains very little step-by-step instruction.

Since painting and drawing can be such an exploratory medium, we thought we would leave most of this lesson to your imagination. Using the various tools and techniques you learned in this chapter, create a nonrepresentational digital art piece—an art creation that may not make reference to anything in nature or reality. See Figure 7–48.

As described in the book *Artforms* (revised seventh edition), by Duane Preble and Sarah Preble (revised by Patrick Frank), "Nonrepresentational art (sometimes called nonobjective or nonfigurative art) presents visual forms with no specific references to anything outside themselves. Just as we can respond to the pure sound of music, we can respond to the pure visual forms of nonrepresentational art."

1. In Photoshop, use the toolbox to set the background color to any color of your choice.

2. Create a new file about 500 by 500 pixels in size. Set Color Mode to RGB Color, and the resolution to 150 ppi. For Background Contents, choose Background Color, which is the color you specified in the first step.

figure | 7–48 |

An example of nonrepresentational art using Photoshop. See also the chapter opening image.

3. Open the Layers panel.

4. Make a new layer and name it **painting**.

5. Select the Brush or Pencil tool. Set the brush style to your liking and start to paint on your canvas—it does not matter what you paint . . . and, if you do not like it, there is always the History panel. Open the Brushes panel (Window > Brushes) to explore more options.

6. Create another layer and name it **shapes**.

7. Create any number of fill shapes using the Shape tool.

8. Make other shape styles, using vector shape layers and paths.

9. Save your file, if you have not already (save often!).

10. Add some text as a graphic design element to the canvas.

11. Use Layer styles on any of the layers you have created, such as Drop Shadow, Bevel and Emboss, and Pattern Overlay. To do this, highlight the layer you want to affect in the Layers panel, and choose Layer > Layer Style from the menu bar.

12. If you recall how from previous lessons, place blending effects and filters on any of the layers you have created. (For more specifics on the "what" and "how" of blending effects and filters, see Chapter 9.)

13. Create another layer and name it **frame**. Draw or construct (using the Shape tool options, such as Subtract or Intersect) a frame around your masterpiece.

14. Save your file in the JPEG format, set the quality amount to about 8, and e-mail your art creation to a friend.

SUMMARY

After this chapter, there is no such thing as a blank Photoshop canvas. Usually it only takes a quick introduction to the drawing and painting tools and processes in this program to initiate a creative spark.

in review

1. What is the main difference between the Pencil and Brush tools?

2. Name at least three features in the Brushes panel.

3. Does the Eraser tool erase with the foreground color or background color?

4. Why would having some vector support in Photoshop be useful for drawing and painting?

5. Name three areas (features/tools) in Photoshop that incorporate the use of vector technology.

6. What is the difference between a "click" action and a "click and drag" action when you are using the Pen tool?

7. What are paths in Photoshop? How do you make them? What tools do you use to select a complete path or parts of a path?

8. What file formats preserve vector data?

9. In what three styles (ways) can you create shapes in Photoshop?

10. Describe nonrepresentational (nonobjective) art.

exploring on your own

1. Create your own custom brush out of your signature. See Figure 7–49.

   - Make a new document. For Background Contents, choose Transparent.

   - Select the Pencil tool in the toolbox.

   - Choose a brush style with a small diameter (1 to 5 pixels in size).

   - Choose a foreground color.

   - Write your signature on the document.

   - Choose Edit > Define Brush Preset, and name your custom brush.

- Set your brush settings in the Brushes panel (look for your custom brush in the Brush Tip Shape area).

- Paint with your signature.

2. In the Photoshop Help files (Help > Photoshop Help), do a search for "brush dynamics" and find out what this feature does.

3. In the Help files, find out what the Convert Point tool does.

4. Using the Pen tool, trace around the images (**goose.tif** or **peacock.jpg**) provided in the **chap07_lessons/samples** folder.

5. Practice creating some type on a path.

- Using the Pen tool, draw a simple path on your document.

- Select the Type tool, and set the font and font size in the Options bar.

- Click with the Type tool (the little I-beam) on the path and start typing some text.

- Adjust the type by selecting it and modifying its formatting options in the Options bar.

- Adjust the path the type is on and the starting point of the type by using the Direct Selection tool. See Figure 7–50.

6. Discover the wonder of kaleidoscopes. Visit these sites:

- Amazing Software Kaleidoscopes: *http://bindweed.com/kaleidoscopes.htm*

- Kaleidoscopes Heaven: *http://kaleidoscopeheaven.org/*

- Kaleidoscope Collector (how they work): *http://www.kaleidoscopesusa.com/how.htm*

- Make your own Kaleidoscope: *http://familycrafts.about.com/cs/toystomake/a/blconnkaleid.htm*

figure | 7–49 |

Use the Scattering option in the Brushes panel with your new custom signature brush.

figure | 7–50 |

Text on a path—yeah!

dodge and burn

In darkroom photography, "dodge and burn" is a technique whereby, using light, a photographer can selectively darken (burn) areas in a photograph and selectively lighten (dodge) shadowed areas to bring out details. In glorified form, this technique is provided for you in Photoshop as the Dodge and Burn tools. Using any selected brush tip, these tools offer the artist localized and precise tonal control of the pixels in an image. See Figure A–1.

figure A–1 The Dodge and Burn tools (along with the Sponge tool) offer localized tonal control on a photograph.

In the toolbox, the Dodge and Burn tools are grouped with another tonal control tool: the Sponge tool. These tools are great for localized manipulation of the highlights, mid-tones, and shadows in a photograph. However, for more global control use the Levels or Curves command. It is a wonderfully advantageous thing to be able to use the Dodge and Burn tools to adjust subtly the brightness and contrast in a photograph, as well as a simple way to paint more spatially enhanced objects. With these tools you can paint dimensional illusions quickly, as you will see in the next section.

PROFESSIONAL PROJECT EXAMPLE

If you have ever taken a traditional drawing or painting class (which we wholeheartedly recommend!), you have probably been assigned the onerous task of rendering an egg—in all its proportionally rounded splendor—using hard and soft lead pencils, charcoal, or a paintbrush. It sounds easy enough—after all it is only an egg. However, after some initial sketches, you might realize—at least Annesa did—that rendering an egg involves a very subtle play of dark and light pencil strokes and finger smudging to make the egg look somewhat realistic, rather than flat or oddly

deformed. Using the Dodge and Burn tools in Photoshop, the digital art professional has found a more, shall we say, quick and dirty solution to putting the life into a flat image or photograph.

Figure A–2 is a photograph of some eggs. There are obvious lights and darks in the photo, but what happens if we enhance these tones for an even more dimensional look? With the Dodge tool and a soft-tipped brush (or airbrush), areas of the eggs can be further lightened. See Figure A–3. Moreover, with the Burn tool and a soft-tipped brush (or airbrush), areas of the egg can be further darkened. See Figure A–4. The result is two "golden-looking" eggs. See Figure A–5. This same technique can be applied without a photo reference. Start with a gray-toned elliptical shape and build the shadows and highlights with varied brush strokes and tip sizes. See Figure A–6.

figure A–2 A digital photograph of some eggs without photo retouching.

figure A–3 With a soft-tipped brush, lighten areas of a photograph with the Dodge tool.

continued

ADVENTURES IN DESIGN

continued

figure A–4 With a soft-tipped brush, darken areas of a photograph with the Burn tool.

figure A–5 A photograph of two eggs made more "golden-looking" using the Dodge and Burn tools.

figure A–6 Go from flat to spatial. Draw a dimensional-looking egg shape using the Dodge and Burn tools.

YOUR TURN

Using the sample file **eggs.psd** in the **aid_examples** folder, you will paint your own realistic eggs with a metallic sheen. If you would like, you can further enhance the image with layer styles and/or artistic brush-stroke or sketch filters.

Self-Project Guidelines

1. Open the **eggs.psd** file in the **aid_examples** folder.
2. View the Layers panel, and be sure **overlay_adjustment_layer** is selected. See Figure A–7. This

figure A–7 Select the **overlay_adjustment_layer**.

is the layer you will paint on with the Dodge and Burn tools. It is a special layer filled with a 50% gray background and set with an Overlay blending mode, located above, thus protecting the original photo you will enhance.

3. Select the Burn or Dodge tool in the toolbox, and set your brush tip size. For starters, we suggest a soft brush with a diameter of about 45 pixels, and for Range in the Options bar of the tool, select Midtones. See Figure A–8. You can also play with the Exposure setting to adjust the amount (or intensity) of lightness or darkness applied with each brush stroke.

4. After enhancing the egg photo on the **egg1** layer, save your file in your lessons folder. Then hide **overlay_adjustment_layer** and **egg1** in the Layers panel. This reveals another egg example: flat, elliptical shapes.

5. Expand the **other_egg_samples** layer set by clicking on the triangle next to the folder icon, and select the **hand_drawn_egg1** layer.

6. Use the Burn and Dodge tools with soft-tipped brushes to bring the egg to dimensional life.

7. Add a drop shadow for further spatial impact via Layer > Layer Style > Drop Shadow.

8. Enhance the other egg example in the **hand_drawn_ egg2** layer.

9. Save your golden eggs.

Things to Consider

For future explorations with drawing and painting, as featured in this "Adventures in Design," consider the following:

- Whenever possible, use an adjustment layer to work on over your original image to protect it. When working with localized tonal control tools, create a new layer with a 50% gray fill and set to the Overlay blending mode (as in the **egg.psd** file). To make global tonal adjustments, such as Levels and Color Balance, choose Layer > New Adjustment Layer.

- There are hundreds of artist's tips and techniques for using Photoshop. Step-by-step instructions are plentiful on the World Wide Web. Do a global search for "Photoshop tips and techniques" or a more refined search for the name of a Photoshop tool or function, such as "dodge and burn."

figure A–8   Set options for the Dodge or Burn tools, such as Brush Size, Range, and Exposure.

| masking |

charting your course

When the power of masking in digital illustration and design was first discovered, people wondered how we managed so long without it. Masking is a technique for hiding or revealing areas of an image. Similar to how masking tape protects window trim as you paint around it, a digital mask protects areas of an image as you apply effects to unmasked areas.

Masks are used a lot in animation and digital video editing. A scene transition where one frame wipes away another is a moving mask. A computer-generated character co-acting with a human actor is superimposed into a scene using masks. There are several types of masks in Photoshop for use in digital imagery. Each contains specific attributes for different purposes. In this chapter, we cover how a mask works and the several types of masks that can be created in Photoshop, including layer and vector masks, type masks, clipping masks, and quick masks.

goals

In this chapter you will:

- **Learn what a mask is and discover how it works and is used in Photoshop**
- **Explore the types of masks available in Photoshop**
- **Paint full and partial selections using quick masks**
- **Hide and reveal content with layer and clipping masks**

UNMASKING MASKS

How does a mask work? First, we will give you an overview, and then we will describe it in depth. Examine the four steps in Figure 8–1. Step 1 shows an original photograph taken at the rustic Palmela castle in Portugal. Step 2 shows part of the photo with a layer mask applied. Annesa's face in the cardboard character was selected with the Elliptical Marquee tool, and then Layer > Layer Mask > Hide Selection was chosen. Step 3 indicates the layer (a picture of Max from Chapter 4) that will be affected by the mask created in Step 2. In Step 4 the "Max" layer is placed below the mask layer, whereby Max's face replaces Annesa's. All of this magic was done without damaging the original photo.

To clarify a few things for you—or maybe to confuse you further—let us give you a closer look at the characteristics of a mask. Remember, masks get easier to grasp when you actually play

figure | 8–1 |

This four-part example shows how a mask can replace an area of a photograph with another photograph behind it. The mask "protects" the original image—so it appears as if you have cut out (deleted) selected parts of an image without actually destroying it. It is just an illusion.

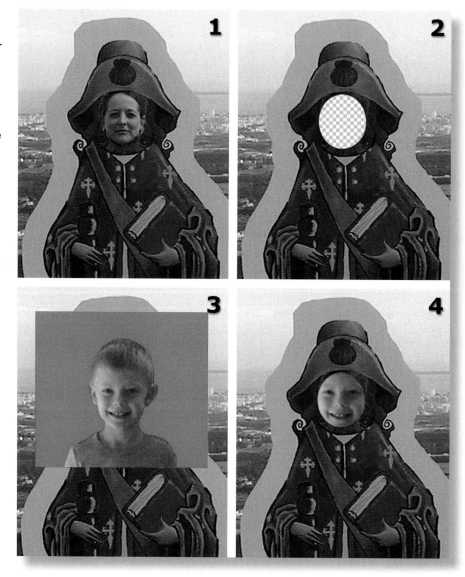

with them (like anything else, of course!). So when you reach the end of this chapter and have had some experience with them, you might want to review this section.

When Step 2 was executed on the photo example (see Step 2, Figure 8–1), the mask became part of the photo's layer in the Layers panel. Now note the mask thumbnail in the layer **cardboard_ character** in Figure 8–2.

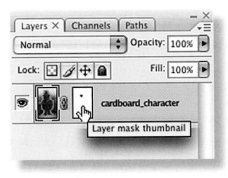

figure |8–2|

The layer mask thumbnail located on the same layer in which the mask is applied.

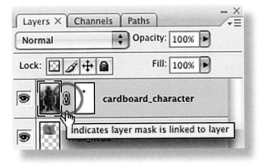

figure |8–3|

Unlink the mask layer from the original object it was masking.

Check it out for yourself! Open **example_mask.psd** in the **chap08_lessons/samples** folder. Then open the Layers panel and take a look. The black dot in the layer mask thumbnail shows the part of the mask to be transparent—in other words, the selection is hidden. An important distinction to make here is that the mask is not "deleting" the selection but "hiding" it. You can disable or delete a mask and still have the original photo or artwork intact. To do this in this example, click on the mask thumbnail in the Layers panel, and then choose Layer > Layer Mask > Disable (a big X appears over the thumbnail). To turn it back on, choose Layer > Layer Mask > Enable. Here are a few other things to do with masks:

- Unlink and move a mask to hide other areas of an image or photograph: In the example layer mask, unlink the mask thumbnail in the Layers panel from the photo it was masking by clicking the link icon, selecting the layer mask thumbnail, and moving it to a different location using the Move tool. See Figure 8–3 and Figure 8–4.

figure |8–4|

Move an unlocked mask elsewhere on the image.

figure | 8–5 |

Disable or delete a mask without damaging the original image.

- Disable or delete a mask without damaging the original work. See Figure 8–5.

- Make masks out of any selected shape. See Figure 8–6.

- Load and save a selection from a mask: You can store and reload selections as alpha channels. Alpha channels are located in the Channels panel and there is a lot to them. See "Note" on page 157. When you examine an alpha channel in Photoshop (see Figure 8–7), the black indicates the area you can see through the mask (like a window, it is transparent), and the white is the opaque area. Figure 8–8, shows how the black and white areas of an alpha channel can hide or reveal (mask) areas of an image. There can also be semitransparent masks at all different levels of transparency, which is indicated by varying shades of gray. See Figure 8–9. You will learn how to create these soft transparency effects using a quick mask in the section "Quick Masks."

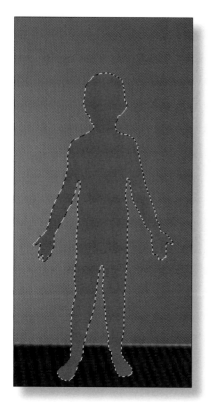

figure | 8–6 |

Make masks out of any selected shape, like that of Max's body.

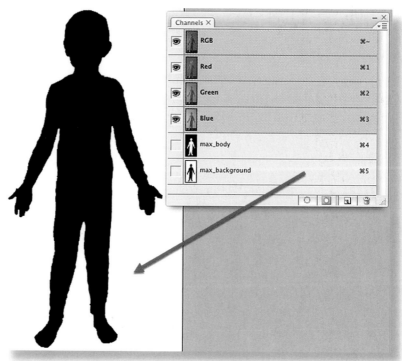

figure | 8–7 |

An alpha channel, saved in the Channels panel, can be used to mask out areas of an image.

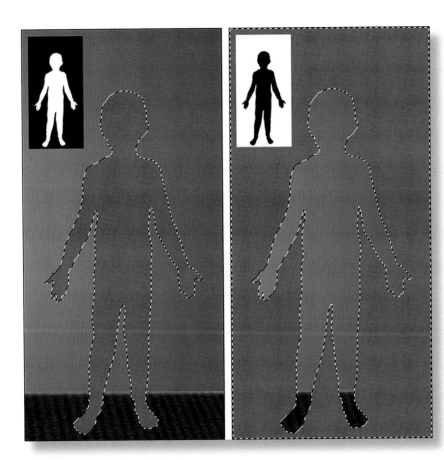

figure | 8–8 |

On the left, the background is revealed (black) and Max remains isolated from the mask. On the right, the background is revealed through Max (black) and the rest of the background remains protected.

figure | 8–9 |

A gradient of grays can become a mask—each level of gray creating more or less transparency. Here, the ostrich is softly being revealed through the gradient mask.

Some file formats, such as TIFF, will support an alpha channel in an image. This is useful when you want to use an alpha channel (i.e., to mask) in another program (other than Photoshop) that supports the use of alpha channels, such as Adobe InDesign, Illustrator, or After Effects. See Figure 8–10.

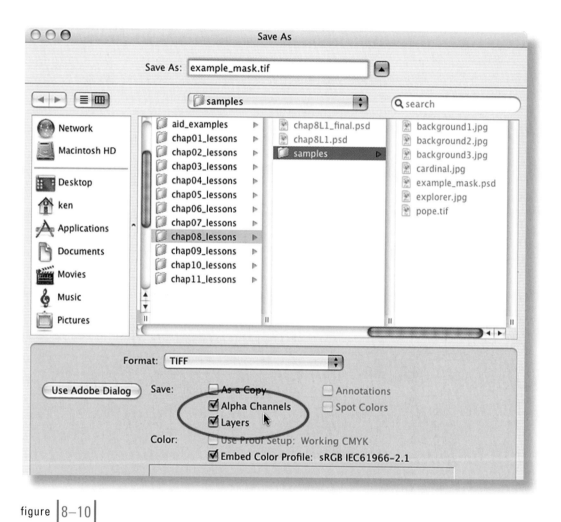

figure | 8–10 |

The option to preserve an alpha channel appears when you save a file to the TIFF format.

TYPES OF MASKS

Although the masks work pretty much the same in Photoshop, there are different types you can use, including layer and vector masks, clipping masks, type masks, and quick masks.

Note: A little more about alpha channels: You can get into some sophisticated image editing and manipulation with alpha channels—something to look into in your more advanced studies of Photoshop. For now, keep in mind that channels, and alpha channels in particular, have these properties (taken directly from the Photoshop Help files):

- Each image can contain up to 56 channels, including all color and alpha channels.
- You can specify a name, color, mask option, and opacity for each channel. (The opacity affects the preview of the channel, not the actual image.)
- All new channels have the same dimensions and number of pixels as the original image.
- You can edit the mask in an alpha channel using painting tools, editing tools, and filters (see Figure 8–11).
- You can convert alpha channels to spot color channels.

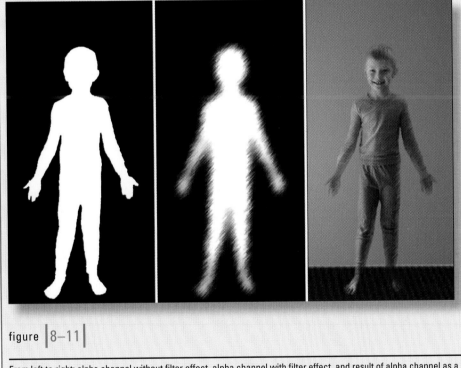

figure | 8–11 |

From left to right: alpha channel without filter effect, alpha channel with filter effect, and result of alpha channel as a mask on the Max photograph (the edges of his body are transparent and appear "alien-like").

Layer and Vector Masks

Layer masks let you create a mask that is linked to an object on the same layer, which, therefore, directly affects the object. A layer mask was used in our first example, shown in Figure 8–1. Vector masks are a variation on layer masks. They are created similarly. However, because vector masks consist of vectors the edges of a selection being used for the mask are much more crisp and clean-looking. To quickly make and edit a layer or vector mask:

1. Select an area on an image or photograph using the shape Marquee tools or a Lasso tool. Note that if you select the Background layer, you must double-click on the layer to turn it into a standard layer (Layer 0) for the next step to work.

2. Choose Layer > Layer Mask or Layer > Vector Mask, and determine whether you want the mask to reveal or hide the selection.

3. To edit a mask, Command-click (Mac) or Ctrl-click (Windows) on the layer mask thumbnail in the Layers panel to create a selection.

4. Turn on Edit in Quick Mask Mode in the toolbox. Add or subtract from the selection with the painting tools (details to follow in the section on quick masks).

Clipping Masks

Clipping masks are a quick way to attach a sequence of layers to be masked by another layer. Here is how it is done:

1. Decide what item you want to use as a mask—text, shape, any filled object—and place it on its own layer.

> **Note:** When using shapes, be sure the Fill pixel option is selected in the Options bar.

2. Place items you want to be revealed through the mask in their own layers above the mask layer.

3. Hold down Alt/Option and place the cursor between these two layers. A funky icon of two circles, one atop the other, appears. Click on this edge line and the top layer will indent above the lower layer. The clipping mask has been executed. See Figure 8–12. Alternatively, you can select the items you want to be revealed through the mask and choose Layer > Create Clipping Mask.

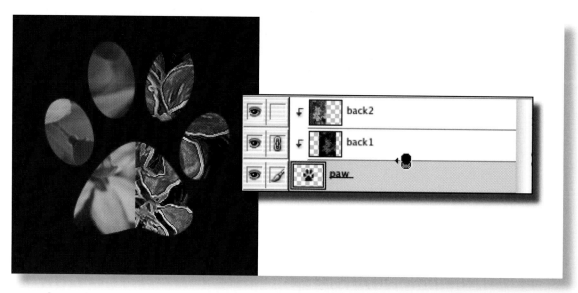

figure |8–12|

Create a clipping mask.

> **Note:** A clipping mask can be applied to several layers.

Horizontal and Vertical Type Mask Tools

You can make masks out of type with the Horizontal Type Mask or Vertical Type Mask tools. It is quite easy:

1. In the toolbox, choose either the Horizontal Type Mask or the Vertical Type Mask tool. See Figure 8–13.

2. Set the type's formatting options (font, size) in the Options bar.

3. Click on the document and type a word or phrase. While you type, you will be sent into Edit in Quick Mask Mode—indicated by the red transparent overlay.

4. Press Enter on the numeric pad (not the main keyboard) or click on a selection tool to create the type selection.

5. Create a new layer in the Layers panel. Note that the type becomes a selection—but only temporarily—on the document for you to fill, add effects to, and use as an object for layer or clipping masks. See Figure 8–14.

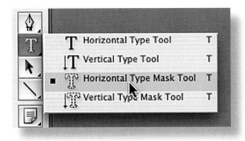

figure | 8–13 |

The Horizontal Type Mask and Vertical Type Mask tools in the toolbox.

figure | 8–14 |

The selected text is filled, has a layer effect added to it, and is assigned a clipping mask that reveals a photographic texture through the letter forms.

Quick Masks

As mentioned in Chapter 4, there is a direct relationship between selections and color in Photoshop. The dynamics of this relationship open the possibility for very versatile and sophisticated mask-making with the use of Photoshop's quick mask feature. A quick mask is not really a mask but a temporary mode in which to define and edit selections with the Painting tools—or even a Photoshop filter effect. Paint with white to select more areas of an image; paint with black to deselect areas; paint with an opacity setting or shade of gray to create a semitransparent mask that is useful for soft-edged, feathered effects. (You can also uniformly soften selection edges with the Feathering option, accessed via the selection tool's Options bar or Select > Modify > Feather.)

> **Note:** When you paint with black and white, the selection is either indicated or not by marching ants. But, when you paint with an opacity setting or a tonal color, a selection may or may not be visible. A dialog box might appear. See Figure 8–15. However, although you cannot always see the marching ants of a semitransparent selection, the selection will be indicated by a level of gray when viewed as an alpha channel (saved mask).

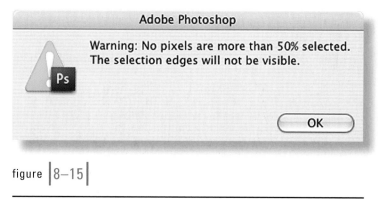

figure |8–15|

The "selection edge not visible" warning.

When Annesa designed the Max lesson in Chapter 4, she used a quick mask to extract the background from the photograph, so she could replace it. The original background was composed of many shadows and highlights, so, regrettably, she could not just click on it with the Magic Wand tool and be done with it. Moreover, she was determined to protect Max's body from the extraction. See Figure 8–16.

To get into Quick Mask Mode, Annesa cursorily selected as much of the background as she could with the Lasso (or Magic Wand) tool. Then she chose Edit in Quick Mask Mode in the toolbox. See Figure 8–17.

Photoshop covers the non-selected areas of the image in a translucent color, which by default is red, like rubylith. She changed this color by double-clicking on the Edit in Quick Mask Mode icon in the toolbox. See Figure 8–18. She then selected the Brush tool in the toolbox. The swatches in the toolbox automatically become black and white, ready to mark out by color her selected or non-selected areas when she paints. She painted with white to add to her selection (remove the translucent color) or black to delete areas of her selection (add the translucent color). Flipping between Edit in Standard Mode and Edit in Quick Mask Mode (the Edit in Quick Mask Mode button toggles between the two modes by clicking on it) lets her see how she was doing—showing what areas were selected. See Figure 8–19.

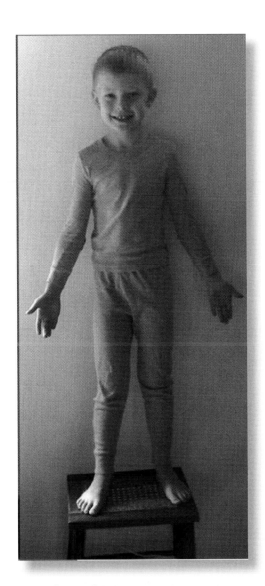

figure |8–16|

The original photo of Max taken near a window with Annesa's digital camera. Admittedly, not the most professional setup.

In Standard Mode, Annesa saved a permanent version of her final selection to an alpha channel (in case she wanted to use it or edit it again later) by choosing Select > Save Selection. Last, she created the layer mask out of the selection, made a new background on a separate layer, and placed it below the mask layer. The result is shown in Figure 8–20.

figure |8–17|

The Edit in Quick Mask Mode option in the toolbox.

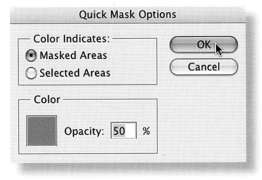

figure |8–18|

Double-click on the Edit in Quick Mask Mode icon in the toolbox to get to its options.

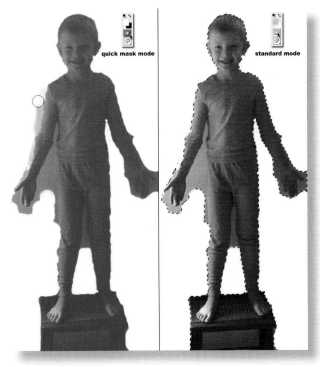

figure |8–19|

Move between Standard and Quick Mask Modes to see how the selection process is going.

figure | 8–20 |

The final Max image used in the Chapter 4 lesson. Compare with Figure 8–16.

Lesson: Lisbon View

In this lesson you will create a new background in a photograph using Quick Mask Mode and a layer mask. See Figure 8–21.

Setting Up the File

1. Open the file **chap8L1.psd** in the folder **chap08_lessons**.

2. Choose View > Actual Pixels.

3. Press Shift-Tab to hide unneeded panels.

Making and Refining a Selection

1. With the Rectangular Marquee tool, draw a rectangle covering the top-left open area of the window—the selection does not need to be perfect. Hold down Shift and keep adding to the selection, defining each window area. For the window with the figure in it, select only the top area with the rectangular shape. See Figure 8–22.

2. Click Edit in Quick Mask Mode in the toolbox. See Figure 8–23.

3. Zoom in close to the window area with the silhouette figure.

4. Select the Brush tool and choose a hard brush about 9 pixels in diameter. See Figure 8–24. Make sure the brush's Opacity setting is set to 100% in the Options bar.

figure | 8–21 |

The lesson before and after a mask effect.

5. Make sure white is the foreground color swatch in the toolbox.

6. Add to the selection by painting away the translucent areas of the open window. You might need to change brush tip sizes to more accurately select the corner crevices of the window. Leave a halo of the translucent color around the head and flying hair strands of the figure. See Figure 8–25.

> **Note:** If you get overly zealous with your painting, you can undo brush strokes in the History panel, or paint with black to deselect areas. Pressing the X key will toggle between the foreground and background colors. This is a great way to switch between black and white at an instant!

7. Click the Quick Mask icon to switch to Standard Mode, so you can see what you have selected.

8. To refine this selection, go to Edit in Quick Mask Mode. Set your brush to a soft, round brush about 9 pixels in size. See Figure 8–26. Adjust its Opacity setting in the Options bar to 92%. Paint carefully around the edge of the figure's head and over the flying strands of hair. You will not see it in the selection, but by using a softer brush and adjusting the opacity setting (or, alternatively painting with a shade of gray), you can create a softer, more realistic mask effect around the hair (you will see this in a later step).

9. Keep refining the selection with the brush tools to your liking. All open parts of the window should be selected.

10. Go to Standard Mode and choose Select > Save Selection from the main menu bar. Enter a name for the new alpha channel. See Figure 8–27.

11. Choose Window > Channels to view the alpha channel mask you just saved.

12. Save the lesson in your **lessons** folder.

figure |8–22|

Select the open window areas with the Rectangular Marquee tool.

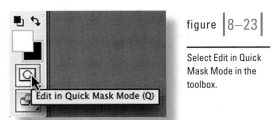

figure |8–23|

Select Edit in Quick Mask Mode in the toolbox.

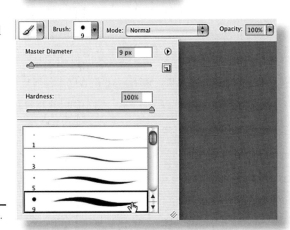

figure |8–24|

Select an appropriately sized paintbrush.

figure |8–25|

Keep part of the translucent color around the figure's head.

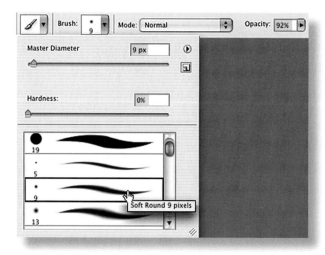

figure |8–26|

Set the brush with a softer tip to produce subtle, semitransparent mask areas.

Create a Layer Mask

1. In the Layers panel, highlight the **lisbon_view** layer. Your windows should still be selected. If not, choose Select > Load Selection and in the options box under Channel choose the alpha channel you just saved.

2. Choose Layer > Layer Mask > Hide Selection.

3. Choose File > Open and from the **chap08_lessons/samples** folder open **background1.jpg**.

4. Move a copy of the background image to the lesson file: with the Move tool, drag the image over the **lesson** file and let go of the mouse to drop the copy.

5. Place **Layer 1** (with the new background image) below the **lisbon_view** layer. Position the background image to your liking behind the **lisbon_view** layer mask.

6. With the background revealed through the mask, you might notice your mask needs a little touch-up. Select the layer mask thumbnail in the Layers panel. Select a brush (set the opacity to 100%) and paint with black to reveal more of the background (the black, transparent area of the mask) or with white to hide more of the background (the white, opaque area of the mask).

7. Save the file in your **lessons** folder. Feel free to try other background images (a couple more are provided in the samples folder).

figure |8–27|

The saved alpha channel mask is located in the Channels panel.

SUMMARY

This chapter uncovered the mystery of masks. Solutions for how to use layer, vector, type, clipping, and quick masks were examined, and practical application for their use revealed.

in review

1. What is the advantage of using masks to hide and reveal content?

2. Name at least four types of masks in Photoshop.

3. When you save a selection, where does it go?

4. Name a the trick (or two) for making soft-edged effects or semitransparent masks in Photoshop.

5. What is the difference between a layer mask and a clipping mask?

6. What is the shortcut key to define a clipping mask in the Layers panel?

7. What first two steps must you do before you can see a quick mask?

8. In Quick Mask Mode, how do black, white, and gray tonal colors affect the selection process?

exploring on your own

1. Explore your own mask effects on the sample cardboard character photographs located in the **chap08_lessons/samples** folder (**cardinal.jpg**, **pope.tif** and **explorer.jpg**).

2. Access the Help > How to Work with Layers and Selections > Soften the edges of selections how-to in the menu options. Read the related topics in the How To.

3. Create textured mask effects with the words earth, wind, and fire, using the Horizontal Type Mask or Vertical Type Mask tool.

4. Do an Internet search for "image masking" and find at least two examples that demonstrate the technique of masking.

Explorer pages

JOSEPH SUMMERHAYS

"If I was starting again right now . . . well, everybody and their dog is learning Photoshop. In fact, Photoshop is being taught in the fourth grade. When I started that I knew Photoshop was huge—someone would find out . . . 'You know Photoshop? Come on in!' So that's the challenge now . . . to be able to distinguish yourself as a quality artist, as an expert user of Photoshop.

 Learn more about this artist via podcast at *http://www.designexploration.com/podcasts.*

About Joseph Summerhays

Joe Summerhays is an award-winning media designer for clients such as HBO, MTV, VH1, AOL, Tribeca Film Festival, Jazz at Lincoln Center, and other innovative media organizations. He has developed more than 30 software titles for children, written over 35 books, and has produced broadband properties for Granada, MTV, and Comedy Central. Additionally, he has guided the production of more than 200 animated short films by young people. His program Animation: Minds in Motion! has been used to teach more than 2,000 elementary school pupils the art of animated film making. Joe has lectured on animation, visual intelligence, and broadband content development. He is currently designing animation workshops for children for the Tribeca Film Festival.

About the Work of Joseph Summerhays

Joe shares his process in creating the "After" animation, a personal project that represents the basic steps he takes in preparing many of his animations:

"The point of the 'After' bit was to have Santa relaxing in front of his TV after a long night of flying, only to be bombarded by infomercials, each addressing his myriad conditions (i.e., balding, wrinkles, abdominal exercise, Viagra). Zamphir and his pan flute is the first commercial he hears, which does not address one of Santa's insecurities, and the bit ends with him dialing the 800 number for a Zamphir album.

"As always, I start with a rough sketch and scan it in. See Figure 1.

Figure 1: The initial idea is sketched on paper.
Joe Summerhay's Productions

Figure 2: Photoshop's Multiply blending mode is used to clean up the sketch.
Joe Summerhays Productions

"Then, in Photoshop, I make a new layer underneath the sketch layer. I turn on the Multiply ink effect on the sketch layer, so the blacks maintain and the whites drop out. I also reduce the opacity of the sketch layer, allowing me to see the painting I'm doing on the layer below. See Figure 2.

"After much painting I turn off the sketch layer and use the smudge tool to blend all my bold color strokes into soft gradients and painterly strokes. I also make new layers for arm positions to be animated later in Adobe After Effects (*http://www.adobe.com/products/aftereffects/*). See Figure 3.

"I want the TV glow on Santa to change colors, so I keep the glow on its own layer above the Santa painting in preparation for color cycling in After Effects. (Color cycling is the process of rapidly changing an object's colors to achieve the illusion of smooth movement.) This glow is painted in with bold brush strokes, then . . . good old Gaussian Blur helps create the haze of late night TV in a dark room. Now it is set; ready to be imported into After Effects for color cycling and animation." See Figure 4.

To see the final version of the "After" animation (see Figure 5) and other eGreetings by Joe Summerhays, visit *http://www.hollysummerhays.com*.

Figure 3: Color effects are painted in. Joe Summerhays Productions

Figure 4: Image is now prepared to be imported into Adobe After Effects.
Joe Summerhays Productions

Figure 5: A single frame of the final animation viewed online with the Quicktime player.
Joe Summerhays Productions

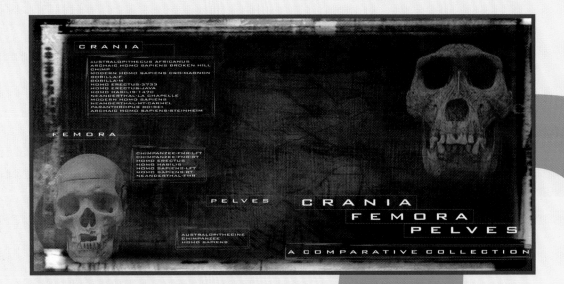

CRANIA

AUSTRALOPITHECUS AFRICANUS
ARCHAIC HOMO SAPIENS BROKEN HILL
CHIMP
MODERN HOMO SAPIENS CRO-MAGNON
GORILLA-F
GORILLA-M
HOMO ERECTUS-3733
HOMO ERECTUS-JAVA
HOMO HABILIS-1470
NEANDERTHAL-LA CHAPELLE
MODERN HOMO SAPIENS
NEANGERTHAL-MT-CARMEL
PARANTHROPUS BOISEI
ARCHAIC HOMO SAPIENS-STEINHEIM

FEMORA

CHIMPANZEE-FMR-LFT
CHIMPANZEE-FMR-RT
HOMO ERECTUS
HOMO HABILIS
HOMO SAPIENS-LFT
HOMO SAPIENS-RT
NEANDERTHAL-FMR

PELVES

AUSTRALOPITHECINE
CHIMPANZEE
HOMO SAPIENS

CRANIA
FEMORA
PELVES

A COMPARATIVE COLLECTION

| layers, compositing, and process |

charting your course

The previous chapters have focused almost exclusively on specific concepts, tools, and ways of doing particular things in Photoshop. You learned how to get around Photoshop's interface, how to manage color, select and transform pixels, retouch photos, draw and paint shapes, use type, and mask areas of an image. Chapter 9 covers the process and methods by which to layer, composite, link, blend, merge, and organize graphic elements into more complex images or graphic layouts. It includes a significant overview of image compositing and the design work process, using layers and alignment tools, merging images with blending modes or filter effects, acquiring content, and producing a CD cover. In this chapter, you can freely utilize all that you have studied thus far in the program.

goals

In this chapter you will:

- **Learn workflow and organizational techniques for developing image compositions and layouts**

- **Cover some specifics using the Layers panel**

- **Review the options for content acquisition and copyright compliance**

- **Composite images together with blending modes, the Liquify effect, and filter effects**

- **Define the sequential steps of a basic design process**

- **Construct a mock CD cover for a client**

ABOUT COMPOSITING AND COMPOSITION

It is important to make a distinction between image compositing and composition in regard to using Photoshop. In his book, *Digital Retouching and Compositing: Photographers' Guide*, David D. Busch describes image compositing as ". . . combining two or more images or portions thereof, to create a new image that didn't exist in that form previously." Other-worldly images by artist Tim Warnock—found found on page 74 of this book—are good examples of images derived by compositing. Also, see the "Adventures in Design: From the Imagination" on page 186.

Composition, on the other hand, ". . . refers to the aesthetic arrangement of elements within a work of art," according to Lois Fichner-Rathus in his book *Understanding Art, Seventh Edition*. It is the artful use of design elements—line, shape, value, texture, and color—in a visual image or design layout, such as a Web site splash page, brochure, or poster. See "Adventures in Design: Wine Box Composition" in this book on page 208. *Exploring Photoshop CS3* does not cover design elements specifically, but *Exploring Illustrator CS3* does in relation to using Adobe Illustrator. *Exploring Photoshop CS3* places more emphasis on image compositing. However, the next section does provide a brief overview of the work process by which a design layout or composition might be constructed.

A DESIGN PROCESS

As much as we might like to snap our fingers in an instantaneous epiphany and have an idea materialize from our heads to reality (that would truly be magic), it does not work that way. Thought to conception, conception to actuality, is a process—there is no way around it. So you might as well make the process your modus operandi. Of course, the process can take shape in numerous fashions. You just need to find the one that is right for you as a graphic designer and for the needs of your clients. (We are assuming your goal is to do work for hire, to actually make money playing with Photoshop.)

In this section, we introduce a general process in which to organize and produce an image composition or layout and share some of the tools available for organization and workflow. There are five parts to this process: start with an idea, make a mock-up, gather content, assemble content, and fine-tune.

Start with an Idea

A design starts with a vision or idea. Sometimes the idea is perfectly realized in your mind and it is simply a matter of putting it into a tangible form. Other times, the idea is further fleshed out as you progress through the design process. Either way, you have to start with an idea, something that drives you to make it "real."

Make a Mock-up

Have you ever made a collage out of magazine clippings? Usually, before you permanently glue everything down, you take your pile of clippings and artfully arrange them on the poster board. You move and rotate things around, group clippings based on topic or color, and inevitably place the most interesting clipping in the center for visual impact. What is hap-

pening at this stage of development is your mock-up; you put thought into the actual design of the collage and the initial placement of elements. At this point, nothing is set in stone, but you thoughtfully consider ideas for how something will look best.

The idea slowly forms into something tangible. Often, it starts out as a cursory sketch or many, many of them (often referred to as thumbnail sketches), and it is then reproduced into a more detailed drawing. Many artists will sketch the idea on paper, scan it, and then use the sketch as a template for constructing the digital version. Others, who feel really comfortable drawing on the computer, construct their vision digitally, utilizing the flexibility of undo and redo and saving multiple copies. See Figure 9–1 and Figure 9–2. When the mock-up is set up to your liking, or to your client's, you move to the next steps: gathering the content to be used in the decided design and assembling it into the final product.

figure |9–1|

Design mock-up 1 of a Web site home page.

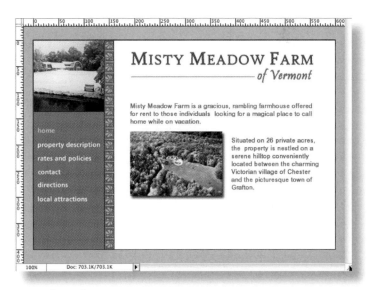

figure |9–2|

Design mock-up 2 of a Web site home page.

Gather Content

The mock-up gives you a better idea of what kind of content you need for the final design. Gathering content for your layout can be the most time-consuming and challenging part of the process, so leave plenty of time for it in your project timeline. You may be in a situation where you must create all of the content—images and copy—yourself, or procure the content from other sources, such as your client or an outside resource (i.e., another artist or writer, image, or font repository). At this point, you must consider the issues of copyright and content format.

Copyright Issues

If you create your own content or use copyright-free material, do not worry about the permission process. However, to re-use other's material, such as a company's logo or a photo of a famous person, you need the correct permissions. As an example, every digital image in *Exploring Photoshop CS3* is protected by copyright law whether explicitly indicated or not. As soon as it is created, copyright is automatically implied—no copyright notices or procedures are required to protect the image from unauthorized reproduction.

It certainly does not hurt, however, to register your work through the U.S. Copyright Office (that is, if you made your creation in the United States) at *http://www.copyright.gov*. You should at least put a copyright notice (©, date, your name) on your work to deter individuals from using it without your permission. We requested permission and/or paid for the artwork and photographs used in this book that we did not create ourselves. We also had to acknowledge that permission was granted (i.e., "Printed by permission of . . ." or "Courtesy of . . .").

Since the proliferation of digital content into our society, copyright protections have been under renewed scrutiny. It has become easier than ever to procure and edit content without giving thought to the original artist. In regard to the protection of digitized content and the use of it for educational purposes, laws have recently been enacted, such as the Digital Millennium Copyright Act (For information, see "Exploring on Your Own").

You should know about a provision to U.S. copyright law called "fair use." Fair use delineates the use of creative works for educational or nonprofit purposes, such as the photographs provided for the lesson project in this chapter.

When determining whether to use someone else's work as part of your own, ask yourself, "Will copying of this image—or text, font, music, video, or data—make me money or take money out of someone else's pocket?" If the answer is "yes," proceed with caution—get permission and credit the artist.

Format

Another aspect of content gathering is getting the content into the right format for your use. For example, if Photoshop is to be used as the medium for assembling your image (see next step), be sure the content can be successfully imported into the program. Are the images and photos you want to use in the correct file format for Photoshop or any other program you might be using? Is the written copy translatable in the digital environment? We are not going to go into great detail about each of the importable file formats supported by Photoshop. However, the available formats appear in Adobe Bridge, the File > Open dialog box, or the File > Place dialog box. The following is an abbreviated list: Photoshop, BMP, Photoshop EPS, CompuServe GIF, JPEG, PCX, Photoshop PDF, PICT file, PNG, Targa, TIFF, and Wireless Bitmap (WBMP).

Assemble Content

Once you have gathered the content, you assemble it in your layout program, which could be Photoshop or a more layout-friendly program (i.e., Adobe Illustrator, InDesign, or QuarkXPress).

There are two parts to integrating content into your final layout design: properly importing content from outside the program; and accurately positioning content into the intended composition using placement and organization tools.

Import

When you have the content in an importable format, you bring it into Photoshop in either two ways: Use the Open and Open Recent commands, or Adobe Bridge (File > Browse); or copy and paste between many applications. You have been taught how to open files in the lessons in this book, but here are the quick steps:

1. Choose File > Open.

2. Select the name of the file you want to open. If the file does not appear, select the option for showing all formats or documents from the Files of type (Windows) or Enable (Mac) pop-up menu.

3. Click Open. A dialog box might appear, letting you set format-specific options. If a color profile warning message appears, specify whether to convert the pixels based on the file's color profile.

> **Note:** For image preview and file compatibility options, choose Photoshop > Preferences > File Handling (Mac) or Edit > Preferences > File Handling (Windows).

Generally when you import native file formats—such as Illustrator (AI) or Flash (FLA)—from one program to another, it is a hit-or-miss proposition. Sometimes the version of the program you are importing the file into will support it, sometimes not. Keeping files in more generic file formats—EPS for vector-based files, or TIFF for bitmap-based files—might prove a better solution, even if—on occasion—you lose some information in translation.

Another importing issue will occur if you attempt to open a newer version of a Photoshop file into an older version (i.e., CS3 to version 7). You usually get a dialog box looking like that shown in Figure 9–3. The conversion will probably work, but you might lose some information. When you go to import artwork and you cannot access the file you want to import, even after you have chosen All Formats from the Files of type (Windows) or All Documents from Enable (Mac) pop-up menu, you know the file has been saved in a format Photoshop cannot read.

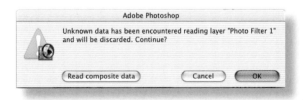

figure |9–3|

Attempt to import a Photoshop CS3 file into Photoshop 7. It will work, but some information might be lost.

Organizing

After importing your content into Photoshop, or creating it in the program, you should organize it. We emphasize the word "should" here, because it is optional whether you want to organize your content. However, we highly recommend it. You cannot leave all of your content in a series of unnamed layers and expect to find what you need quickly and without frustration. Features to keep your work organized while integrating content in a document include Layers, the alignment commands, rulers, the grid, guides, and the Snap feature.

Layers: The Layers panel is your organizational Mecca, as you have probably surmised from working through past lessons. You might be wondering why we have waited until this chapter to impart this important information. Well, the best way to learn how to use this panel is to practice using it, which you have had several chances to do in previous chapters. You have already explored using specific compositing techniques and effects when items are on individual layers, including layer styles (i.e., Drop Shadow, and Bevel and Emboss blending modes, and filters). However these techniques and effects are officially covered in this chapter. The anatomy of the Layers panel (Window > Layers) is visually marked out for quick reference in Figure 9–4.

> Note: By default, every document in Photoshop starts on the Background layer. To change a Background layer into a regular layer (much more versatile), double-click on the Background layer in the Layers panel and give the layer a name. See Figure 9–5.

figure | 9–4 |

The Layers panel is where you keep track of all the images and text elements in a document.

Layers Panel

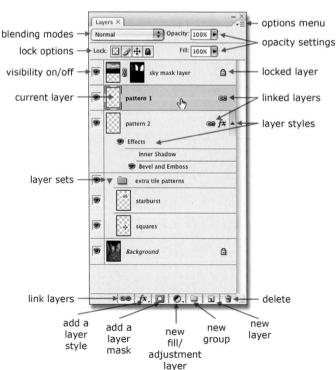

blending modes
lock options
visibility on/off
current layer
layer sets
link layers

options menu
opacity settings
locked layer
linked layers
layer styles
delete

add a layer style
add a layer mask
new fill/adjustment layer
new group
new layer

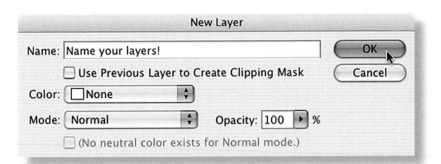

figure |9–5|

Give your layers intuitive names, so you can find what you need in the Layers panel.

Layers are transparent except for any filled content that is placed on them, making it easy to move layers above and below each other for dimensional reasons and for overlapping combinations of images and effects. See Figure 9–6.

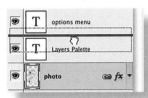

figure |9–6|

Layers can be selected and dragged up and down the layer stack, sending objects in front or in back of each other.

Items can be selected on any layer by highlighting the layer and then Command-clicking (Mac) or Ctrl-clicking (Windows) on the layer's thumbnail. See Figure 9–7.

figure |9–7|

To select all the areas on a layer, Command-click (Mac) or Ctrl-click (Windows) on the layer's thumbnail.

Layers can be selected and linked temporarily to transform or align objects as a group. To select more than one layer, hold down Command (Mac) or Control (Windows). You can also merge selected or visible items into one layer, or group layers in subfolders, called Layer Sets. See Figure 9–8.

For more information on layers, go to Help > Photoshop Help > Contents > Layers.

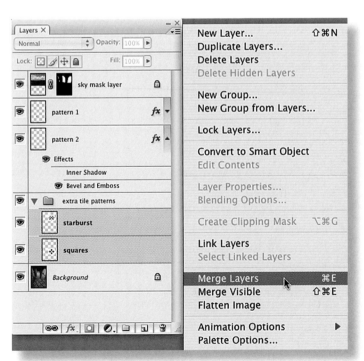

figure |9–8|

You can merge selected or visible layers into one layer, if necessary.

The Alignment Commands: The alignment commands are located in the Move tool's Options bar (select the Move tool to view). They align objects on linked layers horizontally (right, left, or center) or vertically (top, bottom, or center). They also horizontally or vertically distribute linked layers evenly, using the object's edges for spatial reference. You can also get the alignment and distribution options by choosing Layer > Align or Layer > Distribute from the main menu bar. If you are precision-oriented, you will use these commands a lot. See Figure 9–9 and Figure 9–10.

figure |9–9|

The alignment commands are located the Move tool's Options bar.

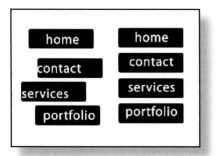

figure |9–10|

Before-and-after example of using the alignment commands. The buttons and text on the right are horizontally centered, with a vertically centered distribution of space between each object.

figure |9–11|

The Ruler Tool and Count Tool in the toolbox.

In addition to alignment commands, there are two tools for measuring precisely: the Ruler Tool and the Count Tool. See Figure 9-11. These tools are found under the Eyedropper tool in the toolbox. The Ruler tool (Analysis > Ruler Tool) analyzes angles and distances across the image with the results in the Info panel (Window > Info). The Count tool (Analysis > Count Tool) counts off with each click of the mouse.

The Auto-Align Layers button (Edit > Auto-Align Layers) is also located in the Move tool's Options bar. This alignment tool analyzes overlapping elements in selected layers to align similar content. This is a great way to create panoramic images (using Auto, Perspective, or Cylindrical options) or piece together scanned segments of a larger image (using Reposition Only option). See Figure 9–12. Once the images are combined, use Auto-Blend Layers (Edit > Auto-Blend Layers) to smooth out any visible seams.

Rulers: Rulers are designed to accurately measure and place objects in the Photoshop workspace. They are toggled on and off by choosing View > Rulers. Both a horizontal ruler and a vertical ruler are made available along the edges of the document. You can change a ruler's measurement by Ctrl-clicking (Mac) or right-clicking (Windows) over a ruler and selecting a new measurement from the drop-down menu. See Figure 9–13. Alternatively, you can go to Photoshop > Preferences > Units & Rulers (Mac) or Edit > Preferences > Units & Rulers (Windows). In the upper-left corner of the document, where the vertical and horizontal rulers meet, you can also set what is called the ruler origin. Setting the ruler origin is useful when, for example, you are working on an object that is 2 by 3 on an 8½-by-11 inch document. You can set the ruler origin at 0, 0 in the upper-left corner of the 2-by-3 area, rather than the 8½-by-11 area, for more precise positioning. To set the ruler origin, you move the cursor into the upper-left corner of the document where the rulers intersect and then click and drag the crosshair to the new origin edge. To restore default settings, double-click on the upper-left corner where the rulers intersect.

Grid: The Grid function is located under View > Show > Grid. A grid of lines or dots appears behind your artwork. The grid can be used to position objects symmetrically. Grids do not print. To adjust grid settings (i.e., color, style, and subdivisions), choose Photoshop > Preferences > Guides, Grid, Slices & Count (Mac) or Edit > Preferences > Guides, Grid, Slices & Count (Windows).

Guides: Guides are incredibly useful for aligning your work. To quickly create guides, choose View > Rulers and drag guidelines from the horizontal and vertical rulers on the sides of the document. See Figure 9–14. Alternatively, choose View > New Guide. You can lock/unlock and clear guides in the View menu, and show guides under View > Show > Guides. Guides do not print. To adjust guide colors and style, choose Photoshop > Preferences > Guides, Grid, Slices & Count (Mac) or Edit > Preferences > Guides, Grid, Slices & Count (Windows).

Snap: Snap allows for exact positioning of selection edges, shapes, and paths. Often, however, the Snap feature—on by default—is more a hindrance than a help, preventing you from properly placing items. Luckily, snapping can be enabled or disabled under View > Snap. With Snap enabled you can snap to particular elements, such as the grid (when visible), guides (when visible), and document bounds. Choose View > Snap To Guides, Grids, Layers, Slices, or Document Bounds. To position things more accurately while Snap is enabled, use the arrow keys on your keyboard.

figure | 9–12 |

Options for the Auto-Align Layers feature.

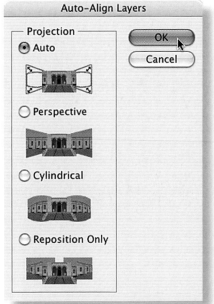

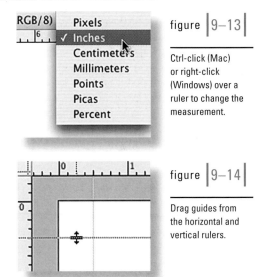

figure | 9–13 |

Ctrl-click (Mac) or right-click (Windows) over a ruler to change the measurement.

figure | 9–14 |

Drag guides from the horizontal and vertical rulers.

Fine-Tune

The fine-tuning stage is where you fix the fine details of your image or layout, including adjusting colors, incrementally aligning items, and playing with subtle formatting of text (such as line and character spacing). In short, you make the document look as perfect as possible. At this time, you also prepare your work for its intended output, such as choosing the proper color mode and settings for either screen or print.

BLENDING MODES, STYLES, AND EFFECTS

If you have spent any significant time playing in Photoshop, you have probably already found and delved into the blending modes, layer styles, filter effects, and Liquify function. These are easy-to-use features with high visual impact (addictive, really) that work miraculously with image compositing.

Blending Modes

Blending modes work with layers and layer sets. A blending mode is specified for a selected layer that affects (blends with) the layer below it or within a layer set.

Blending modes are true compositing of images on different layers, determining how pixels blend with underlying pixels in an image. See Figure 9–15.

> **Note:** Blending modes are also available for the Brush options, found in the Brush tool's Options bar.

To experience pixel blends, open **chap09_lessons/samples/blend.psd**.

1. Open the Layers panel.

2. Two layers are already created for you. Highlight the layer **painted-image**. From the blending mode drop-down menu in the Layers panel, choose the Multiply blending mode—a blend that simulates a look of transparent markers. See Figure 9–16. Explore the other modes. (Alternatively, you can get to the blending modes under Layer > Layer Style > Blending Options.) If you are using Photoshop on Windows, you can also click on the blending mode drop-down menu in the Layers panel and use the up and down arrow keys to cycle through the list of blending modes.

3. For an overview of what each blending mode looks like and its description, examine Figure 9–15 and see Painting > Blending Modes > Blending Mode Examples in the Photoshop Help files.

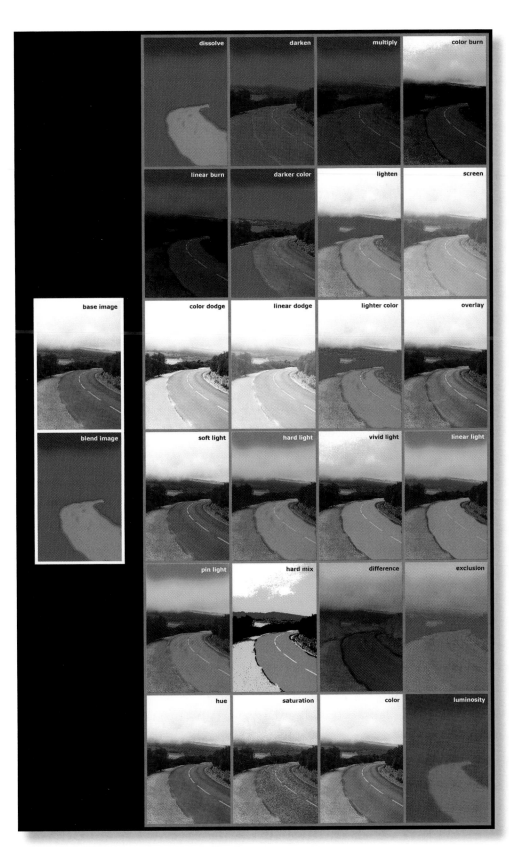

figure | 9–15 |

The blend image is on a layer above the base image, and it contains the specified blending mode. There are many blending modes to choose from.

figure | 9–16 |

Multiply blending mode.

Layer Styles

A layer style can be applied to items on any selected layer, such as a Drop Shadow, Inner and Outer Glow, Bevel and Emboss effects, and Strokes. Go to Layer > Layer Style to choose a style. A dialog box comes up, where you can modify and add or remove a style. To get to the options of any style, click on the style name on the left—not just the check mark, but the actual name—and the options for that style will appear on the right. See Figure 9–17.

figure | 9–17 |

The Layer Style dialog box—a lot to tinker with in here!

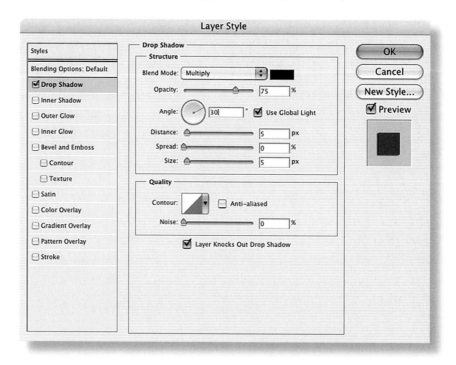

Filter Effects

One thing Photoshop is famous for is its extensive gallery of filters. Filters directly distort and manipulate the pixels in an image. See Figure 9–18. Keep your image in the RGB Color mode to have the full range of filters available. (Once the filter is applied, you can change to another color mode.) To view all the filter choices and preview what they will look like on your image, choose Filter > Filter Gallery from the menu bar. See Figure 9–19. A sample file is provided for you to try out filters: **chap09_lessons/samples/filter.psd**.

figure |9–18|

Filter examples—
there are many to
choose from!

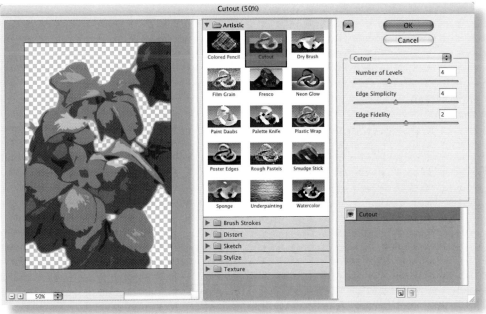

figure |9–19|

The Filter Gallery.
Take your pick and
preview.

The Lighting Effects filter is used often by artists and photographers and is not to be missed. It allows you to create different light styles and properties for your image. To check it out, choose Filter > Render > Lighting Effects. See Figure 9–20.

If there comes a time when you wish you could change how your filters were applied to a layer, the answer is Smart Filters. See Figure 9–21. Smart Filters let you apply filters non-destructively to a layer. This allows you to change the stacking order of filters by clicking and dragging and changing any filter setting simply by double-clicking on the appropriate filter. To add Smart Filters, select the layer and choose Filter > Convert for Smart Filters. If a warning message appears, click OK to accept. A small icon appears in the corner of the layer's thumbnail to show it is now a Smart Object. Now, feel the freedom of adding and experimenting with different combinations of filters!

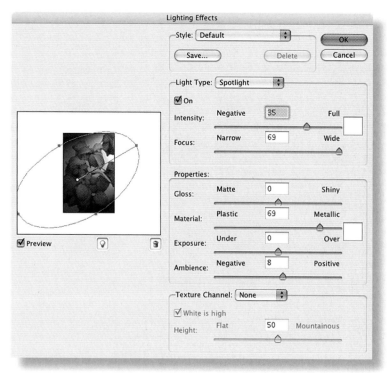

figure |9–20|

The ever-popular Lighting Effects filter.

figure |9–21|

Use of Smart Filers in the Layers panel.

Liquify Function

Last in our tour of special effects is the Liquify feature—it is sweet. With Liquify you can distort pixels with various Liquify commands, such as Bloat, Pucker, and Warp. To open the Liquify menu, choose Filter > Liquify. From the menu select tools on the toolbox to the left of the window and adjust options to the right. See Figure 9–22 and the sample file under **chap09_lessons/samples/liquify.tif**.

Lesson: CD Jacket Project

Now that you have got a handle on using Photoshop, here is your chance to break from the step-by-step study, explore some of the blending and filter effects, and begin to stretch your artistic muscle.

You have been approached by PaleoExcavators Inc., to design a CD jacket (a cover, both front and back) for its new comparative collection CD of skeletal remains. See Figure 9–23. The client has provided a few guidelines and some content (text and photographs) for the project but, in general, it is open to the possibilities of what can be done. The client has also provided some examples of its previous CD jacket designs. See Figure 9–24 and Figure 9–25.

figure | 9–22 |

The Liquify tools in action.

figure | 9–23 |

Skeletal remains to be incorporated into a CD jacket design. All photographs are courtesy of Joel Hagen, graphics design instructor at Modesto Junior College, Calif.

Project Guidelines

1. Required text and a selection of photographs are provided in the folder **chap09_lessons/assets/ CDproject**. Photographs are categorized in folders for what each contains: crania, femora, and pelvic skeletal remains. The text for the front and back covers is provided. You need to include and format the text. For text-formatting options in Photoshop, choose a Type tool to bring up its Options bar, and make use of the Window > Character and Window > Paragraph panels.

> Note: For your viewing fun, some Flash SWF movies have been provided in the **assets** folder as an example of what will be on the mock CD. You will need the Flash Player (free from *http://www.adobe.com*) to view the movies on your computer.

2. You are welcome to use a combination of your own acquired raster- and vector-based images.

figure |9–24|

CD cover project example 1, designed by a Photoshop student at Modesto Junior College, Calif.

figure |9–25|

CD cover project example 2, designed by a Photoshop student at Modesto Junior College, Calif.

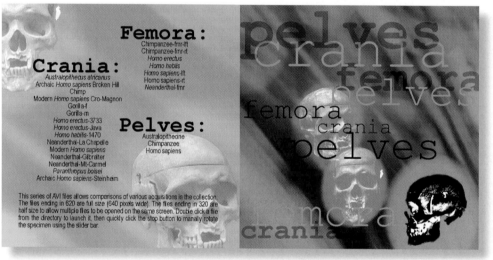

3. Dimension specifications for the jacket are:

- *Width:* 9.5 inches
- *Height:* 4.6875 inches
- *Resolution:* 200 pixels/inch
- *Color mode:* RGB Color (eventually to be converted to CMYK for printing)

4. Before assembling the final designed piece, hone your design ideas by sketching them by hand or mocking them up digitally. Provide an overall potential "look and feel" for the jacket, including font and color possibilities and a general layout of text and images.

5. Save your final work in both PSD and TIFF format.

SUMMARY

Chapter 9 offered the big picture of the image compositing and design composition processes. In addition, it went over often-used organizational and workflow features of Photoshop, and got you hooked (in all hopes!) on its unique blending, Liquify, and filter effects. Work out that imagination muscle!

in review

1. Describe image compositing. Describe composition in design.

2. Define five steps in the design process.

3. What question should you ask yourself when deciding whether to use someone else's work?

4. Name at least five features of the Layers panel.

5. How do you change a background layer to a regular layer?

6. To align items on separate layers, what must you do?

7. Most filter effects are only available in what color mode?

exploring on your own

1. Study about copyright online:

   - U.S. Copyright Office (copyright basics): *http://www.copyright.gov/circs/circ1.html*

   - Specifics of the Digital Millennium Copyright Act: *http://www.copyright.gov/legislation/dmca.pdf*

   - Copyright Web site: *http://www.benedict.com*

   - Stanford University Libraries, Stanford Copyright & Fair Use Center: *http://fairuse.stanford.edu/*

   - Copyright Clearance Center to access copyright permission for millions of publications worldwide: *http://www.copyright.com/*

2. Design a CD cover or promotional poster for a band or theater company in your area.

3. Create a home page design for a Web site.

from the imagination

Photoshop can bring out the mad scientist in us all. It is a digital laboratory where instruments are used to piece together pixels, rather than strands of DNA, into new life forms that come alive on screen or paper, tabloid covers, DVD or video game splash screens, or in this book's Explorer Pages. Enter an adventure in design for the wild imagination.

PROFESSIONAL PROJECT EXAMPLE

Our experiment begins with an example brought to you from the digital artist—aka, "Mad Scientist"—Jeffrey Moring. Jeffrey reveals the secrets used to bring about his optical vision titled *Yesterday, Today, Forever*. See Figure B–1.

figure B–1 Artist Jeffrey Moring's altered self in his image *Yesterday, Today, Forever*. Printed with permission of Jeffrey Moring.

"The first step in creating this piece was getting the right digital images to work with," said Jeffrey. "I took some photographs of myself, then photographed many different skulls. (The biology department of your school should have such skulls.) After picking the right digital photos, I brought them into Photoshop. See Figure B–2 and Figure B–3. The most important techniques for this kind of digital manipulation are selecting areas and your ability to blend two different images together. The tools that I used were the Smudge tool, the Eraser tool, and the Clone Stamp tool." See Figure B–4.

"Getting a good selection of the image you are using is critical," said Jeffrey. "Each picture should be on a different layer when building such images. This is also critical. See

figure B–2 A self-portrait was taken and imported into Photoshop. A black background was added.

figure B–3 Photographs of skeletal remains were taken, brought into Photoshop, and their background pixels selected and removed.

Figure B–5. Being able to change one part at a time is a time-saver and gives great effects. I then scaled down each skull and began placing them over the face layer, changing the opacity and using the blending tools. I left many of my own facial features but also used the main skull features and blended the two. Feathering the selections can help soften an image, but be careful not to feather a selection too much. The tool I probably used the most is the Eraser tool. After you place one layer on top of the other, you can erase (with a soft-tipped brush) what you do not want. See Figure B–6. The more comfortable you get with the mouse, the better you can blend the images."

figure B–4 Tools used to blend the images: the Smudge, Eraser, and Clone Stamp tools.

YOUR TURN

Using some of the tools and techniques recommended by Jeffrey, create your own freak of nature or other-worldly vision of yourself.

figure B–5 Each item—including each bone selection—is placed on its own layer.

figure B–6 Choose the Eraser tool with a soft brush tip to create a seamless blend between layered images.

Self-Project Guidelines

1. Import a photograph of yourself into Photoshop.

2. With the Selection tools or Quick Mask feature, extract the background from the photograph and replace it with a solid color or fantasy-like backdrop.

3. With their backgrounds already removed, bring in other images (with either hard or feathered edges) to composite with the self-portrait. Put each image on its own layer. Duplicate and flip images you might like to use on both sides of the portrait (like the bat wings on Jeffrey's image).

4. Hide and reveal areas of images using Layer Masks or the Eraser tool.

5. Blend images with the layer-blending modes, if needed.

6. Add Liquify or filter effects to individual layers for more distorted and/or textured looks.

Things to Consider

For this "Adventure in Design" and future experimentations such as this, consider the following:

- For photographs of objects where the background will eventually be removed, shoot the picture against a matte-finished, even-colored backdrop. This, of course, will make it easier to remove the pixels in Photoshop.

- Take high-resolution digital photos or scan in photos at a high resolution, so you have plenty of pixels to work with.

- Sketch some of your creature designs on paper.

- Practice mastering the tools (and their many options) you think you will use—such as the Smudge, Eraser, Dodge, Burn, and Clone Stamp tools—on a separate, blank document.

- Save your work often and back it up.

swing.psd

| print publishing |

charting your course

Eventually, you will want to format your artwork so you can share it. Chapters 10 and 11 help you do that. There are many possibilities for where your digital images can appear—including on screen, such as in a Web page, an interactive learning environment, a kiosk, or mobile device (see Chapter 11); and on paper, such as in a glossy magazine ad, a flyer, brochure, or poster. Print media publication is what we explore in this chapter.

goals

In this chapter you will:

- **Learn about the different methods of printing**
- **Discover why color management can make a difference**
- **Understand the halftone and color separation process**
- **Learn the right questions to ask when consulting a print service bureau**
- **Get familiar with the Print command**

PRINTING METHODS

There are several ways to get your artwork onto paper: directly from a desktop printer or digital printing press, from a film negative that is used to create a metal plate for a mechanical press, or in the form of a Portable Document File (PDF) or PostScript file.

Let us briefly describe each of these output methods, and then in the section, "Output Compatibility," we will show you how to set up your print job in Photoshop's Print window.

Desktop Printing

Without a doubt, you will want to print your work from a desktop printer—if not the final version, at least some paper proofs for mock-up and revision purposes. Desktop printers differ by manufacturer and have different levels of printing capabilities. A low-end ink jet printer, for example, deposits ink onto a page much differently than does a high-end laser printer. You should read the specifications for your particular desktop printer, so you can accurately gauge whether a printer issue is something you can fix on the Photoshop side of things, or is an unavoidable product of your type of printer.

You also need to know what resolution your printer will support and what will give you the best quality, which can vary depending on the type of printer and the paper used. Much of the process of determining this is trial and error—print it off and see what it looks like. In general, laser printers have a resolution of about 600 dots per inch (dpi). For printers, dpi is usually the resolution measurement, whereas for computers the measurement is pixels per inch (ppi). Ink jet printers have a resolution of between 300 and 2880 dpi.

> Note: If you need to review the subject of resolution, or want to know more about it related to Photoshop, go to Help > Photoshop Help and do a search for resolution. Also, see Chapter 3.

Digital Printing

A digital printing press is a beefed-up version of a typical desktop computer. As digital printing technologies improve, digital printing services are becoming a more prevalent alternative to traditional offset printing. Digital printers can yield quality output with a quick turnaround, because they rasterize PostScript data—print directly from a computer file, rather than go through the intermediary film or metal plate stage (see next section, "Mechanical Printing"). Digital printing is ideal for targeted printing jobs and short-run projects that need to be done quickly, but at a much higher quality than produced on a desktop printer. The resolution needed to properly print off a digital printing press is the resolution of the particular output device. Consult the printing service for the resolution at which your document should be set.

Mechanical Printing

The traditional mechanical method for getting virtual work to hard copy is termed offset printing. A digital file is transferred to a film negative, which is then used to "burn" a metal printing plate. The metal plate carries the image the press transfers to paper. If you are printing a photograph or illustration with more than one or two colors in it, things get a little more complicated and expensive. To simulate a full range of colors (four-color process printing), mechanical printers deposit the four ink colors (CMYK) dot by dot, called halftones. See Figure 10–1.

To create continuous-tone color using the halftone method, each color must be inked and pressed separately to the paper. In short, the colors are separated and then layered back together. To do this, each color must have its own metal plate (one plate inked with cyan, one with magenta, one with yellow, and one with black). The plates are produced from four separate files or film negatives. This is the process of color separation.

figure | 10–1 |

Magnifying a section of the parrot, you see its color is produced by halftone dots composed of CMYK ink colors

The individual colors produced by the mixing of CMYK colors are called process colors. You can also identify spot colors or custom inks. Spot colors are special colors composed of premixed inks that require their own printing plate other than the one used for four-color processing.

For printers using the halftone procedure, Photoshop provides options in the Print dialog box for preparing your image for color separation and the subsequent printing process.

Portable Document File (PDF)

With Photoshop you can also print a file as a Portable Document File (PDF)—a popular, PostScript-based format developed by Adobe that supports vector and bitmapped data. Printing to

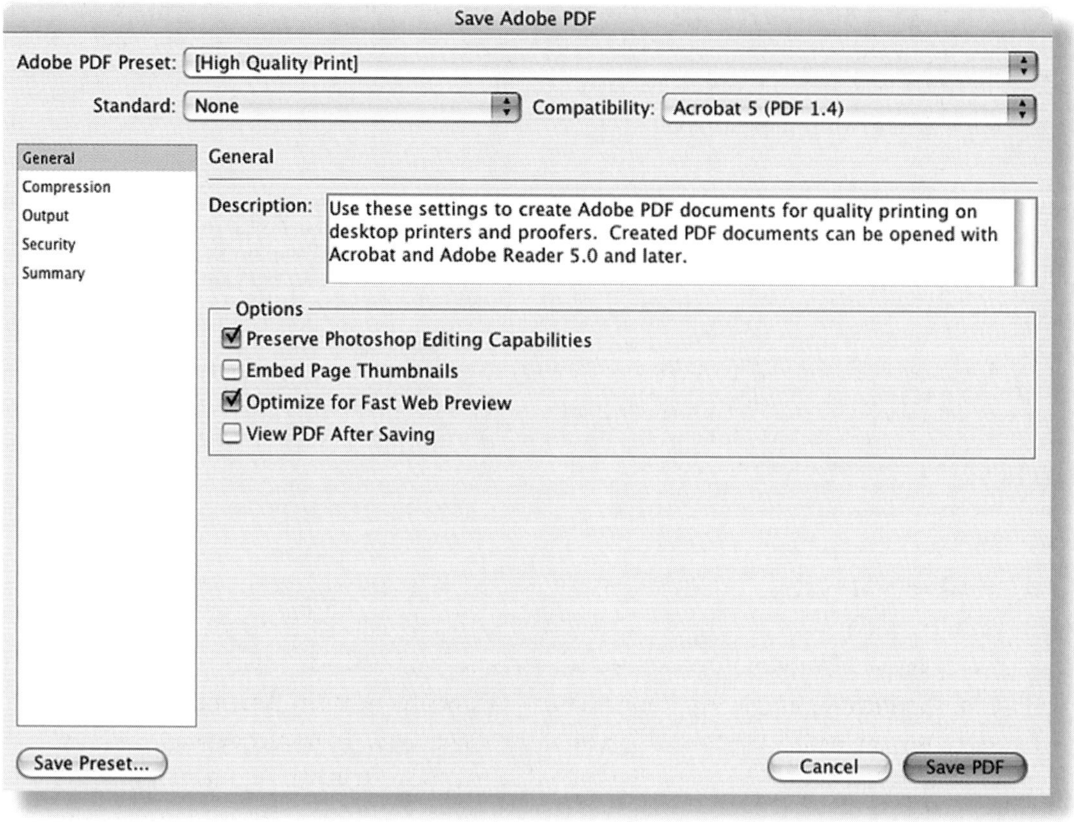

figure |10–2|

The Save Adobe PDF dialog box.

PDF is a convenient way to maintain all attributes of your original Photoshop file into a cross-compatible format. Often, print service bureaus will request a PDF version of your file. To set the PDF options, choose File > Save As, specify a file name, and choose Photoshop PDF as the file format. Click Save and the Save Adobe PDF dialog box appears (see Figure 10–2) where you can indicate compression, output, and security options. For information on these settings, visit the Photoshop Help files, Saving and exporting images > Saving PDF files.

OUTPUT COMPATIBILITY

Have you ever gone to the moon? Well, if you have or you would like to, you need to prepare for the change in atmosphere. This means wearing a special space suit with weighted boots so you stay on the moon's surface, as well as a pressurized helmet shaped like a fish bowl so you can breathe. Just as you must give consideration to the outer space environment, you must assess the printing environment when you decide to take your Photoshop work and land it on a piece of paper, so to speak. In general, three areas need to be considered when you are going to print: the image's color, resolution (size and quality), and format. This applies if you are outputting to a printer device (see the section "Printing Methods") or are importing into another program first (i.e., one that works with layout design, such as Adobe InDesign or Illustrator and QuarkXPress.

> **Note:** Programs specifically designed for layout design are quite savvy in setting up your document properly for print. Although Photoshop is able to do this, programs such as Adobe InDesign and Illustrator are more adept at this kind of translation.

We have discussed color, resolution, and formats in previous chapters, but understanding them is so important we need to mention them again (and again in Chapter 11) as they relate to the printing process.

Color

If you recall from Chapter 5, different devices (whether screen- or print-based) have different color gamuts—the range (or limits) of color that can be reproduced. Therefore, it is important to prepare your image to match the specific color profile of whatever device or other application to which you are going to output. This workflow process is called color management. Admittedly, it is impossible to match colors between a monitor and a printer perfectly—one is using light to make colors, the other using ink. However, you can get close by creating profiles for your monitor, printer, and printer papers. With these color spaces set, Photoshop's built-in color management system can correctly transform the color from one working color space to another. You can explore the fine points of color management to a great extent in the Photoshop help files (you can even purchase complete volumes on the subject), but for now, you will be well on your way if you learn how to set up color profiles and calibrate your monitor.

About Color Profiles

A printer's output quality is determined by its color profile—sometimes called destination profile or output profile. This profile determines how many colors and to what degree of color accuracy it can produce. There are many types of color profiles you can work with, usually identified by the name of the company that designed them or the country that has standardized them, such as Adobe RGB (1998), U.S. Web Coated (SWOP) v2, or Euroscale Uncoated v2. You determine what profile you need by consulting the specifications of your particular printer or, if you are printing commercially, ask your prepress specialist. If you are not sure what to do, stick with Photoshop's default working color space. When working in RGB, and eventually converting to CMYK and going to print, this would be the Adobe RGB (1998) setting. Use this space when you need to print work with a broad range of colors. See Figure 10–3.

figure | 10–3 |

To set your specific working space, choose Edit >Color Settings.

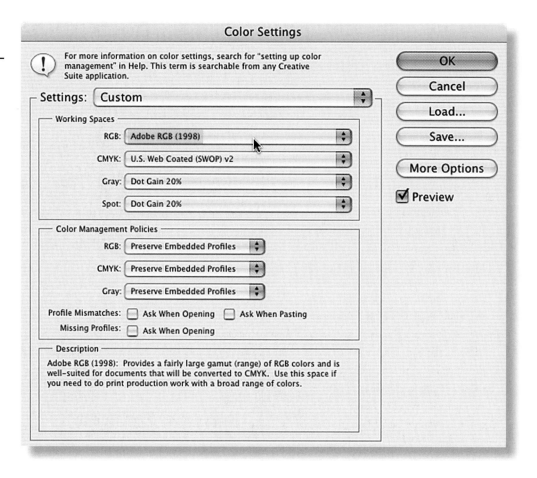

Color Settings

For more information on color settings, search for "setting up color management" in Help. This term is searchable from any Creative Suite application.

OK

Cancel

Load...

Save...

More Options

☑ Preview

Settings: Custom

Working Spaces

RGB: Adobe RGB (1998)

CMYK: U.S. Web Coated (SWOP) v2

Gray: Dot Gain 20%

Spot: Dot Gain 20%

Color Management Policies

RGB: Preserve Embedded Profiles

CMYK: Preserve Embedded Profiles

Gray: Preserve Embedded Profiles

Profile Mismatches: ☐ Ask When Opening   ☐ Ask When Pasting

Missing Profiles: ☐ Ask When Opening

Description

Adobe RGB (1998): Provides a fairly large gamut (range) of RGB colors and is well-suited for documents that will be converted to CMYK. Use this space if you need to do print production work with a broad range of colors.

There are several places in Photoshop where you will encounter options for setting color profiles. Let us open an image and visit each place.

1. In Photoshop, open the file **swing.psd** in the folder **chap10_lessons/ assets**. Note that the status bar at the top of the image indicates that it is already set in the RGB Color mode. See Figure 10–4.

2. Choose View > Print Size to see what dimensions the image will be when printed. To get an idea of this size proportionally to an 8.5-by-11-inch sheet of paper, click on the status bar in the lower-left corner of the program window. See Figure 10–5. And, for exact dimensions and resolution, choose Image > Image Size, Document Size. See Figure 10–6.

figure | 10–4 |

At the top of any open file you can check what color mode it is in.

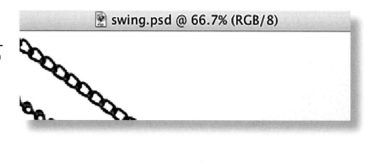

swing.psd @ 66.7% (RGB/8)

3. Let us indicate global color settings for the current document and any new document
you create. Go to Edit > Color
Settings. Choose the More
Options button, then under the
Settings option, choose North
America Prepress 2. Note in this
pop-up window the other presets
available. See Figure 10–7.

4. Under Working Spaces, note that
each color mode (RGB, CMYK,
Gray, and Spot) has its own profile. As mentioned previously,
when in doubt about where your
document will eventually be
printed, keep your file in RGB
Color mode with the Adobe
RGB (1998) setting. To read a
description of this mode and any
other setting in the Color Settings
dialog box, move your cursor over
the item you want described and
view the description at the bottom of the dialog box. Click OK.

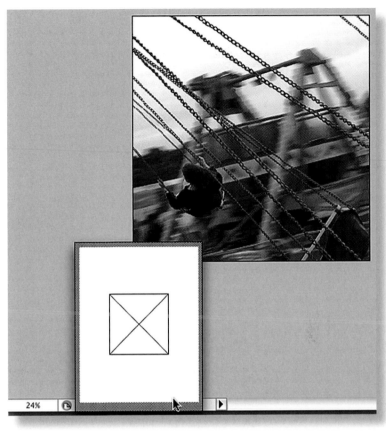

figure |10–5|

In the status bar, you can see how an image fits onto an 8.5-by-11-inch piece of paper.

Image Size

Pixel Dimensions: 4.12M

Width: 1200 | pixels

Height: 1200 | pixels

Document Size:

Width: 4 | inches

Height: 4 | inches

Resolution: 300 | pixels/inch

☑ Scale Styles
☑ Constrain Proportions
☑ Resample Image:
  Bicubic (best for smooth gradients)

OK
Cancel
Auto...

figure |10–6|

To get the exact dimensions of a document, dependent on its resolution, go to Image > Image Size.

figure |10–7|

Indicate a color profile preset in the Color Settings dialog box.

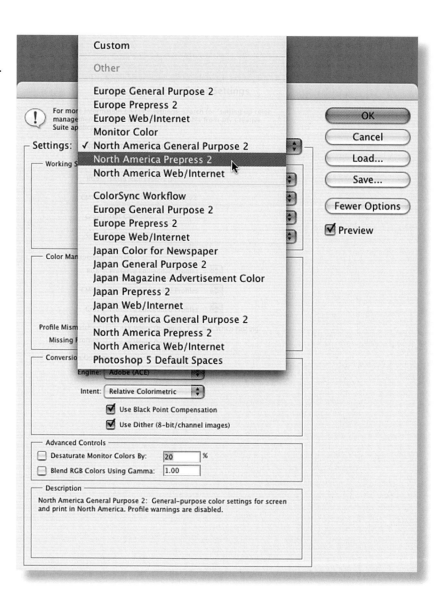

5. Choose Edit > Assign Profile to open the Assign Profile dialog box. See Figure 10–8. In this box you can choose color management options specific to the selected image. The options include using the Don't Color Manage This Document, keeping it at the setting you chose in the Color Settings dialog box, or selecting a specific profile for the particular printer and paper quality you are going to output to. For now, keep the profile the same as what was chosen under Color Settings—Working RGB: Adobe RGB (1998). Click OK.

> **Note:** If you choose to embed a different profile in Assign Profile than what is indicated in Color Settings, be aware that a dialog box will come up the next time you open this document reminding you of this setting and asking what you would like to do next. See Figure 10–9. If no Color Settings have been indicated (Missing Profile), you will get another type of dialog box asking what you would like to do with the documents settings. See Figure 10–10.

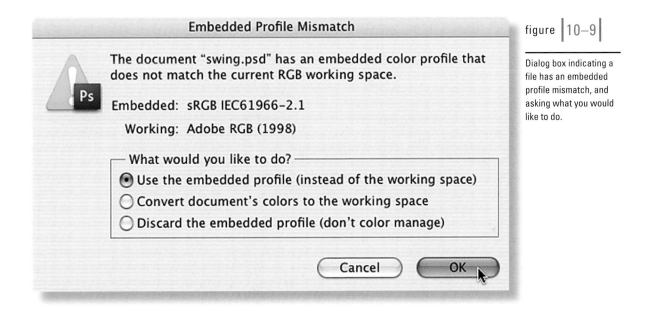

figure |10-8|

Assign a profile for your selected document. Note here that one profile Annesa can choose has been added as part of her EPSON printer software (EPSON Stylus Color 740 Glossy Film). Depending on your brand of desktop printer, there will be different profiles in.

figure |10-9|

Dialog box indicating a file has an embedded profile mismatch, and asking what you would like to do.

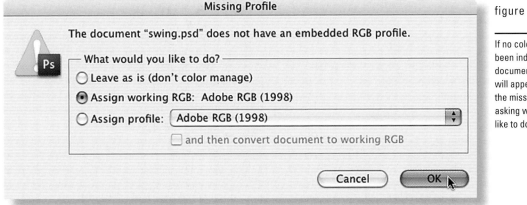

figure |10-10|

If no color settings have been indicated for a document, a dialog box will appear indicating the missing profile and asking what you would like to do.

6. To set your document to print a preview of a specific color profile other than the image's assigned profile, choose File > Print. Under Color Management on the right side, choose Photoshop Manages Colors under Color Handling. Then make a selection under Printer Profile. (See section "Print Command.")

7. Close **swing.psd**. Hopefully, now you have a better idea of the color profile settings in Photoshop.

> Note: Keep in mind that there are also color profiles for input devices (sometimes called a source profile), such as digital cameras and scanners. Creating an input profile to match your working space can get complicated, and there is the question of whether it is essential for producing consistent color. For information on this topic, see Help > Photoshop Help > Contents > Color Management > Working with color profiles > About monitor calibration and characterization.

Monitor Calibration

Monitors are the lighted windows in which you view your digital work. Like printers, they need to be identified with a particular color profile that, preferably, is consistent with the profiles you have set within Photoshop. Although identifying and changing the color profile of your monitor—through calibration—was not the first thing we talked about in the color management process (we wanted to explain what a color profile was first), it should be the first profile you create—even before choosing color settings in Photoshop. To do this you use a visual calibrator provided as part of your computer's operating system. Such calibrators include Adobe Gamma (Windows), Monitor Calibrator (Mac OS), and products from other manufacturers. See Figure 10–11.

Resolution

Argh! Here we are again on the topic of resolution—that illusive concept that pretty much determines everything about your image's final quality and size (both dimensionally and in file size). For output to printers using halftone dots to render images (see the section "Mechanical Printing"), consideration must be given to the number of dots to be printed within a given area or screen—or in other words, the "resolution." This consideration is like working with the resolution of bitmap images, which, similarly, are composed of a given amount of pixels on a bitmapped grid. In Photoshop, you specify halftone screen attributes before producing a film or a paper output of the image. This particularly applies when you are working with commercial printers. Consult your print specialist for the recommended resolution and screen (frequency, angle, and dot) settings.

Halftone dots are deposited on paper based on a screen ruling—the amount of lines or rows within a given screen. Screen rulings for halftones and separations are measured in lines per inch (lpi). The frequency, angle, and size of dots are determined by the screen ruling. More lpi creates smaller, tighter dots, like those seen in a glossy magazine or slick brochure. Fewer lpi creates larger, rougher-looking dots that are easier to print, such as on newspaper. A general rule is

figure |10–11|

Example of the calibrating program provided as part of Annesa's Mac's operating system. These programs will take you through the calibration process.

that the resolution, ppi, or dpi, when referring to halftone printing, of a given piece of artwork is about 1.5 times and no more than 2.0 times the screen frequency. Did we just lose you here? Let us clarify. After consulting your print specialist, you discover that the screen ruling for the glossy flyer you want to print is 150 lpi and needs to be in the TIFF format (an uncompressed bitmap format). This information gives you an idea of what resolution your TIFF file should be in, which would be somewhere between 225 and 300 dpi or ppi (hence, 150 lpi x 1.5 = 225 and 150 lpi x 2 = 300). Keep in mind that the resolution of an image and its screen frequency directly relate to what kind of paper it will be printed on and at what quality.

- Newspapers, or similar highly porous, coarse papers use screens of 85 to 100 lpi. Therefore the artwork resolution should be at least 128 to 150 dpi or ppi.

- News magazines or company publications with medium coarseness use screens of 133 to 150 lpi. Therefore the artwork resolution should be at least 200 to 225 dpi or ppi.

- Fine-quality brochures and magazines with slick paper surfaces use screens of 150 to 300 lpi. Therefore the artwork resolution should be at least 225 to 450 dpi or ppi.

> Note: Photoshop has a nifty little feature that will automatically suggest a resolution for an image based on a screen frequency. Go to Image > Image Size and choose the Auto option. Enter a Screen frequency and Quality setting (Draft, Good, Best) and the resolution will be updated for the document. This option only specifies a resolution for a suggested screen frequency. To determine the final halftone screen ruling for printing, use the Halftone Screen dialog box, accessible through the Print command—select Output from the drop-down on the top right side (the default is set to Color Management), then select Screen.

Format

Final output compatibility should be in the format in which the image is saved. Most likely you have been working on the image in Photoshop's native PSD file format, which maintains all of your layers and effects. Now, you must save a copy of the file in a format specific to its output needs. For bitmapped images, TIFF is the best bet because it uses minimal or no compression on the image (resulting in a higher quality), flattens your layers in a more conveniently sized package (TIFF also gives the option to preserve layers), and will preserve alpha channel information. To preserve both vector and bitmapped data that might be in an image, the EPS format is a good choice. This format is especially useful when you plan to import an image into a vector-friendly program, such as Adobe Illustrator. More recently, print specialists prefer to save their images in the cross-compatible PDF format (see the section "Portable Document File").

You will quickly find there are many different formats in which to save your image. Each format has specific characteristics, depending on where it is going. As for the Web-based formats, that is reserved for Chapter 11. An overview of common formats is also provided in Chapter 3. For practice, here are the steps for saving an image in the print-friendly TIFF format:

1. Open the file **swing.psd** from the folder **chap10_lessons/assets**.

2. Choose Image > Mode > CMYK Color to set the image into the CMYK color space. You will set your image to the CMYK color space if you plan to print the image using the traditional print process. However, if you simply want to make a quick print off a desktop printer, you can stay in RGB color mode.

3. Choose File > Save As and name your file. Under Format choose TIFF (take note of the other formats you can save to). Save the file to your **lessons** folder. Be sure the Embed Color Profile option is selected (if you assigned a profile to the image, this option should be checked automatically). Click Save.

4. A TIFF Options dialog box will appear. Here, you can choose a form of image compression. If the file size of the image is not an issue, stick with a compression setting of NONE to maintain the highest-quality image. LZW is another good choice for image compression, since it is a lossless form of compression (see section on "Compression" in Chapter 11). LZW works best on grayscale images or images with large areas of uniform color. However, LZW compression is not universally used by all programs, so if there is any doubt, keep it set to NONE.

> **Note:** Depending on the image attributes, the choice of options in the TIFF Options box will vary. If, for example, your image contains more than one layer, you have the option Layer Compression. If your image has layers, you can choose the RLE or ZIP compression options and preserve the Photoshop layers in the TIFF or reduce the file size of the image and discard the layers (flatten) and save a copy.
> Preserving the Photoshop layers in TIFF format will increase the file size.

5. If you choose to flatten the layers of the image—which is going to happen in any case when you open the file in another program—be sure you save a version with the layers. You never know when you are going to need to reopen the image in Photoshop and make changes.

6. Click OK to close the TIFF Options dialog box. Out of interest, compare the file size of your PSD version to the TIFF version. To do this, find the saved files in your **lessons** folder (or wherever you saved them), right-click (Windows) or Ctrl-click (Mac) over each file icon and choose Properties (Windows) or Get Info (Mac).

CONSULT THE PROFESSIONALS

If professionally printing your artwork, either via a digital or mechanical press, is a definite "must," alleviate undue headaches and find yourself a reliable print specialist. A good specialist can identify your printing needs and offer appropriate solutions for getting the best-quality print job for your specific situation. However, do not underestimate the necessity of you knowing the printing process and its terminology—what was just covered in this chapter. Properly setting up your Photoshop file before handing it to the printer can save you time and money. Also, have a clear idea of what kind of paper the job will be printed on. For instance, do you envision your creation on porous newsprint or slick, heavy card stock? Different types of paper produce varying color effects and require different specifications.

> **Note:** Your print specialist can provide paper samples and color swatches to aid you in your decision.

During the final output stages of your document, consult your printing service bureau to find out how best to prepare your file (i.e., color mode, resolution, and format). Also, be aware that the complexity of your artwork determines a lot about what you need to know to prepare it for print. Transparencies, alpha channels, spot colors, gradients, fonts, vector graphics, and duotones, for example, might require extra attention to print properly.

SETTING UP THE PRINT JOB

The easy way out of the printing process is to choose File > Print > Print and be done with it. Yeah, right. If you want your print job to look professional, it can get more complicated than choosing Print. (So, if you skipped the rest of this chapter and came directly to here, we are assuming you already know about the quirks and conundrums of printing.) As previously covered, you first need to know where you are going to print your work (desktop printer, commercial printer, PDF). Second, you need to understand output compatibility, and third, you need to contact a print specialist. With that in mind, you can go to the proper setup command in Photoshop—do not simply go to File and choose Print, first consider the options under File > Print.

Print Command

OK, you are ready to see your work on some papyrus material. In Photoshop, choose File > Print and see what is available. See Figure 10–12. (Note: If you want to do this right now, open **swing.psd** in the folder **chap10_lessons/assets** to use as an example.)

1. The first thing to notice is the option to scale your image (Scaled Print Size) to a print size other than what was originally specified under the image size area (Image > Image Size). You might want to do this if your original image is larger than the paper you are printing it on, or if you want a smaller, quicker printable proof for markup purposes.

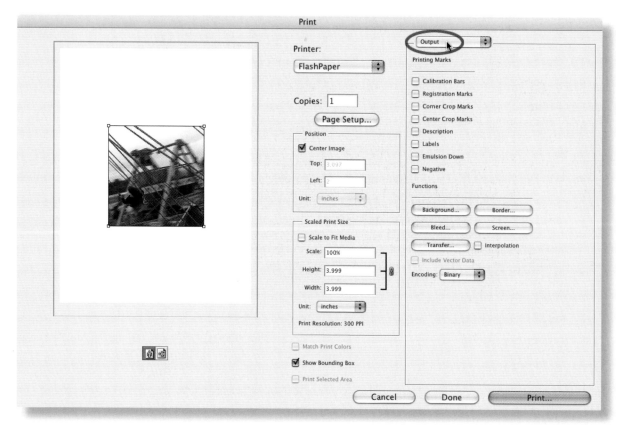

figure |10–12|

Output options in the Print command window.

2. To the right of the image preview, designate Output as your option choice. See Figure 10–12. For output, you can specify numerous goodies (i.e., a background color or border treatment). You can also make specifications necessary for a seamless printing endeavor, such as bleed amounts (if you have color blending right to the edge of your document), screen and transfer measurements, printer marks for proper registration of an image's color plates (see Figure 10–13), and film output options. For kicks, select the Border option and specify a border width. Also, choose Calibration Bars, Registration Marks, Corner Crop Marks, Center Crop Marks, and Labels. Note that each selection is shown on the image in the preview window.

3. Still in the Print window, switch the Output options selector to Color Management. Under the Print option you can choose a Document Profile or a Proof Profile. For each selection, set the options in the Options area. In the Options area, you can set Color Handling to Printer Manages Colors or Photoshop Manages Colors based on a specific Printer Profile.

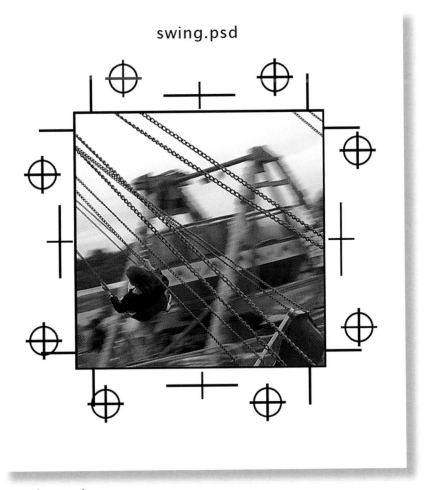

figure |10–13|

A PDF version of the file **swing.psd**. Registration, cropping, border, and bleed specifications were indicated in the Print command output area.

> Note: Proof Profile, which we have not discussed, can be indicated for your document under View > Proof Setup. Consult the Help files for more on soft and hard proofs.

4. If you are not ready to print but want to preserve your settings, choose Done. If you are ready to print, choose Print, and then specify the desktop printer you would like to print from or the Save as PDF option under the PDF button. See Figure 10–14. If your printer does not support PostScript data, a dialog box will come up indicating that some options chosen might not be available with the printer indicated. See Figure 10–15.

figure |10–14|

Options on Ken's Macintosh for printing to a desktop printer or PDF document.

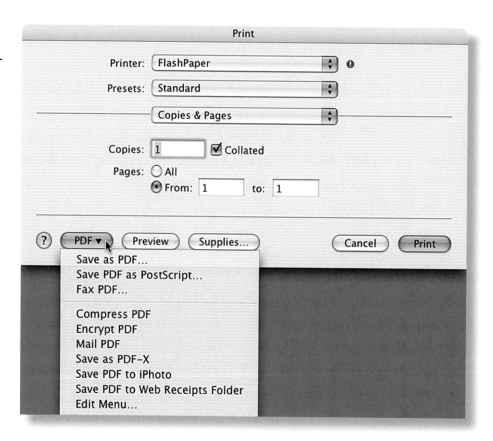

figure |10–15|

Conflict dialog box that could come up if your printer does not support PostScript information.

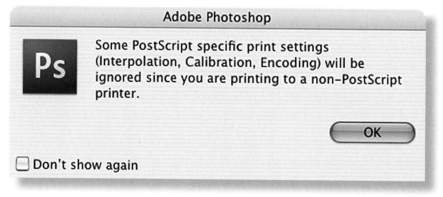

5. If you have printed a copy of your image to a desktop printer or saved it as a PDF document (which you can view using the Acrobat Reader), you will see the specifications set on the image, such as registration and cropping marks. See Figure 10–13 for an example.

▶ **Don't Go There!**

As you roam through the various print dialog boxes, you might discover that you can set scaling options for your image in the print specifications dialog box of your particular desktop printer. See Figure 10–16.

The recommendation is to not set the scaling options in this specific area, but rather in the Print window as reviewed previously.

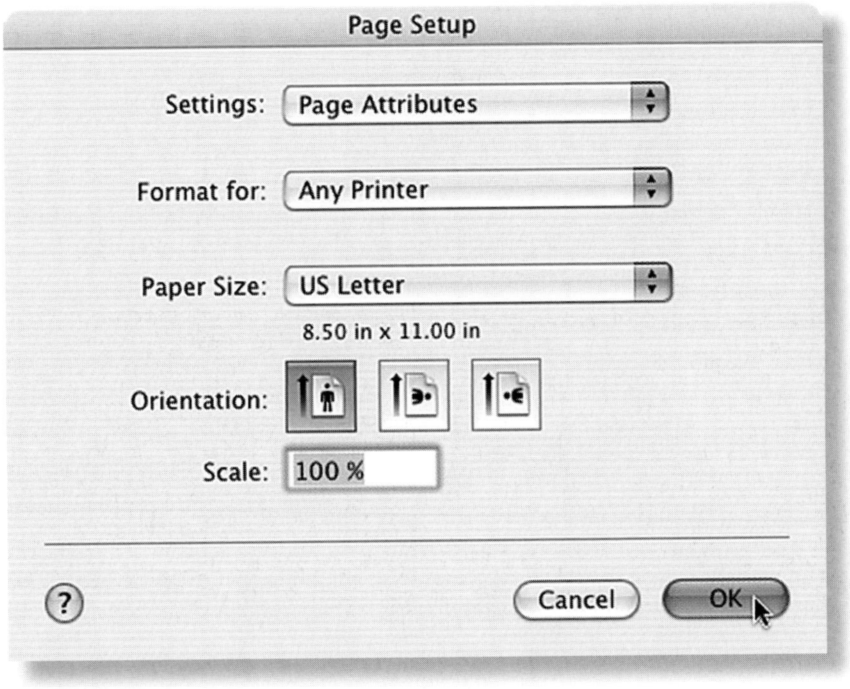

Page Setup

Settings: **Page Attributes**

Format for: **Any Printer**

Paper Size: **US Letter**

8.50 in x 11.00 in

Orientation:

Scale: 100 %

Cancel   OK

figure | 10–16 |

Page Setup for printers specifically installed on Ken's Macintosh. To scale to print size, use the options under the Print command, rather than the Page Setup box for your particular printer.

SUMMARY

With the wave of a wand, we wish we could make the printing process for your digital imagery totally seamless and stress free. But, as you learned, there are many variables to this. It is unlikely your print job will come out perfectly the first time, so be prepared to waste a few (or dozen) sheets of paper trying to get everything "just right." And, of course, it does not hurt to consult the professionals, get a proof or two created of your final work, and meticulously edit before printing the job in full.

in review

1. Briefly describe the four printing methods.

2. What are process colors?

3. Why might you output your image into PDF?

4. What are the three areas that should be considered when preparing an image to go to print?

5. Describe color management and why it is important to understand.

6. What do you do in the Color Settings dialog box (Edit > Color Settings)?

7. Why calibrate your monitor?

8. What does halftone printing refer to? What are halftone dots?

9. Describe what happens when an image is flattened.

10. Where is a good place to set alternate scaling options for a printed image?

exploring on your own

1. Access the Help > Photoshop Help menu option. Under Contents, read the following topics related to printing: "Printing" and "Color Management > Keeping colors consistent." A word of caution: This is a ton of information to wade through—not necessarily bedtime reading, but rather on a "need to know" basis.

2. Find out if your desktop printer supports PostScript and if you have the ability to specify options for color separations in the Print dialog box. If so, print separations for a document that has been saved in the CMYK Color mode (Image > Mode > CMYK Color).

3. For proofing purposes, make a contact sheet that conveniently creates thumbnail versions of multiple images. To explore this feature, choose File > Automate > Contact Sheet II. See

Figure 10–17. There are other (many automated) features, such as Picture Package, Web Photo Gallery, Photomerge, and Merge to HDR. When the moment strikes you, explore these cool options.

4. Open up the sample file **swing.pdf** in the folder **chap10_lessons/assets**. Take a look at the printer marks that have been specified around the artwork. In the Help files, do a search for "setting output options" or "to set output options." Investigate what each printer mark represents.

5. Call a printing service (or search online) and inquire about the printing services it offers and what file specifications it requires. Be specific with your questions and try out some of the terminology you learned in this chapter.

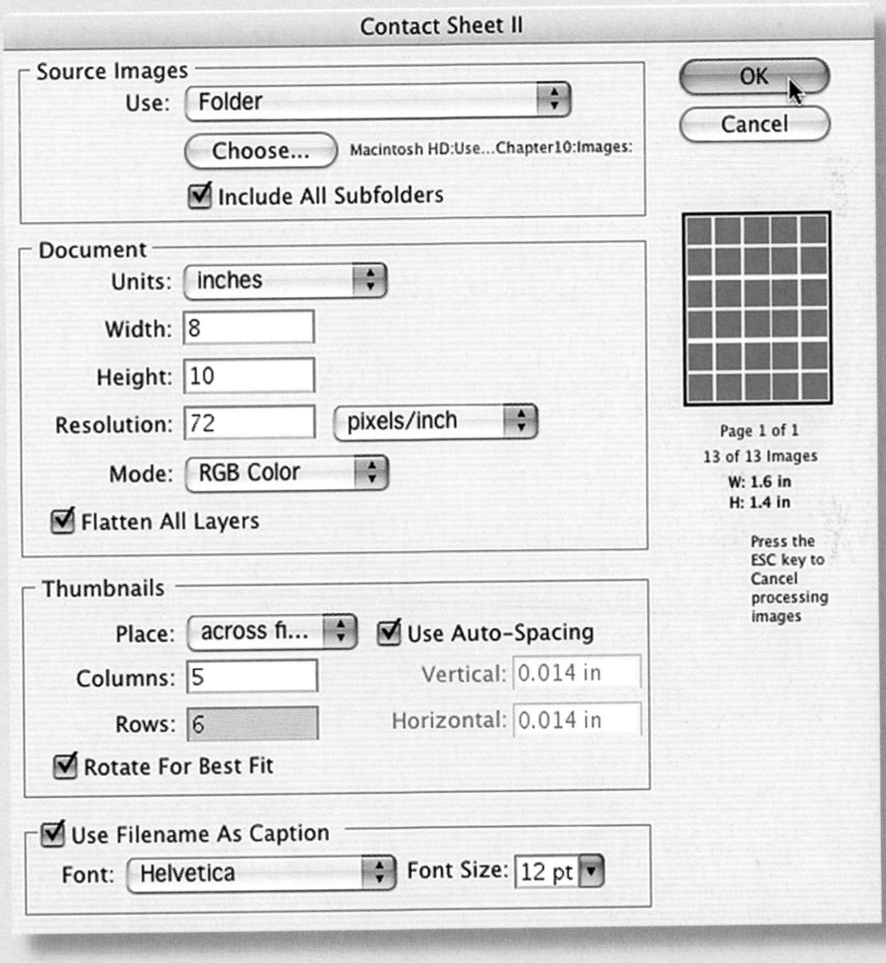

figure |10–17|

The Contact Sheet II dialog box. Here you can specify a folder with images that you would like to print and view as smaller, thumbnail versions.

ADVENTURES IN DESIGN

wine box composition

As you learned in Chapter 9, the assembling of artwork pieces—photos, illustrations, and text—into an aesthetically pleasing whole is the art of composition. An experienced art director or graphic designer can envision the larger scope of attractively arranging elements, while subsequently and just as importantly, narrowing in on each element's minute design details. Moreover, a good handle on current computer graphics software programs and their tool sets is crucial for bringing an inspired vision to actuality. The work of art director Dave Garcez and the graphic artists at E.&J. Gallo Winery in Modesto, Calif., is a good example of how composition is not just the bringing together of elements in one program, but also the

coordination of elements among two or more programs. See Figure C–1.

PROFESSIONAL PROJECT EXAMPLE

The 5-liter wine box label shown in Figure C–1 was created for Gallo Winery using a combination of Photoshop and Illustrator. First, in Photoshop, photographs of glasses of wine were incorporated to achieve the most appetizing look. The final wine glass was then layered with a basket and some grapes. See Figure C–2 and Figure C–3. The logo was created in Illustrator. A hand-drawn sketch was scanned and placed as a template into Illustrator. The final logo design and photographic images were incorporated into Photoshop and then saved and imported into Illustrator, where additional typographic elements were added and the whole file was prepared for print. See Figure C–1.

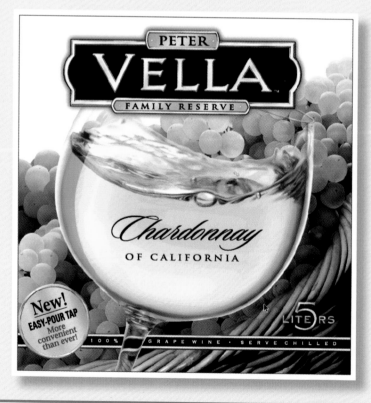

Figure C–1 A 5-liter wine box label was produced using Adobe Photoshop and Illustrator. Used with permission of E. & J. Gallo Winery.

Figure C–2 Photographs were taken and layered in Photoshop.

Figure C–3 The photographs were then incorporated into a complete image.

This same project is used as an "Adventures in Design" in *Exploring Illustrator CS3*, emphasizing the parts of the project (i.e., the logo design) that were done in Illustrator. Now, we want to share the techniques used to achieve the perfect look for the wine glass image.

The pixels of two of the wine glass photos were selected, transformed, and blended to produce the most active and realistic looking "swirl" of wine. See Figure C–2 and Figure C–3. The glass was then retouched to produce a more appetizing glow and give it more roundness. To enhance it the highlights on an empty glass were outlined and then saved into an alpha channel. Using a combination of the Dodge, Burn, and Airbrush tools, the selections (alpha channels) were then used to lighten highlighted areas and darken shadowed areas. See Figure C–4.

continued

ADVENTURES IN DESIGN

continued

Figure C–4 Alpha channels were used to highlight and darken selections, creating more brightness and roundness to the glass: 1. The original wine glass photo; 2. Highlight outlines are drawn; 3. Alpha channel masks are created; 4. Final retouched photo.

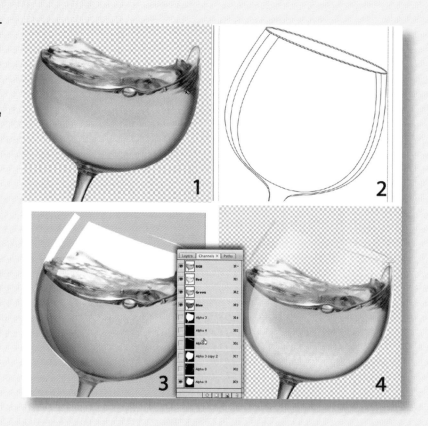

The grapes were also enhanced. The lower-right corner was darkened for more light contrast, and many berries were retouched to remove imperfections. They were then placed within the basket. See Figure C–5.

Another subtle improvement was done to the image. To make the stem of the glass appear in front of the stripe element at the bottom of the final design, another photo of the stem was taken. Then a color print of the grapes and basket was distorted and placed behind it. The areas around the stem were deleted. See Figure C–6.

Your Turn

Putting to practice your image compositing skills, it's your turn to create an attractive image that could be used on a wine box, label, or advertisement. The original photos for the Peter Vella wine box label are provided for your educational use in the **aid_examples** folder (**basket.tif**, **grapes.tif**, **chard_glass1.tif**, and **chard_glass2.tif**), or you can photograph or find your own images.

SELF-PROJECT GUIDELINES

1. Find a selection of images you might like to use in your image composition. They can be photographs you have taken or borrowed for educational purposes, scanned illustrations, or the photos provided in the folder **aid_examples**. Some image ideas could include pictures of wine bottles or barrels, grape vineyards, other styles of wine glasses, or someone enjoying a

glass of wine. Try to get the highest quality images possible.

2. On paper, sketch some ideas of how you see the images assembled into a completely new image.

3. Determine what techniques you know in Photoshop to design the sketch you like best.

4. On a new document with a resolution of at least 150 pixels, import the photos into Photoshop. Put each image on its own named layer.

5. Work your pixel magic on the images using what you have learned in Photoshop. Adjust tonal levels and color, select and transform pixels, blend layers, and add effects and filters.

6. Save the file in PSD format and in a print-ready TIFF format.

Things to Consider

Here are some things to consider when working on your image compositions for this lesson and in your professional work:

- A design is never finished. Leave time to do revisions.

- Save often, and back up your work. We suggest saving different versions of your work, as in **wine_imagev1**, **wine_imagev2a**, **wine_imagev2b**, **wine_imagev3**, etc. You never know when you might want to refer to an earlier version.

- Get your document organized. In other words, use layers and name them intuitively.

- Print your image from a desktop printer (preferably color) to get a good idea of the image size and overall look.

- If you "borrowed" from another's work, or used another's image as a template in the creation of your own composition, resolve any copyright issues.

Figure C–5   The grapes were retouched and incorporated with the basket.

Figure C–6   An effect is created on the stripe element at the bottom of the design. The stripe is reflected through the wine glass stem.

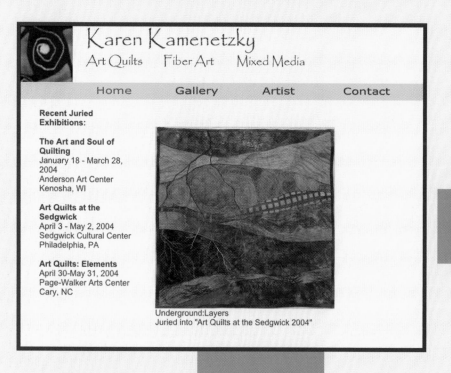

Karen Kamenetzky

Art Quilts   Fiber Art   Mixed Media

| Home | Gallery | Artist | Contact |

Recent Juried Exhibitions:

The Art and Soul of Quilting
January 18 - March 28, 2004
Anderson Art Center
Kenosha, WI

Art Quilts at the Sedgwick
April 3 - May 2, 2004
Sedgwick Cultural Center
Philadelphia, PA

Art Quilts: Elements
April 30-May 31, 2004
Page-Walker Arts Center
Cary, NC

Underground:Layers
Juried into "Art Quilts at the Sedgwick 2004"

| web publishing |

charting your course

Preparing images for the Web or screen-based publication is an important task in today's online world. Lucky for us, Web development tools come packaged with Adobe Photoshop and alleviate many of the headaches that occur when we try to find the right balance between an image that looks good but can also quickly download over the Internet for efficient viewing. For the avid Web designer, there is much to explore in Photoshop's Web tools, and it is not uncommon to find instructional books specific to this part of Photoshop. This chapter offers an overview of three of the main features Web designers use in Photoshop: the Save For Web & Devices command (see the section by the same name); the ability to slice images for fast rendering and create button and rollover effects (see the section "Image Slicing"); and the Animation panel (see section "GIF Animation").

goals

In this chapter you will:

- **Optimize images like a pro**
- **Get a handle on Web file formats, including saving files in SWF format**
- **Understand the interrelationship among image color, format size, and compression in the Web publication process**
- **Get hands-on experience with the Save for Web & Devices options**
- **Slice a Web page**
- **Create an animated GIF using the Animation panel**

WEB PUBLISHING

ABOUT OPTIMIZATION

In part, Chapter 9 discussed the process of designing a print or Web page layout—the integration of many elements (such as text and graphics) into a pleasing visual display. We want to reiterate that the layout process usually involves working in more than one graphics program. For Web page design and development, this most likely includes the use of an image manipulation program to optimize images (i.e., Photoshop) and a layout program that assembles Web elements and codes them into a Web page fit for a browser to read (i.e., Adobe Dreamweaver or Flash).

When it comes to publishing graphics for the Web, it is all about optimization. Optimization, when referring to online artwork, is the process of preparing a functionally optimal graphic, which is an artful balancing act between the visual quality of an image and its quantitative file size. There are three interrelated areas to consider in the Web optimization process: image format, image color, and image size. These areas directly relate to image compression, which refers to reducing an image's file size, so it looks good on screen and downloads quickly over an Internet connection.

Compression

An image's file size can be reduced by compression. If you compress a bitmap image too much—to make it smaller in file size—you can lose visual quality. For instance, it might lose its antialiased effect, which is the smoothing of pixilated edges through a gradation of color.

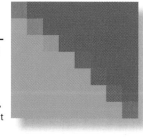

figure | 11–1 |

Close-up antialiasing creates a stair-step effect of color gradation. When viewed at a distance, the edge of the object looks smoother.

It could dither, which occurs when colors that are lost during the compression are replaced by colors within the reduced color palette. See Figure 11–1 and Figure 11–2.

There are two basic types of compression: lossy and lossless (or "nonlossy"). Lossy compression discards data to make a file smaller. Let us say you are optimizing a line of pixels into the JPEG format, which uses lossy compression. Ten of the pixels are white, followed by a gray pixel, and then five more white pixels. With lossy compression the computer reads the line as 16 white pixels; the gray pixel, being the odd one in the sampling area, is converted to white.

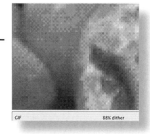

figure | 11–2 |

Dithering attempts to simulate colors that are lost in the compression process.

Lossless compression does not eliminate detail or information. Instead it looks for more efficient ways to define the image, such as through the use of customized color tables (see the section "Image Color"). Ultimately, how compression is applied to an image varies greatly depending on the image's format, color, and size.

Image Format

Traditionally, most Web images are saved in the bitmap formats GIF, JPEG, or PNG. Bitmap images rely on resolution to determine their file size and quality. Therefore, bitmap images are generally larger in file size than vector graphics, and when it comes to "the Web," that means a much bulkier download. Vector-based file formats—including Adobe's SWF and Scalable Vector Graphics (SVG) formats—have emerged that allow us to save and view graphics as streamlined paths, shapes, text, and effects in the online environment. Such graphics are scalable in size and easier to download. However, Photoshop does not handle these file types because it is the master of pixels not vectors. Adobe Illustrator does a much better job at creating vector images. It also can support export of both the SWF and SVG formats.

> **Note:** Adobe Flash and After Effects also have the ability to export bitmap images and animations to the SWF format. In the SWF format, the graphic can be posted directly to the Web or be opened in Adobe's Flash. For information on SWF, do a search for SWF in the Photoshop Help files.

The file format you choose for an optimized image depends on the color, tonal, and graphic characteristics of the original image. In general, continuous-tone bitmap images (images with many shades of color, such as photographs) are best compressed in the JPEG or PNG-24 formats. Illustrations or type with flat color or sharp edges and crisp detail are best as GIF or PNG-8 files. The following lists run down the characteristics of each Web-friendly format you can save in Photoshop including GIF, JPEG, PNG-8, PNG-24, and WBMP. Further clarification of these characteristics is presented in the next two sections.

GIF (Graphics Interchange Format) Format

- Supports an 8-bit color depth. Bit depth determines the amount and range of color an image can contain. A 1-bit image supports two colors, black and white; an 8-bit image supports up to 256 colors. A customized 256-color palette is referred to as indexed color.
- Works best compressing solid areas of color, such as in line art, logos, or illustrations with type.
- Is supported by the most common Web browsers, such as Internet Explorer, Netscape, Safari, and Firefox.
- Can be animated.
- Traditionally uses a lossless compression method. Lossless compression occurs when no data is discarded during the file-reduction process (see the section "Compression"). You can save a GIF file multiple times without discarding data. However, because GIF files are 8-bit color, optimizing an original 24-bit image as an 8-bit GIF will generally degrade image quality.

> **Note:** Illustrator and Photoshop also allow you to create a lossy version of a GIF file. The lossy GIF format includes small compression artifacts—similar to those in JPEG files—but yields significantly smaller files.

- Can be interlaced, so images download in multiple passes, or progressively. The downloading process of interlaced images is visible to the user, ensuring the user the download is in progress. Keep in mind, however, that interlacing increases file size.
- Includes dithering options: the process of mixing colors to approximate those not present in the image.
- Supports background transparency and background matting: the ability to blend the edges of an image with a Web page background color.

JPEG (Joint Photographic Experts Group) Format

- Supports 24-bit color (millions of colors) and preserves the broad range and subtle variations in brightness and hue found in photographs and other continuous-tone images (such as gradients).
- Is supported by the most common Web browsers.
- Selectively discards data. Because it discards data, JPEG compression is referred to as lossy (see the section "Compression"). The compression is set based on a range between 0% and 100% or 1 and 12. A higher percentage setting results in less data being discarded. The JPEG compression method tends to degrade sharp detail in an image, particularly in images containing type or vector art. Because of the nature of JPEG compression, you should always save JPEG files from the original image, not from a previously saved JPEG.
- Can be interlaced, so images download in multiple passes.
- Does not support transparency.
- Does not support animation.

PNG-8 (Portable Network Graphics) Format

- Uses 8-bit color. Like the GIF format, PNG-8 efficiently compresses solid areas of color while preserving sharp detail, such as that in line art, logos, or illustrations with type.
- Has not traditionally been supported by all browsers, but this is changing. It is advisable to test images saved in the PNG format on browser platforms that you and your audience might be using to view Web pages.
- Uses a lossless compression method, in which no data are discarded during compression. However, because PNG-8 files are 8-bit color, optimizing an original 24-bit image as a PNG-8 can degrade image quality. PNG-8 files use more advanced compression schemes than GIF, and can be 10% to 30% smaller than GIF files of the same image, depending on the image's color patterns.
- Can be indexed, like the GIF format, to a specific 256-color palette (such as Adaptive or Restrictive).
- Includes dithering options: the process of mixing colors to approximate those not present in the image.
- Like the GIF format, it supports background transparency and background matting: the ability to blend the edges of the image with a Web page background color.

PNG-24 (Portable Network Graphics) Format

- Supports 24-bit color. Like the JPEG format, PNG-24 preserves the broad range and subtle variations in brightness and hue found in photographs. Like the GIF and PNG-8 formats, PNG-24 preserves sharp detail, such as that in line art, logos, or illustrations with type.
- Uses the same lossless compression method as the PNG-8 format, in which no data is discarded. For that reason, PNG-24 files are usually larger than JPEG files of the same image.
- Like PNG-8, is not necessarily supported by all browsers.
- Supports multilevel transparency, in which you can preserve up to 256 levels of transparency to blend the edges of an image smoothly with any background color. However, multilevel transparency is not supported by all browsers.

WBMP format

- Supports only 1-bit color, which means images are reduced to contain only black and white pixels.
- Standard format for optimizing images for mobile devices in the past, such as older cell phones and PDAs, devices that did not support viewing complex images in color.

Image Color

Photographs and artwork to be viewed on-screen, such as on a Web page, must be saved in the RGB Color mode. (To review, read the characteristics of the RGB Color space in Chapter 5.) To convert artwork to the RGB Color mode, choose Image > Mode > RGB Color. When it comes to the topic of image color you need an understanding of color-reduction algorithms, covered in the following section.

Color-Reduction Algorithms

"Color-reduction algorithms" is the name Adobe gives the methods used to generate a specific color table for an optimized image. You get a better idea of how color tables work in a lesson later in the chapter. Color-reduction algorithms only apply to the GIF and PNG-8 formats. Because these two formats support the 8-bit format (i.e., an image with 256 colors or fewer), the color tables determine how the computer calculates which 256 colors out of the image to keep.

> Note: If the original image has fewer than 256 colors, you can adjust the maximum number of colors that are calculated, further reducing the size of the image.

Each color reduction palette produces slightly different results, so it is a good idea to understand how each type works its magic. The descriptions of the color tables that follow are taken from the Photoshop Help files. (Photoshop categorizes the color tables as dynamic, fixed, or custom.) Reading descriptions, however, will not give you the full effect of what these color tables do. That you only will get when you see how the tables affect an actual image, which you will experience in the lessons.

Dynamic options use a color-reduction algorithm to build a palette based on the colors in the image and the number of colors specified in the optimization setting. The colors in the palette are regenerated every time you change or re-optimize the image.

- *Perceptual:* Creates a custom color table by giving priority to colors for which the human eye has greater sensitivity.
- *Selective:* Creates a color table similar to the Perceptual color table, but favoring broad areas of color and the preservation of Web colors. This color table usually produces images with the greatest color integrity. Selective is the default option.
- *Adaptive:* Creates a custom color table by sampling colors from the spectrum appearing most commonly in the image. For example, an image with only the colors green and blue produces a color table made primarily of greens and blues. Most images concentrate colors in particular areas of the spectrum.

Fixed options use a set palette of colors. In other words, the set of available colors is constant, but the actual colors in the palette will vary depending on the colors in the image.

- *Restrictive (Web):* Uses the standard 216-color color table common to the Windows and Mac OS 8-bit (256-color) palettes. This option ensures that no browser dither is applied to colors when the image is displayed using 8-bit color. (This palette is also called the Web-safe palette.) If your image has fewer colors than the total number specified in the color palette, unused colors are removed. Using the Restrictive palette can create larger files and is recommended only when avoiding browser dither is a high priority.
- *Black & White:* Builds a color table of only two colors—black and white.
- *Grayscale:* Creates a custom table of only grayscale pixels.
- *Mac OS and Windows:* Builds an 8-bit palette, capable of displaying 256 colors, using the color table of the system you select. If your image has fewer colors than the total number specified in the color palette, unused colors are removed.

The *Custom* option uses a color palette that is created or modified by the user. If you open an existing GIF or PNG-8 file, it will have a custom color palette. When you choose the Custom color palette, it preserves the current perceptual, selective, or adaptive color table as a fixed palette that does not update with changes to the image.

> **Note:** For future reference, you can lock, add, sort, delete, and shift colors in the generated color tables. You can also save and load color tables to apply to images.

Image Size

To discuss image size is to reintroduce the concept of resolution. For online display, an image's resolution need only match a standard monitor's resolution, which is 72 pixels per inch (ppi) for Mac and 96 ppi for Window. This is a welcome relief to what you learned in Chapter 10—the resolution of artwork going to print varies depending on where it is being printing and on what kind of paper stock.

Resolution is a mute point when working with vector-based graphics. These types of images are unique in their application to the Web. They are inherently scalable and compact in size. So, keep in mind that much of what we are talking about in regard to file size and compression applies to bitmap (or rasterized) images. Until more Web designers advance to using the latest online vector graphic formats, such as SWF and SVG, much of the graphics you see on the Web will be in bitmap format.

A bitmap image's size is directly related to its resolution. Image size can be referred to in two ways, and both impact optimization: the actual dimensions of an image (e.g., 5-by-5 inches or 400-by-600 pixels); and the image's file size (its actual amount in digital bits). This is measured in bytes, kilobytes, megabytes, or gigabytes. A byte is 8 bits, a kilobyte (KB) is 1,024 bytes, a megabyte (MB) is 1,024 kilobytes, and a gigabyte (GB) is 1,024 megabytes. How big is too big for a Web image? Well, it depends on how many images you have on a single Web page, whether they are bitmap or vector based, and whether they are dimensionally large or small.

We prefer to keep our Web images, especially bulky bitmap ones, to no more than 10 to 20 KB each in file size. In fact, when we build Web pages it is not uncommon that a client will ask that we keep the total file size of everything on a Web page under 30 KB for those viewers with slow Internet connections. The ultimate, of course, is to actually post your optimized images to the Web and test how long it takes for them to download on different Internet connections.

SAVE FOR WEB & DEVICES

Think of the Save For Web & Devices option (File > Save For Web & Devices) as a fitness program for your graphics. Depending on your image's body type (format), you can try out various fitness regimes (compression schemes) to produce the best looking and most lean image possible in the Optimized window view. A 2-Up or 4-Up window view lets you compare and contrast an image's optimization settings next to the original file. See Figure 11–3.

In Save For Web & Devices you also can view your image and its selected specifications in a browser window of your choice (e.g. Safari,

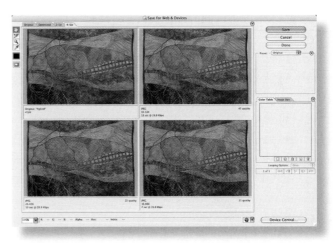

figure | 11–3 |

The Optimized window view with the 4-Up window tab selected.

figure | 11–4 |

Select a browser to view your image. If you do not have a browser selected, choose Other and find the browser of your choice installed in your applications folder, such as Safari, Firefox, or Internet Explorer.

Firefox, Internet Explorer, whatever is installed on your computer). In the Save For Web & Devices window, this option is located in the lower-right corner of the box, next to the Device Central button. See Figure 11–4.

As discussed in the section "Image Format," there are general guidelines for what kind of artwork to save in the various kinds of formats—photos as JPEGs, line art as GIFS. However, to find the right size and quality, you need to subtly adjust the options in the Save For Web & Devices dialog box. A simple adjustment to the bit depth of a GIF image, for example, can reduce the file size of an image immensely, resulting in a much more efficient Internet download. There are a lot of options to choose from in the Save For Web & Devices dialog box, but do not let that overwhelm you. When you are ready to learn about these options, review that information in the Photoshop Help files. For now, just learn some of the basics and trust your visual instincts when you start comparing and contrasting settings in the Save For Web & Devices dialog box—something you get the opportunity to do in "Lesson 1: Preparing an Image for the Web."

Optimization Workflow Techniques

If you understand how optimization works and how to save an image with proper optimization settings, you know 90% of the Web image publication process. However, for purposes of workflow—producing more efficient ways of doing a task—there are several features related to optimization that might prove beneficial for you sooner rather than later. First, this includes the ability to save and edit optimization settings (see Figure 11–5) and resize the image (pixel size) at export (see Figure 11–6).

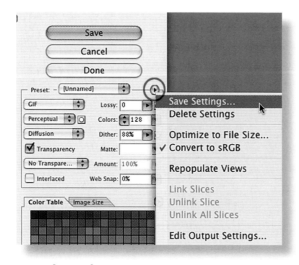

figure | 11–5 |

Save and edit your optimization settings.

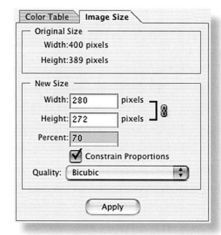

figure | 11–6 |

Create a new size for the optimized image at export.

Second, for more precise control and higher quality results when you optimize potentially critical areas, use weighted optimization. "Weighted optimization lets you smoothly vary optimization settings across an image using masks from text layers, shape layers, and alpha channels," according to the Photoshop Help files. When you create text or shape layers, masks are created automatically and, as learned in Chapter 8, you can save your own masks using alpha channels. These masks can be used for weighted optimization. See Figure 11–7.

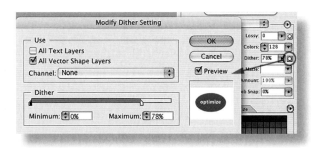

figure |11–7|

To find the weighted optimization options for particular color tables, look for the Mask icon and click it to view the masks available for editing.

Finally, when you have many images that need to be saved with the same optimization setting, you can create a clever timesaver called a "droplet." A droplet is a small application that automatically applies specific settings to a batch of images you drag over a droplet icon. Let us say you just received 50 high-resolution photos that need to be resized and converted to JPEG format, with a 60% compression. Moreover, the project needs to be done fast because the Web developer has to get the photos online (today) as part of the company's new spring catalog. With a droplet action, you record the optimization specifications on one of the photos and then have Photoshop diligently execute the steps on the rest of the images (while you take a long lunch break, of course).

To make a droplet with specific optimization settings, record your optimization settings into an action. Then, to execute the action, choose File > Automate > Create Droplet. See Figure 11–8. When ready to execute the droplet action on images, drag a folder of images over the saved droplet.

We do not cover the topic much in this book, but Photoshop has an Actions panel (Window > Actions) where you can record a series of individual actions (commands)—like the steps for saving an image to a particular size and format— and then automatically run the action on

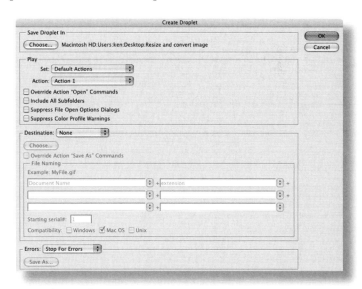

figure |11–8|

The Create Droplet options dialog box.

batches of images. To practice creating a droplet in Photoshop, see the section "Exploring on Your Own" at the end of this chapter.

Lesson 1: Preparing an Image for the Web

In this lesson, you optimally save a colorful photograph, originally in the TIFF format, of a quilt created by Karen Kamenetzky. You use the settings in Photoshop's Save For Web & Devices dialog box to prepare the image for Web publication.

Setting Up the File

1. In Photoshop, choose File > Open and open **chap11L1.tif** in the **chap11_lessons** folder.

2. Press Shift-Tab to hide unneeded windows.

3. Select View > Actual Pixels to be sure you are viewing the image at 100%.

4. Familiarize yourself with the file's specifications. Choose Image > Mode and be sure it is saved in the RGB Color mode.

5. Choose Image > Image Size and note the document size and resolution. Right now the image is saved at 150 ppi. When optimized it will be reduced to 72 ppi—the standard resolution for screen-based graphics. Do not make any changes, just click OK.

6. Make a color adjustment to the image. Choose Image > Adjustments > Auto Levels, and then Image > Adjustments > Auto Color. Note the subtle but significant changes in the brightness and contrast (the vibrancy) of the image.

Setting the Save for Web Options

1. Choose File > Save For Web & Devices, and select the 4-Up option on the tab in the upper-left corner of the window. A four-window view of the image becomes available. See Figures 11–9 and 11–10.

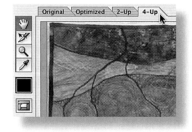

figure |11–9|

2. Click on the first window to highlight it. A colored box appears around the image. Note that the first window shows the original image at a file size of 456 KB. Also, note that Preset is set to Original in the information area to the right of the dialog box,.

Choose the 4-Up option to compare and contrast the image in four different windows.

3. Click on the window to the right of the first window. A colored frame will appear around the image and the settings for the image become available.

4. The viewing annotations at the bottom of the selected window provide valuable information about the optimization settings for that particular window. Those settings include format type, size, estimated download time, and Color table specifications.

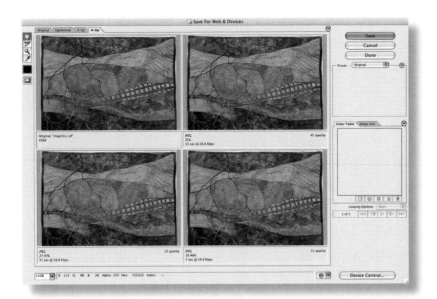

figure | 11–10 |

The full 4-Up
window view.

5. Note that the download time is determined by a specified Internet connection speed. By default, this is set to the lowest possible modem speed, 28.8 kilobytes per second (Kbps). To adjust this setting to a more standard 56 Kbps modem speed, click on the arrow right above the selected window and from the menu choose Size/Download Time (56.6 Kbps Modem/ISDN). See Figure 11–11.

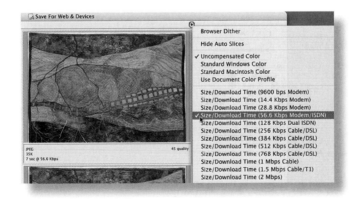

figure | 11–11 |

Change the Internet
connection speed
to see how it
affects the image's
download time.

6. Under Preset, leave it [Unnamed]. Then select the following options (see Figure 11–12):

- *Optimized file format:* GIF
- *Color-reduction algorithm:* Adaptive
- *Dither algorithm:* No Dither
- *Transparency:* Uncheck
- *Interlaced:* Uncheck
- *Lossy:* 0
- *Colors:* 256 (the maximum number available)
- *Matte:* None
- *Web Snap:* 0%

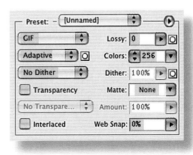

figure | 11–12 |

Set the optimization
options.

7. The Color Table for the selected window indicates the colors being used in the image, which is determined by the color-reduction algorithm (Adaptive) and the maximum number of colors in the algorithm setting (256). Hover—do not click—your cursor over a swatch to reveal the color's attributes. See Figure 11–13.

8. Select the third (bottom-left) window and adjust the settings differently, as follows:

   - *Optimized file format:* GIF
   - *Color-reduction algorithm:* Restrictive (Web)
   - *Dither algorithm:* Diffusion
   - *Dither:* 100%
   - *Transparency:* Uncheck
   - *Interlaced:* Uncheck
   - *Lossy:* 0
   - *Colors:* Auto (the maximum number available)
   - *Matte:* None
   - *Web Snap:* 0%

figure | 11–13 |

Hover over a swatch to reveal the color's numeric attributes.

9. In the Color Table for the selected window, the swatches with a diamond in the middle indicate Web-safe colors. (For more information on Restrictive [Web], see the section "Color-Reduction Algorithm.") The others are in the general RGB color space. Hover—do not click—your cursor over one of the diamond swatches, and the hexadecimal color number is revealed.

10. Select the fourth window and alter its settings, as follows:

    - *Optimized file format:* JPEG
    - *Color-reduction algorithm:* Maximum
    - *Quality:* 100
    - *Progressive:* Check
    - *ICC Profile:* Uncheck
    - *Blur:* 0
    - *Matte:* None

Comparing and Contrasting Settings

1. Take a close look at what each optimization setting has done to the image. Magnify each window with the Zoom tool (located to the left of the Save For Web window) and really examine the artifacts of each compression scheme. Use the Hand tool to move the magnified image around in a window.

2. Double-click on the Zoom tool icon to set the view of each window to the original image size. Which version looks best to you?

3. Compare and contrast the viewing annotations at the bottom of each window. What are the size differences? Is the one that looks best to you a reasonable size for a quick download from the Internet (i.e., under 20 KB)?

Getting Picky

1. OK, let us fine-tune and reduce the file size of the image even more. It definitely needs it. It is a beautifully complex image that could be worth the download wait time, but let us make a version a user would be able to view relatively fast, even on a slower connection (i.e., 56 Kbps). Select the second window (top right side).

2. Change the color-reduction algorithm to Selective, and reduce the colors to 128. The file size is reduced, but it does not look any better, and the file size is still too large. The gradients of color on the rock formations are getting splotchy. This is because gradients are composed of several shades of color, so when the color palette is reduced, so is the amount of color that makes the gradient look smooth.

3. Look at window 4—the JPEG. The gradient here looks good, but the file size is too big. How to fix it?

4. Select window 4 and change the JPEG compression quality to Medium. Great! The file size is smaller and the image still looks relatively acceptable (compare it to the first window—the original file). It is still pretty big, however. Let us get it under 20 KB.

5. Click the Image Size tab (below the optimization settings), reduce it to 75%, and hit Apply. See Figure 11–14.

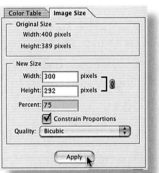

figure | 11–14 |

Scale down your optimized image to lower its file size.

6. Select the Select Browser Menu option (bottom of window) and choose a browser to view the optimized image. This is the ultimate test of how good it looks. See Figures 11–15 and 11–16. Close the browser window.

> Note: You might need to choose Other in the Browser menu to find a browser you have installed on your computer. We like to check my image in several browser types—Internet Explorer, Safari, and Firefox—because you never know which browser a viewer will be using to view the image.

figure | 11–15 |

From the Select Browser Menu, select the browser in which you want to view the image.

7. Select Save to save this version of the file. Name it **webimage.jpg** and for format, (Save as type) choose Images Only. Save the file in your folder **chap11_lessons**.

> Note: If you do not want to save the file right away, choose Done rather than Save. This will close the Save For Web window but maintain your optimization settings.

8. Save and close the lesson.

figure | 11–16 |

Examples of details revealed when an image is viewed in a browser window.

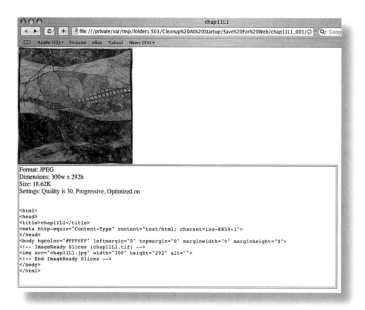

IMAGE SLICING

Image slicing is dividing up areas of an image or a complete Web page layout into smaller, independent files. If you are familiar with constructing Web pages, and working in HTML, you probably have an understanding of the benefits of slicing. If you are new to Web page design and development, this might seem like a somewhat crazy thing to do to your artwork, but slicing is useful for the following reasons:

- Creating accurate HTML table placement
- Creating independent files, each containing its own optimization settings
- Creating smaller, independent files for faster download
- Creating interactive effects, such as button rollovers

Lesson 2: Slicing a Web Page Navigation Bar

In this lesson, you prepare a navigation bar for placement in a Web page. Using Photoshop's Slice tool, you will slice and optimize areas of the layout for optimal Web performance.

Setting Up the File

1. Open **chap11L2.psd** located in the folder **chap11_lessons**. If a "Missing Color Profile" warning appears, click OK.

2. Choose View > Actual Pixels.

3. Press Shift-Tab to hide unneeded panels, if not already hidden.

4. Choose Window > Layers. Note that there is one layer available, called **nav_bar**.

5. To turn the guides on, choose View > Show > Guides, if not already checked. Guides have been created for you to indicate where the slices will be made. See Figure 11–17.

figure |11–17|

The guides help to accurately create image slices.

Making Slices

1. To turn the slices on, choose View > Show > Slices, if not already checked.

2. Select the Slice tool in the toolbox. See Figure 11–18.

3. Position the pointed end of the Slice tool in the upper-left corner of the image and click and drag to the right, defining a box around the swirl logo and top header section (do not include the yellow bar of "nav" buttons at the bottom). See Figure 11–19. Note that a number for the slice is indicated in the upper-left corner of the defined box. To hide/show slices, choose View > Show > Slices.

figure |11–18|

Select the Slice tool.

> Note: When you make slices you do not actually "cut up" your artwork. Instead you create an overlay of divided areas that determines how the individual files will be created when saving the document. Slicing always occurs in a grid-like pattern. Even if you do not define a slice in a particular area, Photoshop automatically creates one to maintain the table structure necessary for exporting into an HTML page.

figure |11–19|

Define a slice with the Slice tool.

4. With the Slice tool, slice around each button area in the lower part of the navigation bar. There will be six slices across the bottom: a slice defining each of the four buttons and on the two edges. Use the guides to get accurate placement. See Figure 11–20.

> Note: Do not worry if you make a mistake. Just Edit > Undo (a few times, if necessary) and try your slice again.

figure |11–20|

Create six more slices, using the guides for accurate placement.

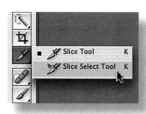

figure |11–21|

Choose the Slice Select tool to select and modify slices.

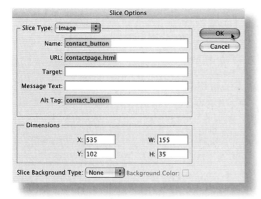

figure |11–22|

The Slice panel options to modify individual slices.

figure |11–23|

Select the Slice Select tool.

figure |11–24|

Option to toggle the Slices Visibility.

5. Each individual slice can be modified. From the toolbar, choose the Slice Select tool (under the Slice tool, as shown in Figure 11–21), and then click on the slice you want to alter. You can resize it with the handles in each corner of the selection, move it, or delete it.

6. With the Slice Select tool, select the Contact slice area.

7. There are also options for selecting individual slices. Double-click on the Contact slice area. In the Slice Options window, change the name for the sliced area to **contact_button**, make up a link (URL), such as **contactpage.html**, and an Alt text **contact_button**. See Figure 11–22.

8. Choose File > Save for Web & Devices. Select the Select Browser Menu option (bottom of window) and choose a browser to view the sliced image. Place your cursor over the word Contact to reveal that the area is now being considered a button link (the little hand icon shows up). This occurs when you add a link name to the slice in the Slice Options panel. Close the browser window and the Save for Web & Devices window.

9. Choose File > Save As, and save your file in your **lessons** folder.

Optimizing and Saving the Slices

1. To optimize and save the images, choose File > Save for Web & Devices.

2. Choose the 2-Up window option.

3. Select the Slice Select tool located on the left side of the window. See Figure 11–23.

4. Select slice number 1 in the second (top-right) window. It will highlight in yellow or appear with a lightened screen. Adjust the optimization settings of this sliced area. We chose JPEG, Medium, Quality 50 because of the many gradations of color in the header and logo graphics.

5. Select the first button area (Home) and adjust the optimization settings. We chose GIF, Selective, No Dither, and reduced the Colors to 16, producing a very efficient graphic.

6. Select each of the other slices and optimize them to your liking. Balance the image file size with visual appeal.

7. To view the final, optimized work, turn off the Toggle Slices Visibility in the tools area to the left of the window. See Figure 11–24.

8. OK, we are almost there. Choose Save in the Save For Web & Devices window.

9. In the Save Optimized As box, enter the following:

- *Save As:* **mynavbar.jpg**
- *Format (Save as type):* Images Only
- *Where:* Your lessons folder
- *Settings:* Default Settings
- *Slices:* All Slices

10. Wait—before you hit Save, we want to show you something. Under Settings, choose Other. In Output Settings, choose the Saving Files option. In the Optimized Files options, make sure Put Images in Folder is checked and that **images** is indicated for the folder name. Then click OK. See Figure 11–25.

11. Hit Save to save the individually divided files to the images folder you indicated previously. The images folder will be located in your **lessons** folder. Minimize the Photoshop program and go find this folder. Open it up and, amazingly, all of your sliced images are there and ready to be placed into an HTML Web page. See Figure 11–26.

GIF Animation

Photoshop offers features to create simple animations for Web publication.

Lesson 3: Creating a Web Animation

In this lesson, you are preparing an animated GIF for a vintage aircraft Web page. Using the Animation panel, you will move a number of elements to give the illusion of motion and flight.

Setting Up the File

1. Open **chap11L3.psd** located in the folder **chap11_lessons**.

2. In the toolbox, double-click on the Hand tool to expand the working window.

3. Double-click on the Zoom tool in the toolbox. Now, you have plenty of space to work in. See Figure 11–27.

4. Be sure View > Snap is checked. This option will allow you to snap the layers easily to the sides of the canvas.

5. Choose > Animation to open the Animation panel. By default, the Animation panel opens up at the bottom of the screen. Here you will see two frames: the first frame shows all of the layers and the second frame shows only the Sky layer. See Figure 11–28.

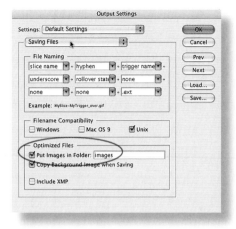

figure | 11–25 |

The Saving Files options in Output Settings.

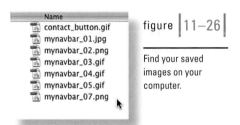

figure | 11–26 |

Find your saved images on your computer.

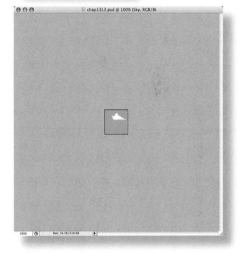

figure | 11–27 |

Zoomed out version of the file—now, lots of room to work!

figure | 11–28 |

Animation panel shows two frames.

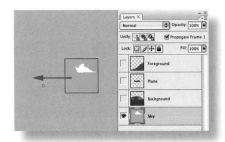

figure |11–29|

Move the sky image to the left until it snaps.

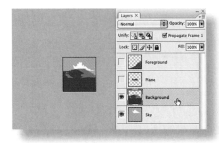

figure |11–30|

Make the Background layer visible and select it.

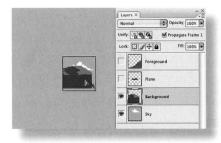

figure |11–31|

Snap the Background layer object into position.

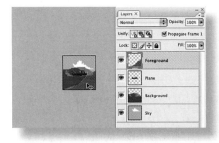

figure |11–32|

Snap the Foreground layer object into position.

Animating the Layers

1. Select the Move tool in the toolbox.

2. With the Sky layer highlighted in the Layers panel, and your Move tool selected, click and drag the sky image in the working window to the left. As you position the layer, you will notice the image moves to the left and eventually snaps to the right edge. When it snaps, you are done with the layer. Holding down Shift will keep it aligned top to bottom. See Figure 11–29.

> Note: If you are thinking, "It looks exactly the same . . . what's going on?" Remember, looks can be deceiving. The reason for making them look exactly the same has to do with making the animation loop. Looping an animation is a great way to catch the attention of a viewer and minimize the file's size. You will soon find out what we mean.

3. In the Layers panel, turn on the layer visibility (the eyeball) of the Background layer and highlight the layer. See Figure 11–30.

4. Using the Move tool, click and drag the purple mountains to the left like the Sky layer previously. It may take multiple click and drags to move the layer until it snaps to the right edge. If the Background layer suddenly disappears and all you see is blue sky, choose Edit > Undo and move the layer again but not as far to the left. You want to snap the bottom-right corner of the Background layer to the bottom-right corner of the canvas. See Figure 11–31.

5. In the Layers panel, turn on the layer visibility for the Plane layer and Foreground layer.

6. Click on the Foreground layer to highlight it.

7. Again, using the Move tool, click and drag the brown foreground cliffs to the left and snap the bottom-right corner of the layer to the bottom-right corner of the canvas. This is a long drag and may take multiple click and drags to move the cliffs all the way to the left. See Figure 11–32.

8. In the Animation panel, you will notice the two frames are identical. Now, we are ready to create the animation. See Figure 11–33. To do this, you will have Photoshop create more frames between the two frames. This is called "tweening" in the animation industry. Traditional animations, created by such studios as Disney and Warner Brothers, had many frames drawn in between key frames (the two frames in the Animation panel would be considered "key frames") to create the illusion of motion. These "tween" frames were drawn by artists called "in-betweeners."

9. In the Animation panel, click on the Tweens animation frames icon. See Figure 11–34.

figure |11–33|

Frames 1 and 2 are identical and ready to be animated.

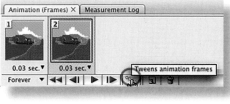

figure |11–34|

Click the Tweens animation frames icon.

10. In the Tween window, Tween With should be set to Previous Frame, Frame to Add is 58, Layers is All Layers, and all Parameters (Position, Opacity, and Effects) should be checked. See Figure 11–35. Click OK.

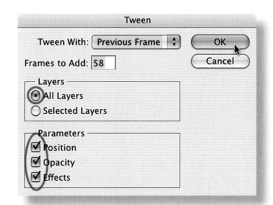

figure |11–35|

Select options in the Tween window.

11. You will notice a lot more frames appear in the Animation panel. Those frames are created by our in-betweener—Photoshop. See Figure 11–36.

figure |11–36|

Photoshop creates all the in-between frames – alright!

12. Want to see how it looks? In the Animation panel, click the Plays animation button. See Figure 11–37. There goes your plane flying through a canyon. Pretty nifty! Click the Stops animation button (same location as the Plays

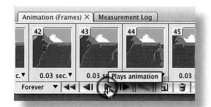

figure |11–37|

Click play to view your animation.

animation button). To learn more about the animation feature of Photoshop, choose Help > Photoshop Help > Contents > Video and animation.

Saving the Animated GIF

1. Choose File > Save for Web & Devices.

2. Under Preset, leave it [Unnamed]. Then select the following options (see Figure 11–38):

- *Optimized file format:* GIF
- *Color-reduction algorithm:* Selective
- *Dither algorithm:* No Dither
- *Transparency:* Uncheck
- *Interlaced:* Uncheck
- *Lossy:* 0
- *Colors:* 16
- *Matte:* None
- *Web Snap:* 0%

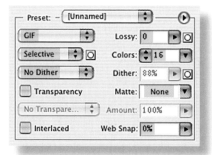

figure |11–38|

Save options for the animated GIF.

3. Select the Select Browser Menu option (bottom of window) and choose a browser to view the animated GIF. See Figure 11–39. Close the browser window.

4. Click Save. Name it **plane.gif** and for Format (Mac) or Save as type (Windows) choose Images Only. Save the file in your **chap11_lessons** folder.

figure |11–39|

View the animated GIF in a browser.

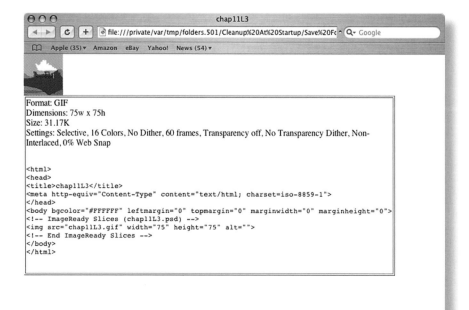

SUMMARY

Yeah, we know, you are probably all excited now—at least, we hope so—about using Photoshop. Creating, adjusting, and preparing images for print and Web publication is no longer such a deep, dark secret. Now that we are at the end of this book, it is up to you to continue exploring the magic of Photoshop. As you undertake this graphic design adventure, keep in mind the words of the great magician Harry Houdini, "Don't lose confidence in an effect because it has been presented many times before. An old trick in 'good hands' is always new. Just see to it that yours are 'Good Hands.'"

in review

1. Describe image optimization. What three interrelated areas must be considered in the Web optimization process?

2. What is dithering?

3. Photographs are best saved in what format? What about graphics with solid colors and line art?

4. What image formats use color-reduction algorithms and why?

5. When would you use the WBMP format?

6. How many bytes are in a kilobyte? Why is that important to know?

7. Name at least two things you can do in the animation panel.

8. Name three useful things about slicing images.

9. Where do sliced images go once you save them?

10. What is so useful about a droplet?

exploring on your own

1. For information about Web graphics with Photoshop, spend some time in the Help files (Help > Photoshop Help > Contents > Web graphics).

2. Using what you have learned about the Save for Web & Devices window, decide which optimization settings are best for the example artwork, **fig1.tif**, located in the folder **chap11_lessons/samples**.

3. Automate the optimization process by learning how to make a droplet in Photoshop. For more information about droplets and automating tasks, refer to Help > Photoshop Help and search for Droplet and Automating tasks. Use the batch of images located in the folder **chap11_lessons/samples**. See Figure 11–40.

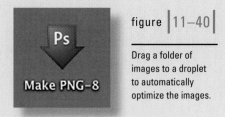

4. Using the Automate feature in Photoshop, create a Web photo gallery. We admit it, this is a really cool thing! A photo gallery is an quick way to create a working little Web site that showcases a series of digital images or photos. You can send the whole gallery package to family, friends, and clients and all they need to do to view it is open the **index.html** in a browser window. Choose File > Automate > Web Photo Gallery. In the options window, choose a Style, enter an e-mail address you want to display as the contact for the gallery, and under Source Images, identify the folder of images you want to transform into the gallery and a destination (for practice purposes, you can use the images located in the folder **chap11_lessons/samples** folder). See Figure 11–41 and Figure 11–42.

Web Photo Gallery

Site

Styles:	Centered Frame 1 – Basic
Email:	galleryowner@whatever.com

OK
Cancel

Source Images

Use: Folder

Choose...   Macintosh HD:Users:k...ap11_lessons:samples:

☑ Include All Subfolders

Destination...   Macintosh HD:Users:k... Files:chap11_lessons:

Options: Banner

Site Name:	Adobe Web Photo Gallery
Photographer:	Karen
Contact Info:	
Date:	3/30/07
Font:	Helvetica
Font Size:	3

figure |11–41|

The Web Photo Gallery options window. Choose File > Automate > Web Photo Gallery in Photoshop.

figure | 11–42 |

Example of a Web photo gallery viewed through a browser window.

Explorer pages

GLENN MITSUI

"Learn aggressively. Make the technology end of what you do go away with your skill in the programs. This will allow you to create freely because you know what is possible. This is when the real magic happens. Think of the obvious, then throw it away. Your ideas have to be better, be two steps ahead, that's when you surprise people, that's when you surprise yourself."

About Glenn Mitsui

Glenn Mitsui was born and raised in Seattle, Wash.. He attended Seattle Central Community College studying graphic design/illustration. With one class short of graduating, Glenn took the graveyard shift at Boeing where he learned technical illustration on the computer. After earning enough money to buy a Datsun 280Z, he left Boeing and opened Studio MD in Seattle with friends Jesse Doquilo, Randy Lim and Cindy Chin. Glenn became the studio illustrator, doing work for various magazines, newspapers and corporations. Studio MD flourished for 10 years until 1.5 million gallons of water flooded the entire business in 1998. Since then, Glenn began looking at things differently as a close friend comforted him with these words, "This is a baptism, baby, time to start over."

Glenn continued to work as a freelance illustrator. His work concentrated on editorial illustrations for clients such as the *New York Times*, the *Wallstreet Journal*, the *LA Times*, the *Atlantic Monthly*, *PCWorld*, *Time* and *Discovery Magazine*. His work has been honored by the Society of Illustrators, HOW, Graphis and Print. In 2002 he was inducted into the NAPP Photoshop Hall of Fame. In his spare time, Glenn is president and co-founder of a program called LINK. Its aim is to bring various artists in the community together, connecting them with inner city high school students to help expand their art awareness in monthly Saturday workshops. For the past 11 years, LINK has helped fund over 50 students to go to college.

Glenn's work has evolved from editorial illustration to fine art. It is used in concert settings, church services and installation pieces. His latest venture, the Organica project, is a collaboration with musicians to visually score their music. It includes a full length DVD of moving pictures set to the ambient music of Dan Phelps. Visit Glenn's Web site to learn more about his exciting work: *http://www.glennmitsui.com/*.

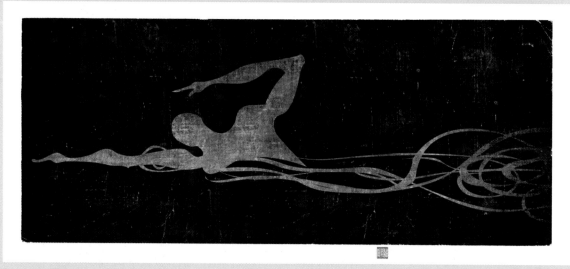

Upstream. Compliments of Glenn Mitsui.

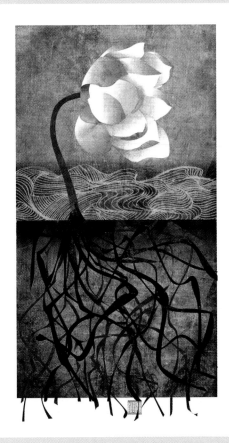

Family. Compliments of Glenn Mitsui.

About the Work of Glenn Mitsui

Glenn shares his process for creating the Family image:

"The *Family* image is homage to a good friend's father who passed away. He was an amazing man who enjoyed life to the fullest and left behind a legacy of a wonderful family. His stem was not strong enough to support his petals, but his roots will grow forever.

"This piece was done entirely in Photoshop. The process is quite simple, no filters, no real amazing techniques. A lot of this piece is grounded in what feels right. The flower and roots were drawn with the Pen tool in Photoshop. The petals were also drawn using the Pen tool, then filled with a gradation. The wavy lines were drawn with a regular pencil on paper, then scanned. The textures are layered on top of each other till they look right. Cement, paper, linen, papyrus, rusted metal, paint, graphite streaks all combined till it feels right. I love the different variations you go through to get something you like. The trick is knowing when it is done, when can you walk away and feel satisfied. Then all you have to do is find someone who shares your sense of beauty."

Gesthemene. Compliments of Glenn Mitsui.

| index |

INDEX

C